KYOTO CSEAS SERIES ON ASIAN STUDIES 2
Center for Southeast Asian Studies, Kyoto University

POPULISM IN ASIA

T0345508

KYOTO CSEAS SERIES ON ASIAN STUDIES 2
Center for Southeast Asian Studies, Kyoto University

POPULISM IN ASIA

Edited by
Kosuke Mizuno and Pasuk Phongpaichit

NUS PRESS

Singapore

in association with

KYOTO UNIVERSITY PRESS

Japan

NUS Press
National University of Singapore
AS3-01-02, 3 Arts Link
Singapore 117569
www.nus.edu.sg/nuspress

ISBN 978-9971-69-483-8 (Paper)

Kyoto University Press
Kyodai-Kaikan (Kyoto University Hall)
15-9 Yoshida-Kawaramachi, Sakyo-ku
Kyoto-city 606-8305
Japan
www.kyoto-up.or.jp

ISBN 978-4-87698-351-3

National Library Board Singapore Cataloguing in Publication Data

Populism in Asia / edited by Kosuke Mizuno and Pasuk Phongpaichit. –
  Singapore: NUS Press in association with Kyoto University Press, c2009.
  p. cm. – (Kyoto CSEAS series on Asian studies; 2)
  Includes index.
  ISBN-13: 978-9971-69-483-8 (pbk.)

  1. Populism – Asia – Congresses. 2. Asia – Politics and government –
  21st century – Congresses. I. Kosuke Mizuno.
  II. Pasuk Phongpaichit. III. Series: Kyoto CSEAS series on Asian studies; 2.

JQ24
320.95 – dc22   OCN336932970

Note on Name Order: The names of the volume editors and the authors of individual articles are given with their surnames last to avoid confusion in cataloguing. However, within the articles some names are given with the surname first, depending on the convention of the country concerned.

Typeset by : Scientifik Graphics
Printed by : Mainland Press Pte Ltd

CONTENTS

Part II Populism in Northeast Asia

LIST OF TABLES AND FIGURES

Tables

Figures

List of Tables and Figures

ABBREVIATIONS

ABAC	Assumption University (originally, Assumption Business Administration College)
AD	Acción Demócrata
APRA	Alianza Popular Revolucionaria Americana
CDR	Council for Democratic Reform
CNN	Cable News Network
DPP	Democratic Progressive Party
DPRD	Dewan Perwakilan Rakyat Daerah
EDSA	Epifanio de los Santos Avenue, a Manila highway
EOI	export-oriented industrialization
FPJ	Fernando Poe, Jr.
ILO	International Labour Office
IMF	International Monetary Fund
ISI	import substitution industrialisation
JSP	Japan Socialist Party
KMT	Kuomintang Party
LAMMP	Laban ng Makabayang Masang Pilipino (Struggle of the Patriotic Filipino Masses)
LDP	Liberal Democratic Party
NCCC	National Counter Corruption Commission
NGO	non-governmental organisation
PACC	Presidential Anti-crime Commission
PAD	People's Alliance for Democracy
PDIP	Indonesian Democratic Party of Struggle
PJ	Partido Justicialista
PPIB	New Indonesian Association Party (Partai Perhimpunan Indonesia Baru)
PRC	People's Republic of China
PRI	Partido Institucioal Revoulucionario
ROC	Republic of China (Taiwan)
Rp	Rupiah
RRI	Radio Republik Indonesia

SBY   Susilo Bambang Yudhoyono
SMS   short messaging service
SWS   Social Weather Stations
TDRI   Thailand Development Research Institute
TRT   Thai Rak Thai Party
UMNO   United Malays National Organisation

PREFACE

This book has grown out of academic collaboration under the JSPS-NRCT Core University Programme between Thammasat University and the Center of Southeast Asian Studies (CSEAS), Kyoto University that started in 1998.

A project on "Entrepreneurship in East Asia: Political, Economic, Social and Cultural: Towards a New Paradigm of Political Economy in East Asia", headed by Pasuk Phongpaichit from the Thai side, and Kosuke Mizuno from the Japanese side, was launched with an international workshop in October 2005.

A two-day international workshop was held on "The Thai Coup d'Etat and Post-Authoritarian Southeast Asia: The Shifting Balance of Social Powers" at Kyoto in March 2007 with participants from Japan, Thailand, Malaysia, Indonesia, and the Philippines. This workshop debated whether the coup in Thailand six months earlier signalled a shifting balance of social power that had regional dimensions. The papers examined not only the Thai coup, but appearances of populism around the region. It also drew on international comparisons thanks to Professor Otake's valuable contribution on Japanese periodic waves of populism, and Professor Matsushita's discussion on populism in Latin America.

As a result of the enthusiasm at these sessions, it was decided to hold another conference focusing on populism in Asia. This session took place a year later in March 2008 with the title "Populism in Asian Clothes: Thailand and Southeast Asia in Comparative Perspectives". Most of the chapters in this volume were presented at this session. Professor Ben Anderson gave concluding remarks at the event, and his contribution is included in this volume.

We are very grateful to many people who have helped to bring this volume into existence. First and foremost, we wish to thank all those who participated in the two workshop sessions. We are indebted to the Publication Committee of CSEAS, to Tetsuya Suzuki of Kyoto University Press, and to Paul Kratoska of NUS Press for accepting this collection for publication. We acknowledge the work of two anonymous and erudite reviewers for their valuable comments on an earlier draft, and also the commentary of guidance of Professor Akira Suehiro of the University of Tokyo. Chris Baker assembled the papers and edited the language. Without his assistance, this volume would not have reached publication. Finally, the publication of this book was aided by Grant-in-Aid for Publication of Scientific Research Results, Japan Society for the Promotion of Science (JSPS).

Most of all we would like to thank the authors of the chapters whose enthusiasm for the subject has resulted in this volume.

Kosuke Mizuno & Pasuk Phongpaichit
March 2008

CHAPTER 1

Introduction

Kosuke Mizuno and Pasuk Phongpaichit

Starting in the years around the millennium, the word "populism" began to appear in Asia. In the Philippines, it was used to explain Joseph Estrada's political image as a hero of the poor and his dramatic election as president in 1998. In Thailand, it was applied to describe Thaksin Shinawatra's successful courting of the electorate in 2000–1, positioning himself as an economic nationalist and saviour of Thailand from globalisation. In South Korea, Roh Moo-hyun's rise to the presidency in 2002 against the opposition of the established political elite was explained in terms of his nationalist and populist appeal. Similarly in Taiwan, the success of Chen Shui-bian, son of a poor tenant farmer, in capturing the presidency against the party which had ruled Taiwan since its foundation, was attributed in part to his populist appeal. In Japan in 2001, the surprising rise of the maverick politician, Jun'ichiro Koizumi, to head the ruling party and the government, was explained in terms of his extraordinary personal popularity and populist allure.[1]

The drift of the term "populism" into the Asian political atmosphere is rather new. Of course there have been sporadic sightings in earlier years. But we think this is the first book in English that has put "Asia" and "populism" together in the title.

Why has this word been adopted in Asia, both in day-to-day political commentary, and in academic analysis?

Populism in the World

A first explanation lies in the fact that populism has enjoyed a resurgence, both in political practice and academic analysis, on a world scale. This has had (at least) three streams.

First, in Latin America there was a wave of "neoliberal populism" from the 1980s onwards, followed by a wave of more radical populism in the last decade. In very general terms, though in very different ways, these can both be seen as adaptations as well as reactions to the era of globalisation, neo-liberalism, and renewed US dominance.

Second, in western Europe there has been a spate of movements expressing frustration at the unresponsiveness of the state and the limitations of electoral democracy as a form of representation. Often they have been right-wing in nature.[2] In Italy and Austria, they successfully captured power.[3] In very general terms, these movements can be seen as reactions to the increased power of the bureaucratic state.

Third, there has been a wave of movements in the former states of the Soviet Union and East European countries, often emerging in reaction to the initial phase of liberalisation and de-sovietisation.

All of these three trends have taken place in the aftermath of the Cold War, when leftist organisations and leftist debate was in disarray.

Alongside this upsurge in movements which were often described as populist there has been increased academic interest in these movements.[4] This new literature has helped to make the term populism more respectable and more widely useable than earlier, when the term was largely confined to late nineteenth-century USA and Latin America since the 1930s. First, it was argued that populism is a useful term to describe challenges to established authority that lay claim to represent the desires and interests of "the people". Second, several scholars argued that it is pointless to tie the term to a particular ideology, or a particular form of political organisation, or a particular social equation. Where the term "populism" was once criticised constantly for being "vague", the broadness of the term is now seen as an asset. Third, especially in the work of Ernesto Laclau and his associates and followers, populism was identified as a *form of political practice* that could appear in varied contexts.

In short, on a worldwide scale, populism is in the air, and populism as a word is more available. But what exactly is it?

What is Populism?

In academic literature, the most intense debate over the word and its meanings has been in the field of Latin American studies. Because of the importance of this literature, we open this book with an Asian review of the debate by Matsushita Hiroshi (Chapter 2). He traces three stages: a classical phase of heroic leaders backed by labour organisations and social movements, pitched against old oligarchies; a neopopulist phase distinguished by leaders who appealed to people through mass media rather than relying on political organisations, and who compromised with the neoliberalism dominant at the time; and a revived classical populism with a return to socialist ideology and open antagonism towards the U.S. The emblematic leaders of these three phases were Juan Perón in Argentina from the 1940s to 1970s, Alberto Fujimori in Peru in the 1990s, and Hugo Chávez in Venezuela over the past decade.

Matsushita makes the important point that the academic interpretation of the word populism has evolved in dialogue with the phenomena it is used to describe. He concludes that perhaps the message of Latin America's history of populism is that populism can become part of a political culture and may change in ideology, organisational style, and leadership over time.

To aid the discussion among members of this project, Otake Hideo compiled a working description,[5] reproduced over the next five paragraphs.

Populism can be right, left, or middle in the political spectrum. It has no common programme such as nationalisation (socialism), privatisation (neo-liberalism), or racism/anti-immigration (Nazism), and may adopt any one of them. All populist movements share a set of core values and a certain distinct rhetoric or discourse. In other words, populist movements, populist regimes, and populist leadership are defined by their ideology, with the following characteristics.

1. Wisdom lies among the ordinary people. This wisdom, that is, common sense, is necessary and sufficient to make political decisions. The people acquire this wisdom through productive works, not by reading books or through speculation. This notion is anti-intellectual, and denies technocratic knowledge in politics. It supports direct democracy, that is, politics by the people themselves.

2. There are no conflicts among the people. They are monolithic, homogenous, and classless. They embody Rousseau's will of the people. This idealised and romanticised image of the people often leads to nationalism. In contrast, internationalism or cosmopolitanism is mostly a characteristics of the elites, who are viewed with suspicion. Thus xenophobia often, if not always, becomes one feature of populism.

3. The ruling elites ("the establishment") are selfish and morally corrupted. The people are not only wise, but morally virtuous. The conflicts between elites and people are not merely clashes of interests, but the moral confrontation of good versus evil. The unity of the people is manifested most clearly through this confrontation with the enemy elites, who are often the representatives of foreign powers. Populism emerges only through the existence of those enemies, and hatred against them.

4.   Once the people eject their enemies, an ideal society will be realised.
     Then there will be no need of politics, which is regarded as essentially
     an unproductive activity. Here lies the inherently anti-political stance
     of populism. Populism ignores the necessities of political institutions,
     political parties in particular, and denies the institutionalisation of
     political representation. It hence necessitates a strong leader in place of
     institutional arrangements. Popularity is, however, unstable and short
     lived. In order to stabilise this personal power, a populist movement
     inevitably strengthens its leadership by more or less authoritarian
     methods. It often leads to an authoritarian populist regime.

Other academic analysts of populism place less emphasis on ideology.
Kenneth Roberts summarised "the essential core of populism" as "the political
mobilization of mass constituencies by personalistic leaders who challenge
established elites". He argued that such movements encompass many shades
of ideology, and various types of organisation.[6] Similarly, Sabatini and
Farnsworth point out that populism is used to describe any movement that
"mobilises those who feel themselves to be disadvantaged by socioeconomic
and political dislocation, as well as a leadership style that draws on a sense
of disaffection from the established political system and elites".[7] Margaret
Canovan argued that populist movements "involve some kinds of revolt
against the established structure of power in the name of the people. Populists
claim legitimacy on the ground that they speak for *the people* ... they claim
to represent the democratic sovereign ... the united people ... as against the
parties or factions that divide it."[8]

The appearance of the term populism in Asia over the past decade is
both a political event and an academic event, and these two aspects cannot
be neatly separated. New things happened in the politics of certain countries
which prompted both political actors and political observers to apply the
term populism. So what happened new and why was this term applied? A
good place to start is the economic crisis of 1997, the most severe and widespread shock to the region's economy in modern times.

The Asian Crisis of 1997

Summarising from the experience of Latin America, Francisco Panizza argues
that crises are often sparks for populism. Crises undermine the legitimacy
of "self-serving political elites",[9] "loosen traditional relations and subordi-
nation and throw up new forms of identification". They create conditions
in which "Populist leaders appeal to both the never-enfranchised and the
newly-disenfranchised."[10]

The appearance of populism in Asia is bound up with the Asian economic crisis of 1997 or, more broadly, with the trends within globalisation that conspired to create the crisis, and with the social impact left in its wake. The Asian crisis was preceded by an unprecedented boom in Northeast Asia and Southeast Asia. Over a generation, Japan was established as the world's prime manufacturing economy. Korea and Taiwan grew at rates that even surpassed Japan in its heyday. Southeast Asian countries seemed to be readying themselves for a similar surge. New wealth, new aspirations, and new pride were created across the region. Against this background, the financial disarray of 1997 was a crisis not only for economies but for ruling oligarchies, and for the state itself. Japan's slowdown and slump into a "lost decade" came earlier but ultimately belonged to the same historical experience. Korea, Thailand, Malaysia, the Philippines, and Indonesia faced not only dramatic reversals in economic growth, but intrusions by the IMF on their economic sovereignty, and wholesale denigration of their economic strategies and political systems at the hands of western analysts.

As existing political elites were discredited, people looked for someone on a white horse to rescue them from hardship, or restore their pride and aspirations. The stage was thus set for the rise of political leaders who had strong personal appeal and an ability to present themselves as somehow different from an old elite. Globalisation, and especially foreign finance capital, had become an "external enemy", while established political parties and leaders had become an "internal enemy". In very different ways, several new Asian leaders blended aspects of nationalism and populism.

As pointed out by Khoo Boo Teik (Chapter 7 in this volume), globalisation in general and the 1997 crisis in particular, undermined economic nationalism and developmentalism, the two most prominent ideologies of successful political movements in Asia in the era of liberation from imperial rule and the pursuit of economic growth. These ideologies had provided the legitimation for "collective action" by governments in the name of the "common good". Both these ideologies and the old political establishments associated with them were discredited in the crisis. In the five years following the financial crisis, virtually every Northeast Asia and Southeast Asian country with an open economy experienced a radical political disjuncture of some kind.

At the same time, the aftermath of the 1997 crisis created pools of discontent, especially among urban labour, peasant farmers, and migrant workers who often bore the brunt of the crisis in the form of unemployment and falling real incomes. There was discontent also among urban middle classes that had become accustomed to rising prosperity, and had often allowed their aspirations to race ahead of reality.

As Francisco Panizza argues,[11] such post-crisis situations, when old political arrangements are widely discredited, and when people from various social segments suffer a loss of welfare and aspiration, create fertile conditions for people to embrace new political identities and offer support to new political leaders or movements that might have gained little attention in calmer times.

The exact form of these disjunctures differed greatly depending on the specific country's background. Japan and the Philippines can be used to illustrate the two ends of a spectrum. In Japan, as Otake Hideo argues (Chapter 11), the disjuncture that brought Koizumi to power was one iteration of a cyclical pattern that had developed over two decades as Japan's political system had become more sclerotic; but, coming in the aftermath of the lost decade, it was a more wayward turn of the cycle than earlier iterations. Still, it was a disjuncture that was contained within the system of the LDP's virtual one-party rule. There was not even a defeat for the ruling party, let alone any challenge to reform the political system, just a new and intriguingly different style of leader. By contrast, in the Philippines as Joel Rocamora describes (Chapter 3), Joseph Estrada rose against the background of the crisis precisely by embodying the aspirations of those social classes that felt excluded from the political arena. His rise was symptom of a political breakdown that allowed politics to flow out of its institutional restraints onto the streets in a series of mass demonstrations. Although Estrada failed, he was seen by his supporters as a vehicle to "change the system", and was perceived by the old ruling oligarchs as a dangerous threat.

This contrast between Koizumi (a maverick within a ruling party) and Estrada (a challenger to the system) encapsulates the contrast between the meaning of populism in Northeast Asia and Southeast Asia respectively. Let us now explore that contrast.

Northeast Asia: Democratic Disillusion

The essays by Otake Hideo, Kimura Kan, and Matsumoto Mitsutoyo in this volume see populism in Northeast Asia primarily as an expression of frustration and distrust at an old political leadership and at the working of electoral democracy. This frustration and distrust was closely connected to trends in the economy. In Japan, Taiwan, and South Korea in the 1990s, the rate of economic growth had slipped down from the high rates sustained for over quarter of a century. The old political leaderships had drawn their legitimacy in large measure from their success in delivering these spectacular growth rates. High growth had allowed the established leaders to claim the mantle of nationalism, leaving little room for oppositions to mount a challenge. The decline in growth undermined this legitimacy, and widened the opportunities for challenge. As Kimura Kan argues in the case of Korea (Chapter 9), this disenchantment extended not only to the government and ruling parties but to the political system as a whole.

In this context, old political leaders were subject to closer scrutiny, especially over corruption and abuse of power. In all three countries, a very dominant party system had developed over prior decades. In Japan, the LDP had effectively created a one-party system. In Taiwan, the KMT had monopolised power for half a century. In South Korea, the end of military rule seemed to be leading towards a similar pattern of dominant factions sharing power. The era of rapid growth in these countries was founded to a large extent on close relations between business and politics. As long as growth remained high, the occasional scandals which emerged from these close business-politics relations were not a threat to dominant parties and leaders. But in the changed circumstances of lower growth, challengers had more success in portraying incidents of corruption and abuse of power as evidence of structural malaise. Challengers could position themselves as tribunes of the people and guardians of the nation. Matsumoto Mitsutoyo (Chapter 10) describes how Chen Shui-bian built support in Taiwan by setting up an antagonism between the "corrupted" "privileged elites" of the KMT and the "common people". In Japan, Koizumi drew mass support by campaigning for privatisation as a way to undercut the cosily corrupt business-politics relations underlying his own party's dominance. In South Korea, a political movement drew support by criticising the domestic relations between the largest *chaebol* and some major politicians, and the international dependence of Korea on the United States.

In such situations, populist challengers situate themselves in opposition to the existing political elites, or "go public" by ignoring political parties and parliament, and embarking on reforms which appeal to the people who are dissatisfied with the existing established politicians. They make the people feel they are doing politics for the people themselves.[12] In Otake Hideo's words, such populism is "political opportunism or flattery of the public, one type of pathology of mass democracy".

To play this role, the challengers had to be "outsiders" so that they were not implicated in the corrupt past, and could be convincing when they promised a new and different future. But significantly, all three of the new leaders featured in the essays on Northeast Asia in this volume were "insider-outsiders" rather than something truly new and different. Koizumi was a maverick within the LDP, but he belonged to an established political dynasty, and was a senior member of a powerful faction in the party. Roh Moo-hyun belonged to a group dubbed "The Outsiders" but he had entered politics under the patronage of a prominent leader of the prior generation, and been a player in Korea's electoral and factional politics for over 20 years. By his origins, Chen Shui-bian was an outsider in Taiwan's Kuomintang-dominated politics, but he also had 20 years of experience in the country's political milieu, and had served as mayor of the capital.

While these three challenged the old political leadership, they did not challenge the political systems in their countries in any fundamental sense. Although Koizumi occasionally surprised his colleagues in the LDP by breaking well-established informal rules, ultimately he conformed to the conventions of LDP politics. Roh and Chen failed to establish any party or movement which changed the political landscape.

Southeast Asia: Image and Programme

The essays on Southeast Asia, in this volume, portray populism as a more dramatic challenge to existing political systems, emerging from more widespread social change.

In all the countries of Southeast Asia, the last three decades of the twentieth century were a time of extraordinary change. For all the severity of the 1997 crisis, the boom that preceded this bust probably has had more long-term impact. Incomes increased. The structure of economies shifted. Countries became more integrated with the outside world. Political systems were creaking, bulging, and cracking in response to these massive changes in the distribution of economic and social power. The fall of Suharto in 1998, and the subsequent re-composition of Indonesia's political system, is the most dramatic example. But Estrada's election as president in the Philippines, Thaksin's landslide election victories in Thailand, and even Mahathir's retirement in Malaysia are all part of the same trend.

As Ben Anderson notes (Chapter 12), the norm of politics in these Southeast Asian countries over the past 30 years has been an oligarchy of wealth and power. "Populism" has become a label for challenges to these oligarchies. As Tamada Yoshifumi (Chapter 5) and Joel Rocamora both note, often the label is applied by the old oligarchs and their supporters as a tactic to discredit and delegitimate these challenges. "Populist" can be simple political abuse. But "populism" may also be a useful term to describe movements that challenge an old order in the name of "the people". Thaksin's political heirs have put the word in their electoral slogan.

Estrada is a perfect — almost cartoon-like — example of one key aspect of such challenges. Almost solely on the basis of his personal image as a heroic outsider — an image constructed partly out of his film roles, and partly out of his public and disorderly lifestyle — Estrada came to embody the frustrations and aspirations of those excluded from the Philippines' tightly oligarchic politics. He had nothing that could be seriously called a political programme. As Ben Anderson archly notes, Estrada probably just wanted to join the oligarchs. To phrase the same sentiment another way, he had no conception of himself as a populist. Once his following realised that fact, his fall was steep. "Estrada the populist" was constructed in the imagination of his followers. He was able to conceal his real self because his followers were captivated by his movie roles as a fighter against evil, and imagined him to be a leader who would fight the oligarchs on their behalf.

Thaksin Shinawatra displays the other side of the same coin. At the outset, he promoted himself as a business leader, and his public image had very little popular appeal. He adopted a populist programme to balance his strongly pro-business agenda. Yet when his government implemented this programme of cheap health care, agrarian debt relief, and village funds, his popularity soared. Thaksin then re-crafted his personal image to meet the expectations of his followers. In the words of Pasuk Phongpaichit and Chris Baker (Chapter 4), he was "swept along" by the force of his following. He remade his personal image by changes in appearance and oratorical style but, more importantly, he became more aggressive in positioning himself as a challenger to the old oligarchs. In short, Thaksin became what his followers imagined.

In Okamoto Masaaki's case study from Indonesia (Chapter 8), image and programme were better aligned from the start. Okamoto argues that the oligarchs managed Indonesia's post-Suharto transition with great skill, and that as a result there is little space for a populist challenger at the national level. But the spread of elective local government has opened up a new political milieu with new rules and new players. One new local politician, Fadel Muhammad, built popularity by constructing his image around the down-to-earth subject of corn. He challenged the local oligarchs of his Sulawesi province by promising to use the new local institutions for mass benefit. Fadel succeeded because his programme delivered enough to justify the image.

In an intriguing parallel, both Fadel in Indonesia and Thaksin in Thailand combined appeals to "the people" with promises to conduct government in the style of business management — in Thaksin's phrase, to run the country like a company. It is difficult to tell whether this combination of populism and entrepreneurialism signifies any wider trend. It certainly reiterates that populism can co-exist with varied ideologies.

Followers and Leaders

Populist challenges in Southeast Asia seem to be part of a process whereby oligarch-dominated politics are forced to respond to new social demands. Leaders as diverse as Estrada and Thaksin can become the embodiment of new political forces in the society. Thaksin does not seem initially to have aspired to this role, and Estrada totally failed to understand it. While the leadership of populism is often a fascinating subject of study — because the leaders themselves are fascinating — these two cases urge us to look deeper into the followership. The advent of populism in Southeast Asia signals a broadening of the political space, and a new assertiveness among the disadvantaged and excluded.

These populist leaders did not spring from nowhere. As Rocamora shows, Estrada's rise was predicated on organisations which already existed among the urban poor in the Philippines. These organisations helped Estrada to win elections. Similarly in Thailand, Thaksin's strongest base developed in an area where the Communist Party of Thailand had been active 30 years earlier, and where NGOs had organised savings group and protest campaigns about natural resource ownership over the prior decade. Neither of these leaders repaid their support base in the long run. But the populist stance adopted by Estrada and Thaksin populisms served as a sort of "political and ideological glue"[13] attaching popular forces to national politics. In the classical era of populism in Argentina, as Matsushita Hiroshi shows (Chapter 2), Peronism acted as an entry point for the Argentinian working class into politics with benefits over the long term.

But how do such leaders serve as "political and ideological glue"? As Matsushita shows, in the era of classical populism, the prominent role of the leader was often explained by reference to Weber's concept of charisma ("the presence of a charismatic leader who can unite the heterogeneous groups"), and this "explains why Latin American populism was named after their leaders such as Varguism, Peronism and Cardenism". Yet as Ben Anderson argued over 20 years ago, this concept of "charisma", used to explain the intrinsic nature an "extraordinary leader", never translated well into the Asian environment and has rather fallen out of fashion on a world scale.[14] None of the Asian anti-colonial nationalists, for all the fervour they aroused in their time, has bequeathed the world an "ism" based on their name. Tellingly, Thaksin's name was crafted into "Thaksinomics", a title for his government's policies, while the form *thaksin-niyom*, Thaksinism, never caught the public imagination. Similar comment could be passed on Koizumi, Roh, and Chen. Interestingly, the only recent Asian leader who has been bestowed with an "ism" of any real acceptance is Mahathir. Perhaps, as Khoo Boo Teik shows (Chapter 7), this was because his appeal was both ethnic-nationalist and class-based — a championing of the rural Malay against the urban Chinese. Perhaps also it was because he vaunted himself as an "extraordinary leader" in Weber's sense, *and because he lasted.*

Nowadays, the dynamics of the relationship between leaders and followers is increasingly facilitated and shaped by mass media. Part of what made Koizumi seem different — and hence a perceived alternative to the old LDP bosses — was simply that he looked so different from the standard image of a Japanese politician in the public media. Estrada's image as a "man of the people" was constructed from his film characters and from press reporting on his lifestyle. This image bore little relationship to his social origins, and turned out to be a poor guide to his politics too. On his first emergence, Thaksin had little that could be mistaken for charisma but, as Nualnoi Treerat shows (Chapter 6), he was able to build an image as an "extraordinary leader" by deliberate, heavy, and strategically apt use of public media under his control.

Populism has evolved in reach and style with the technology of mass media. The anti-colonial nationalists built their base with the help of the press and radio, and often their social base was defined and confined by the reach of these media. Estrada's appeal depended on the mass reach of cinema. Koizumi is a product of television. Over the last half century, the evolution of media has been in the directions of greater reach and more visual content. The audience has widened. With the spread of visual media, image has become at least as important as message. But in the last few years, the evolution of media has also moved towards more interaction. Thaksin's populism was built on this new facility. His policy agendas were put together with the help of opinion polls, surveys, and focus groups. After his overthrow, his attempts at resurrection depended a lot on mobilising the potential of the internet to act not only as a way he could communicate with his followers, but also as a channel for his followers to express their anger at Thaksin's enemies.

Opposition and Decay

For all their novelty and promise, the Asian populists failed to last. This can be ascribed to many different reasons. First of all, their challenges brought forth an equivalent or even stronger response among powerful, established groups. Thaksin was brought down by the naked power of a military coup. Chen was eclipsed in Taiwan in part because the KMT deftly stole his nationalist platform. But besides these powerful reactions, all the populist leaders fell to some extent because of a decay in their base of support. Ernesto Laclau[15] has drawn a formal model of populism which attempts to encompass both the rise and fall.

In Laclau's model, all people have grievances against their rulers, but these grievances are widely different. Populism emerges at a moment when many people realise that their grievances are "equivalent" to those of others. This can happen when there is an organisation, movement, idea, or leader which they believe can represent their grievances. They re-identify themselves as the followers of this organisation, movement, idea, or leader — or, more simply as "the people". In practice, this moment of consensus and re-identification happens when there appears to be a common enemy — a "Them" which makes possible an "Us". This enemy may be an external threat or an internal agent of oppression. In practice, an enemy that combines both these internal and external dimensions may serve the role best. As Ben Anderson notes, the first and probably the most successful populists in Asia were the anti-colonial leaders who faced a foreign enemy acting as an internal agent of oppression. Perhaps the prime example in the region was Sukarno. His enemy was foreign colonialism and neo-colonialism, and also the capitalism that gave birth to colonialism. In contrast to the "Them" of colonialism, he constructed an "Us" centred on an ideology of "marhaenism" — an idealisation of the typical Javanese farmer as self-reliant and independent.

Possibly this insight about external-internal enemies helps explain why populism has spread in parallel with globalisation. Established rulers are inevitably involved in the economic and political relationships of the globalised world. Challengers can portray them as internal oppressors beholden to outside forces. The fact that neoliberal policies so obviously favoured the advanced nations made populist nationalism an appealing and powerful message in the neoliberal era.

Laclau's model goes on to explain what happens once a populist movement takes power. All too easily, the leader fails to deliver, the consensus breaks down, the act of re-identification collapses, and "the people" vanishes.[16] The case of Estrada exhibits such a decay in extreme form. Estrada's real-reel public image, constructed out of his film roles and real-world lifestyle, became a focus of identity and loyalty which allowed an unprecedented challenge to the ruling oligarchy of the Philippines. But Estrada totally failed to understand his historical role as a populist, and seems to have had no conception of any need to deliver anything to his followers. He fell not only because of the concerted opposition by the Philippines elite, but because his core supporters among the poor expressed their disappointment at his incompetence.

As Kimura Kan describes, the case of Roh Moo-hyun in South Korea had some of the same elements. Against the background of the 1997 crisis, the Korean electorate invested their hopes in Roh because he was not associated with the old ruling cliques. But once Roh came to power, the public soon discovered that Roh's agenda was rooted in the old politics of the 1980s and was irrelevant to Korea in the 2000s. Roh's popularity also fell like a stone.

Populist leaders may resort to several techniques to sustain themselves in power. One way is to dramatise a continued external threat. Roh Moo-hyun tried this strategy by promoting nationalist feelings, but with little success. Yet the device can work. Chávez portrays himself as a knight jousting with the U.S. dragon, to great effect. Sukarno vaunted a policy of "smashing Malaysia", engineered confrontations with the U.S. and UK, and withdrew Indonesia from the UN, IMF, and World Bank. Alternatively populist leaders may try to dramatise the continued power of internal threats or enemies. Throughout his five year prime ministership, Koizumi never failed to publicise his continuous fight against powerful LDP faction leaders who tried to protect their vested interests. More often, populists have turned to forms of authoritarianism — suppressing public debate, undermining opposition, corrupting the judicial process, sidelining democratic institutions. In practice, populist leaders may use a blend of these methods. Sukarno did away with parliament and launched his "guided democracy". Thaksin Shinawatra waved a nationalist flag about defying the IMF, while he slid into authoritarian ways and explained to his followers that these were necessary in order to overcome a lingering old elite in order to deliver on his promises to "the people".

All the recent populists in Asia who successfully challenged existing elites or oligarchies were validated by elections. A question thus arises. Since oligarchies usually establish electoral systems designed to favour themselves (by rigging district boundaries and voter qualifications, making room for money politics, and so on), how come they still can be defeated in elections? Two explanations may be advanced. Firstly, oligarchies do not rule through election but through structural power so they do not pay enough attention to the intricacies of electoral politics.[17] Secondly, oligarchies do not feel threatened by elections until some unexpected crisis occurs and creates the opening for a serious challenger. This is clearly seen in the case of Thailand.

For two decades, the old political oligarchs neutralised the potential of elections through money politics, and were returned to power time and again. But the financial turmoil of 1997, by destroying fortunes and destroying complacency, created the conditions for Thaksin's challenge.

Populism's Future in Asia

On the face of it, the populist flurry in Asia over the decade since the 1997 financial crisis would seem to have been a failure. Many observers in Japan feel that Koizumi's zeal for "reform", including the privatisation of the postal services and highway corporation, ultimately seemed to have more style than substance. His retirement saw the immediate return of the LDP's usual distributional politics. In the cases of Roh Moo-hyun in South Korea and Chen Shui-bian in Taiwan, their popularity collapsed before they could achieve anything substantial in terms of policy or structural change. With their retirement, the prior political leadership has returned, perhaps strengthened by this interlude. Not one of these three leaders did anything substantial on the key issue of corruption and the linkages between business and politics.

In Southeast Asia, Estrada's ineffectual rule and rapid collapse are now legendary. He was replaced by a coalition of the Philippines' old ruling oligarchs. Thaksin Shinawatra was removed by coup, bringing the military back to Thailand's political front-line after a long absence. In Indonesia, the fate of Fadel and other popular-populist new leaders in local government is perhaps too early to assess.

But it would be wrong to assume that populism in Asia was an aberration created by the 1997 crisis, and bound to be short-lived because of populism's intrinsic weakness. Ben Anderson's reminder that the anti-colonial nationalists were essentially populist points to a longer tradition in the region. The recurrence and evolution of populism in Latin America testifies to its lasting appeal, and ability to change with circumstances.

The fact that Koizumi, Roh, and Chen failed to make much headway with their popular agendas means that the underlying malaise on which they were borne up to power remains in place. As Otake Hideo notes, there is a kind of cycle in Japanese politics over the past two decades, with the recurrent appearance of outsiders who promise to bring "reform". Perhaps Taiwan and South Korea may slip into a similar pattern. A form of "populist practice" becomes a mechanism within a relatively settled democratic system.

Thaksin won four electoral victories more convincing than victories by any previous leader or party in Thailand. He made promises to his supporters, and implemented more of them than most people expected. He showed people that their vote mattered, and undoubtedly increased the enthusiasm for democracy among people in general. Although he was then removed from power by coup, he was not discredited in the eyes of his supporters, and hence his time in power will linger as a powerful memory.

Thaksin did not fall because of some inherent failing of populist practice. Rather, he was bitterly opposed by people and institutions that felt challenged and threatened. As Tamada notes, whether or not Thaksin deserves the title of "populist", his problem was simply that he was so popular. Thaksin has clarified a deep division in Thailand's politics.

Megawati won election in 1999 largely because people could remember her father, Sukarno, as a contrast to the oligarchy that had dominated Indonesia for 30 years. But when the mass realised she lacked her father's affection for the people and was incapable of delivering any benefits to her supporters, she soon lost popularity.

At first when Estrada's incompetence and mismanagement became obvious, many observers expected that his core support would hold up because of his stature as a "culture hero", and because the poor were assumed to be incapable of properly judging performance. In fact, they judged very quickly. Estrada's behaviour in power revealed himself as no different from the rich and powerful. He blatantly took the side of the rich in many instances and, in Joel Rocamora's nice turn of phrase, he metamorphosed from Robin Hood into the Sheriff of Nottingham, "taking from the poor to give to the rich".

Rocamora reads Estrada's fall to mean that populism, with its emphasis on a single leader and hence vulnerability to that leader's weakness, is no substitute for broad-based popular organisation of a classic sort. Even so, it seems likely that some form of "populist practice" in Laclau's sense will recur in Southeast Asia. As long as societies remain starkly divided, and as long as oligarchies remain jealous of their privileges and resistant to demands of change, the appeal of a leader or movement that promises to empower "the people" will remain.

There is an awkward relationship between populism and democracy. Populism tends to appear when democracy is not working very well, or not working at all. People have expectations about democratic states. When these states fail to fulfil their citizens' expectations, there is an opportunity for leaders or movements which claim to represent that alienation. Historically, populist movements have often challenged oligarchic political systems disguised as democracies, and been instrumental in making political systems more open and responsive. But populism can also be a threat to democracy.

Populist leaders under pressure lapse into authoritarianism and either corrupt or destroy many basic democratic institutions. In the words of Ben Anderson, they lapse into "closed national oligarchies ... queuing for lucrative posts", until their opposition succeeds in plotting to overthrow them. Thaksin was following a well-worn path.

Populism and democracy are two sides of the same coin. Both stress the importance of "the people", but while democracy is almost invariably considered in a positive light, populism is probably most used as a term of abuse. But populism dies hard as long as democratic states provide cover for enduring oligarchies, and fail to fulfil their promise as providers of well-being, citizenship rights, and equality. Studying the many faces and facets of populism in Asian countries provides a window on democracy's successes and failures in the region. As Francisco Panizza concludes, "By raising awkward question about modern forms of democracy, and often representing the ugly face of the people, populism is neither the highest form of democracy nor its enemy, but a mirror in which democracy can contemplate itself, warts and all, and find out what it is about and what it is lacking."[18]

We hope that the studies in this volume contribute towards this contemplation in the context of Asia today.

Notes

[1]   See Kent E. Calder, "Asian Populism and the U.S. Security Presence in Asia", transcript of an October 2001 roundtable in Washington DC, sponsored by the Sasakawa Peace Foundation, at <www.spfusa.org/program/av2001/oct0301.pdf>.

[2]   See for example, Dabiele Albertazzi and Duncan McDonnell, ed., *Twenty-First Century Populism: The Spectre of Western European Democracy* (London: Palgrave Macmillan, 2008).

[3]   In his presidential campaign, Barack Obama took a populist approach: "This election is not about me. It's not about Sen. Clinton. It's not about John McCain. It's about you. It's about your struggles, your hopes, your dream." See "Obama pushes new populist message to NC voters", at <http://blogs.abcnews.com/politicalradar/2008/04/obama-pushes-ne.html>.

[4]   See especially Paul Taggart, *Populism* (Buckingham: Open University Press, 2000); Margaret Canovan, *Populism* (London: Junction Books, 2000); Francisco Panizza, ed., *Populism and the Mirror of Democracy* (London: Verso, 2005); Ernesto Laclau, *On Populist Reason* (London: Verso, 2005); Kenneth M. Roberts, "Populism, Political Conflict, and Grass-Roots Organisation in Latin America", *Comparative Politics* 38, 2 (Jan. 2006); Kenneth M. Roberts, "Neoliberalism and the Transformation of Populism in Latin America: The Peruvian Case", *World Politics* 48, 1 (1995); Kurt Weyland, "Neopopulism and Neoliberalism in Latin America: Unexpected

Affinities", *Studies in Comparative International Development* 31, 3 (1996); M. L. Conniff, *Populism in Latin America* (Tuscaloosa: University of Alabama Press, 1999).

[5] This summary is based primarily on: Guy Hermet, *Les populismes dans le monde* (Paris: Fayard, 2001); Taggart, *Populism*; Pierre-Andre Taguieff, *L'Illusion populiste. Essais sur les démagogies de l'âge démocratique*, revised edition (Paris: Flammarion, 2007).

[6] Kenneth M. Roberts, "Populism, Political Conflict, and Grass-Roots Organisation".

[7] C. Sabatini and E. Farnsworth, "A 'Left Turn' in Latin America? The Urgent Need for Labor Law Reform", *Journal of Democracy* 17, 4 (2006): 63n2.

[8] Margaret Canovan, "Trust the People! Populism and the Two Faces of Democracy", *Political Studies* 47 (1999): 3, 4, 7.

[9] Francisco Panizza, "Introduction: Populism and the Mirror of Democracy", in *Populism and the Mirror of Democracy*, ed. Francisco Panizza (London: Verso, 2005), p. 12.

[10] Panizza, "Introduction", p. 13.

[11] Ibid., pp. 11–2.

[12] Otake, this volume and his research note, "An Attempt to Define Populism", 12 May 2008.

[13] Silvio Waisbord, "Media Populism: Neo-Populism in Latin America", in *The Media and Neo-Populism: A Contemporary Comparative Analysis*, ed. Gianpietro Mazzoleni, Julian Stewart, and Bruce Horsfeld (New York: Praeger, 2003), p. 202.

[14] Benedict R. O'G. Anderson, "Further Adventures of Charisma", in *Language and Power: Exploring Political Cultures in Indonesia* (Ithaca and London: Cornell University Press, 1990), pp. 78–93.

[15] Ernesto Laclau, "Populism: What's in a Name?", in *Populism and the Mirror of Democracy*, ed. Francisco Panizza (London: Verso, 2005); *On Populist Reason*.

[16] Some economists argue that populism destroys itself by fiscal irresponsibility. Dornbusch and Edwards actually built this self-destruction into their definition of "economic populism" as an "approach to economics that emphasizes growth and income redistribution and deemphasizes the risk of inflation and deficit finance, external constraints and the reaction of economic agents to aggressive non-market policies". See Dornbusch Rudiger and Sebastian Edwards, *The Macroeconomics of Populisms in Latin America* (Chicago: University of Chicago Press, 1991), p. 9. This approach ignores the political battle that lies behind the fiscal result.

[17] Thanks to Michael Connors for this thought.

[18] Panizza, "Introduction", p. 30.

CHAPTER 2

The Evolution of Populism in Latin America and Changing Interpretations

Hiroshi Matsushita

Introduction

Once Latin America was called a treasure-house of military coups but nowadays it has become a region in which any possibility of a new military regime has almost completely disappeared since democratisation in the 1980s. Yet, populism which has been another traditional trait of the region's politics, has seemed to gain added momentum. In effect, we have seen a variety of forms of populism in the last two decades. In the 1990s, there was the conservative populism or so called neopopulism led, among others, by Alberto Fujimori in Peru and by Carlos Saúl Menem in Argentina. In the first decade of this century, we have witnessed a different and much more radical populism such as that led by Hugo Chávez in Venezuela, who assumed power in 1999 and who has influenced Bolivia, Ecuador, Nicaragua, and Paraguay where populist leaders of the same stripe are now in power.

Whether all these regimes qualify to be considered as populist depends upon the way the word is defined. Under the definition of Nicolás Lynch, a Peruvian political scientist, who stresses that populism should mean "social democratization" or "access to social and political rights", some Latin American neopopulists such as Albert Fujimori would not qualify.[1] However, if populism is defined as a political movement that tries to build its power from popular support by offering redistributive policies and other measures that directly appeal to popular sentiment, Fujimori's regime can be counted as a kind of populism. Hereafter, we will use the term populism in this broad sense.

Given this definition, it is safe to say that populism appeared in Latin America as early as the first two decades of the twentieth century, initiated by José Batlle y Ordónez, president of Uruguay for 1903–7 and 1911–5, and followed by Hipólito Yrigoyen, president of Argentina for 1916–22 and 1928–30. From then until now, Latin America has exhibited many varieties of populism, and truly does qualify as a treasure-house of different forms of the genre. Although I cannot trace its evolution chronologically in detail here, I shall point out four distinctive periods within its history.

The first period corresponded to the populism of Batlle y Ordoñez and Yrigoyen. Although their populism was moderate, they may be called the forerunners of Latin American populism, because, to bolster their regimes with popular support (especially from the middle class), they introduced some redistributive policies combined with some nationalistic measures for the first time in Latin America.

The second period began in the decade of the 1930s and ended in the 1950s. It was the golden age of Latin American populism because populism became a predominant phenomenon in the region's politics, especially in the big countries of the region such as Brazil (Getúlio Vargas, president 1930–45, 1951–4), Mexico (Lázaro Cárdenas, 1934–40), and Argentina (Juan Domingo Perón, 1946–55, 1973–4). Although there was much difference among them, Vargas, Cárdenas, and Perón all consolidated their power on the base of popular support, principally from the working class and labour organisations, by offering concrete benefits and by appealing to nationalistic sentiment. In addition, all three had a charismatic trait, which was undoubtedly one of the reasons they could attract the mass. In this second era, the combination of concrete benefits for the people, charismatic leadership, and some nationalistic linkages between the leaders and the mass, created the form of populism now generally referred to as "classical". However, this kind of populism became so strong in some countries that it provoked intense criticism especially from conservatives. In Brazil and Argentina (but not Mexico), populism was opposed by the armed forces during the 1950s and 1970s.

This repression was so harsh that populism seemed to disappear from the political scene around the beginning of the 1980s. A book on Latin American populism edited in 1982 in the United States began with the statement that "Populism is dead".[2] However, less than a decade later, populist leaders assumed power in several countries, although they adopted very different policies from those of classical populism. In this third period, debt and financial austerity prevented the leaders from offering the same concrete benefits. There appeared a new kind of populism that tried to gain support even while adhering to strict financial austerity and neoliberal economic policies instead of the free-spending ways of classical populism.

This new form that dominated in the 1990s was dubbed as neoliberal populism or neopopulism. But its time was short-lived. Recently in several countries of the region, neopopulism has been replaced by a kind of populism which has some similarity to classical populism. One typical example of this fourth period of Latin American populism is found in Venezuela under Hugo Chávez. Although some scholars call this new populism as neopopulism,[3] we reserve that term for populism of the third period.

This chronology, albeit brief, demonstrates the recurrent character of Latin American populism. This can be attributed to some extent to the traditional political culture of the region, marked by paternalism and patron-client relations. But undoubtedly, the political culture alone cannot explain why different kinds of populism appeared at different times in the history of Latin America. To explain the recurrent character of populism in this region, we should analyse each period carefully, but that is beyond the scope here. In this chapter, I focus principally upon the third period for various reasons. First of all, the appearance of this new kind of populism required change in the theoretical interpretation of Latin American populism that had previously been based upon classical populism. Second, as the fourth stage of populism appears to some extent to be a reaction against neopopulism, this fourth type has to be understood by comparison between neopopulism and the present form. Third, comparison between classical populism and neopopulism sheds some light on Asian populism, for example, populism in Thailand.

This chapter begins with a description and interpretation of classical populism, then presents neopopulism as a comparative form, and finally looks at the recent resurgence of populism of a more classical type.

What was Latin American Classical Populism?

Although many scholars comment that populism is a vague term, there is a very influential definition of the classical form of Latin American populism by the Argentine sociologist, Torcuato S. Di Tella, in an article written in 1965.

> It may be defined as a political movement which enjoys the support of the mass of the urban working class and/or the peasantry but which does not result from the autonomous organisational power of either of these two sectors. It is also supported by non-working-class sectors upholding an anti-*status quo* ideology.[4]

The reason why this definition was influential is that it illustrates in a concise way several substantial characteristics of Latin American classical populism. First, Di Tella's stress on the importance of anti-*status quo* ideology gained widespread acceptance. Populism is evidently a movement which opposes something, for example, landed elites, an oligarchy, or imperialism. Especially in Latin America, where landed elites ruled in collaboration with foreign enterprises, anti-*status quo* ideology combined opposition to landed elites in the name of social justice, and opposition to foreign economic predominance in the name of nationalism. These are two essential claims of populism. Second, Di Tella points out the multi-class support enjoyed by populism. Populist movements in Latin America tend to be supported by a coalition of workers, peasants, and non-working class sectors, including the middle class. This multi-class character is considered a basic element of Latin American classic populism. Another important trait is the presence of a charismatic leader who can unite these heterogeneous groups. That explains why Latin American populist movements tended to be named after their leaders, such as *Varguismo, Peronismo,* and *Cardenismo.* Thirdly, Di Tella thinks that populism is not an autonomous movement organised from below but basically induced or manipulated from above. As we shall see later, I do not agree with him on this point, because some kinds of populism, especially Peronism, undoubtedly had some autonomous mass participation. Yet it is true that a certain element of manipulation was involved in almost every type of populism including Peronism.

In sum, although I do not intend to attempt any very sophisticated definition, Latin American classical populism had the following characteristics: (1) it was a movement or a government which was opposed to the status quo and which tried to introduce reforms to realise more social justice and more economic and political independence; (2) it was supported by a multi-class coalition led by a charismatic leader; (3) it gained a following among the mass, though generally not acting autonomously.

Controversies over the Interpretations of Classical Populism

Why was this kind of populism born in many Latin American countries between the 1930s and the 1950s? There is a large literature on this issue, but I will highlight only the principal controversies on the causes of classical populism, using Peronism as its typical example. This can be justified because the studies of Peronism have influenced the interpretation of other populist movements in Latin America, as we shall see below.

As is well known, Peronism was a political movement initiated by Colonel Juan Domingo Perón, who participated in a military coup in 1943 and launched a series of pro-labour policies as a member of the military government in charge of labour affairs. Although his policies were rejected by Socialist and Communist-led workers, many others welcomed them with great pleasure, because they met long-held labour demands. With labour support, Perón was elected president in 1946. During his rule until 1955, he continued his pro-labour policies, including nationalising British-owned railways, launching an ambitious industrialisation programme, and conducting a diplomatic policy independent from the United States. These policies reflected very well the three elements of his slogan, namely, "social justice, economic freedom, and political sovereignty". These are considered as fundamental claims shared by almost all classical populisms. Even after he was overthrown in 1955, his popularity remained so strong that he returned to the presidency in October 1973, but died of chronic heart disease in July of the following year.

As this brief sketch illustrates, the key to Peronism was its support from labour, but there are fierce debates over the interpretation of this fact. The pioneering interpretation was made by Gino Germani, who focused on the rapid internal migration from the rural areas to the cities in Argentina as a consequence of the devastation of the rural area after the world depression of 1929, and the accelerated import-substitution industrialisation around the capital and its suburbs. The demand for labour for this new industrialisation was satisfied chiefly by migrant workers, whose numbers increased year by year until they represented an important portion of the working class in the metropolitan areas by the early 1940s. Germani claimed that this labour sector was the most important social base of Peronism. He argued that the mass of rural migrants were not sufficiently integrated into urban society and hence became an "available mass" that was manipulated by Perón. His famous thesis was that the time delay between migration and integration produced an available and irrational mass that became the social base of populism.[5] In short, the basic elements of Germani's argument were the presence of migrants and manipulation by the leader.

This interpretation, elaborated during the 1950s and the 1960s, soon became an orthodoxy in Argentina. More importantly, it was also applied to explain other classical populisms in Latin America because a huge migration from the rural areas to the cities was a common phenomenon in many countries during that period. For example, as a similar migration was under way in Brazil, the birth of *Varguismo* could be understood within this framework. However, in Mexico, although there had no massive migration prior to the rise of *Cardenismo* in the 1930s, Germani thought that *Cardenismo* was a consequence of psychological processes in the rural areas similar to what had occurred in Bolivia, Cuba, and the northern part of Brazil.[6] What he meant was that just as the Cuban revolution of 1959 produced psychological mobilisation effects on the Cuban people, the Mexican Revolution begun in 1910 had the same effects on the Mexican people. In other words, according to Germani, populism could arise without any context of migration provided that a similar psychological mobilisation was present and the mass was not satisfactorily integrated. He wrote that "these national popular movements (populist movements or populism) appeared and continue to appear punctually in all of the Latin American countries, to the extent that the level of mobilisation *exceeds* the capacity of the integration mechanism".[7]

However, this interpretation was criticised in Argentina during the 1970s and the 1980s, by both Argentine and non-Argentine scholars. According to one review essay on Peronism by Mariano Plotkin,[8] the criticism was initiated by a book written in 1971 by the Argentine sociologists, Miguel Murmis and Juan Carlos Portantiero.[9] They argued that during its formative phase in 1943–6, Peronism was supported not only by new migrant workers but also by a lot of existing urban workers, who played a very important role in leading the rank and file of the working class to support Perón in this crucial period. In other words, labour support for Perón came not only from migrant workers but from all segments of the working class. Murmis and Portantiero explained this widespread support by arguing that the working class as a whole had been suffering from the depression, from high unemployment, and from political repression under conservative rule since the military coup of 1930. As I pointed out, the 1930s saw the development of import substitution industrialisation which expanded demand for labour in Argentina. But the conservative governments did not pay much attention to working people, and did not have any policies for distributing income. This kind of industrialisation without distribution increased labour discontent. As not only migrants but also other workers faced the same situation, they naturally welcomed Perón's pro-labour policies and supported Perón, not because they were manipulated but because they perceived their support as "the most appropriate election".[10] This interpretation is clearly quite different from that of Germani, as it rejects the idea of manipulation and denies the irrationality of mass support. Germani's thesis can be called an approach "from above", because he stresses manipulation and initiatives taken by the government, while Murmis and Portantiero's thesis is an approach "from below", because they stress the role of autonomous participation by the working class in the formation of Peronism — not as an object for manipulation but as an autonomous subject.

As the interpretation of Murmis and Portantiero was the most severe criticism of his theory, Germani counterattacked, leading to a very hot debate on the origins of Peronism.[11] Although the controversy continues until now, the Murmis and Portantiero thesis gradually became so predominant that an American historian on Peronism stated in a book published in 1990 that, "in the past two decades the migration hypothesis has been discredited".[12] Torcuato Di Tella, who has constantly supported Germani, had to recognise in his book published in 2003 that the revisionist interpretation initiated by Murmis and Portantiero had become a new orthodoxy, though a mistaken one.[13]

There are at least two reasons for this change of position. One was that the participation of old workers in the formative period of Peronism was an undisputed fact, although some workers undoubtedly also opposed Peron. The other reason was the transformation of Peronism itself. After it was overthrown by the armed forces in 1955, Peronism became a popular and autonomous movement of the working class. The approach "from below" explained very well Peronism as it existed in the 1970s. Besides, this interpretation influenced scholars of populism in other countries who also placed more emphasis on the rationality of the followers of populism rather than on manipulation "from above". In his review essay published in 1982, Paul Drake noted that a political culture characterised by patron-client relationships could be explained in terms of the preferences of the clients based on "quite objective working-class calculations of their viable political alternatives, regardless of cultural traditions".[14]

Controversies regarding Peronism were not limited to the topic of labour participation, but the question whether labour participation was autonomous or manipulated was one of the most important issues. It also has a direct bearing on the interpretation of neopopulism.

Neopopulism and Its Theoretical Implications

Neopopulism here denotes a kind of populism accompanied by neoliberal economic policies. This variant of populism appeared in Latin America around the end of the 1980s, represented by three presidents who curiously had the same name of Carlos: Carlos Salinas of Mexico (who took power in 1988), Carlos Andrés Pérez of Venezuela (1989), and Carlos Saúl Menem of Argentina (also 1989). They shared not only a name but also a political background in the sense that all of them were elected to the presidency backed by a populist party — Salinas by Partido Institucional Revolucionario (PRI), Pérez by Acción Demócrata (AD), and Menem by Partido Justicialista (PJ). In 1990, two persons were added to the list of neopopulist presidents, Fernando Collor de Mello of Brazil, and Alberto Fujimori of Peru. Both of them lacked experience in party politics and owed their election chiefly to the fact that they were political outsiders and took advantage of that fact to appeal to people who were dissatisfied with party politics.

There were thus two kinds of neopopulism, one based upon a previous party structure, and the other without any party structure. These can be defined as party-based neopopulism and non-party neopopulism. This distinction is very important to understanding the emergence of each. The party-based variant arose as a consequence of an old party's failure to cope with economic difficulties, creating an opening for a new leader with a new party strategy. This kind of neopopulism depended greatly on prior party organisation and did not involve any rejection of party politics as such. The non-party variant, by contrast, was motivated and inspired by popular discontent with party politics, and involved to some extent a rejection of party politics. Some scholars such as Steven Levitsky believe that the term neopopulism should be applied only to the non-party type, and insist that Menem should not be considered as a neopopulist president, because he was supported by a powerful political party.[15]

All the five above-mentioned presidents faced serious problems of fiscal deficits, inherited from previous governments. They had to abstain from any excessive spending, and adopt a low-cost form of populism. Within this constraint, they tried to raise popular support through diverse measures which were to some extent similar to classical populism. In other words, neopopulism was a mixture of similarities and differences with classical populism. The similarities were: direct appeal to the people; stance against the *status quo*; and multi-class support base. The differences were: stress on social efficiency through the market; in favour of small state and privatisation; in favour of international cooperation instead of nationalism.

Some analysts who stress the differences have argued that these movements do not qualify as populism, while others (including myself) believe the similarities cannot be denied. In addition there are clear organisational continuities in the case of the party-based neopopulisms. Moreover, by including them within the general framework, we can apply the general framework of interpretation developed for classical populism, as I shall essay now.

As in the case of classical populism, there is an issue of whether these movements were autonomous or manipulated. First, because of the financial and economic restraints which neopopulist governments faced, they could not run financial deficits to finance free-spending redistributive policies. Therefore, they had to utilise other means to gain and maintain popularity. In reality, neopopulist presidents tended to use mass media and public performance. Menem once played football with the world-wide famous soccer player, Diego Maradona. Fujimori sometimes wore a poncho (traditional

Indian sweater) to identify himself with the Indian poor. Second, labour received very few benefits from the neopopulist regimes because of the economic restraint, and hence it is difficult to argue, as was the case with Peronism, that labour supported the movement for economically rational reasons. This does not mean that neopopulism gave no benefits to its supporters. Kurt Weyland, one of the pioneering scholar on neopopulism, pointed out that there were at least three "unexpected affinities" between neopopulism and neoliberalism. First, the sources of societal support were shared, because neopopulism tried to appeal to the poor in the informal sector, bypassing the organised groups in civil society that neoliberalism wanted to destroy. Second, neopopulism and neoliberalism shared political strategies in the sense that both relied on a strongly top-down approach, strengthening the apex of the state in order to effect profound economic reform. Third, both had similarities in their distribution of costs and benefits. Neoliberalism imposed high costs on organised groups and gave benefits to the poorest people by ending inflation, while neopopulism concentrated its benefits on the poorest people.[16] Labour and the mass also received many small-scale benefits that Kenneth M. Roberts, another pioneering analyst, described as "populism at the microlevel".[17] Yet these benefits were indeed small. Under these neopopulist regimes, the benefits which the mass or labour received were not so great as to provoke an autonomous mass movement of support from below. For this reason, some scholars on neopopulism tend to stress its manipulative character. Is there any relation between the interpretations that stress the manipulative character of neopopulism and that of Germani on classical populism?

We can see Germani's theoretical influence on Weyland's work when he points out the importance of "mass mobilization" and a "primary reservoir of people who are nowadays *available for populist mobilization*".[18] But there are also noticeable differences in several aspects. For example, Weyland stresses the importance of the political strategy of populist leaders whereas Germani tended to focus on the social conditions of the mass of followers. Accordingly Weyland defines populism in the following way: "populism is a political strategy through which a personalistic leader seeks or exercises government power based on direct, unmediated, uninstitutionalized support from large numbers of mostly unorganized followers".[19]

Another important difference can be seen in Weyland's use of prospect theory, elaborated by Daniel Kahneman and Amos Tversky in the 1970s. Like Germani, Weyland makes use of psychological theory, but whereas Germani applied socio-psychology, Weyland makes use of later developments

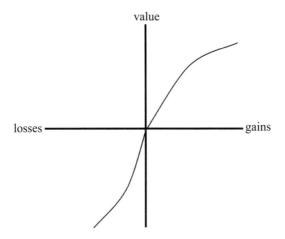

Figure 2-1 A Value Function from Prospect Theory

in cognitive psychology. A full explanation of prospect theory is beyond the scope of this article, but it can be summarised briefly in the following way.

The theory stresses differences in human attitude between when a person is in the domain of gain and when he is in the domain of loss (see Figure 11-1).[20] If people are in the domain of gain, they tend to act on the principle of decreasing marginal utility and therefore tend to adopt risk aversion. On the other hand, if people are in the domain of loss, they are risk-acceptant in the hope of recovering the loss as soon as possible. Weyland applies this theory to neopopulism, especially to explain why neoliberal economic policies were chosen in spite of the high risk that they implied. He argues that risky neoliberal policies were chosen by neopopulist leaders and were accepted by the people because both the leaders and the people were in the domain of loss as a consequence of repeated failures of economic policies, prolonged economic disasters such as hyperinflation, and so on.[21] Although his interpretation remains a hypothesis, Weyland succeeded in theoretically advancing not only studies on neopopulism but also those on classical populism, because according to him, his "political definition of [neopopulism] encompasses both the classical populists of the 1930s through 1950s and the neopopulists of the 1980s and 1990s".[22]

In Kenneth Roberts' works on neopopulism, we can see some influences of Germani, in the sense that Roberts explains the birth of classical populism in the 1930s in terms of industrialisation, urbanisation, and the appearance of "a new urban sector disposed to political mobilization".[23] He also accepts the importance of manipulation in neopopulism as well as in classical populism. But he departs greatly from Germani, because he does not think that the presence of an available mass or a time-lag between mobilisation and integration is a precondition for the birth of populism. Indeed, Roberts argues that "populism should be decoupled from any specific phase or model of economic development".[24] Instead, he stresses the importance of institutional weakness as a principal cause of populism; that is to say, when institutional weakness is evident, a leader can attract the people with simple slogans opposing the oligarchy or the political class.[25] Political outsiders such as Fujimori used this strategy to gain popular support. As institutional weakness occurs frequently in Latin America, he thinks that populism is "a recurrent feature" of this region's politics.[26] Although he recognises that populist leaders use political manipulation and does not deny its psychological effects, Roberts insists that popular support for populist leaders is based upon concrete benefits even under neopopulist rule. To prove this, he points out several strategies which made neopopulism compatible with neoliberalism in Fujimori's regime. One was the microlevel populism mentioned above, a kind of classical populism on a very limited scale with respect to the number of targeted sectors and the quantity of assistance. In other words, it was a selective assistance programme. As Roberts says, "leaders may seek to establish a material foundation for populism at the microlevel even where macrolevel policies are apparently exclusive or antipopular".[27] Another strategy was the personalistic use of funds gained through privatisation for purely political purposes. Steven Levitsky also points to such microlevel populism in the case of Menem, calling it "micro-Peronism".[28] Clearly this microlevel populism is an important component of neopopulism. However, if micropopulism is a necessary condition for neopopulism, it shows its weakness compared with classical populism, because micropopulism is only a kind of classical populism limited in scale.

There are several other studies on neopopulism. For example, Philip Oxhorn thinks that populism is a mode of interest intermediation and agrees with Roberts that it is recurrent. However, as a neo-Marxist Oxhorn stresses the importance of class relations in Latin America, especially their heterogeneous character as a result of the predominance of the informal sector within the working class. The lack of an autonomous identity of the lower class can be exploited by populist leaders who use vague claims to attract the people, but in reality for "their own positions".[29]

Another weakness of labour in the face of a neopopulist leader results from the declining political power of organised labour.[30] Neopopulist leaders tended to seek mainly the support of non-organised, informal, or marginal masses.[31] Organised labour had been weakened by economic crises, and by the neoliberal policies introduced to combat those crises. As Oxhorn says,

> An immediate consequence of the economic crisis and predominant policy responses to it has been the weakening of state corporatist institutions, particularly organized labor. With the passing of the old development model and the introduction of a new neoliberal development model, the centrality of organized labor as a political actor in Latin American politics has been undermined. While it is still an important actor, it frequently remains a passive one in the face of economic policies and trends that further weaken labor's collective strength and well-being.[32]

In sum, neopopulism was a political response to the economic crises of the 1980s and the resulting new social and political situation in which popular confidence in politics was greatly eroded and organised labour, a key factor in classical populism, had lost its power. Neopopulist leaders exploited this situation by targeting their appeal for popular support at informal sectors through the use of various forms of performance. The study of neopopulism has tended to concentrate on approaches "from above"; does that mean that views "from below", similar to those that illuminated Peronism, are irrelevant?

An Argentine political scientist, María Victoria Murrillo, analysed the dilemma faced by labour leaders when their populist parties (AD of Venezuela, PJ of Argentina, PRI of Mexico) adopted neoliberal economic policies, which were so unpopular that they threatened their own positions within the labour movement or within their own union. If they remained loyal to the party, they risked losing leadership within the labour movement especially when there was a rival party or a rival labour leader that opposed neoliberal policies. In Venezuela, the labour movement's opposition to AD-led neoliberal policy was so powerful that President Andrés Pérez resigned in 1993, one year before the end of his term. This example suggests that, although labour's political role had diminished, as Oxhorn points out, labour was still a factor in the success or failure of neoliberal policies.[33]

I also analysed the conflictual relations between government and labour over labour flexibility policies during the first Menem government (1989–95), showing that labour could prevent government enacting anti-labour laws in spite of the government's manipulative strategies against labour.[34] Although organised labour plays a "passive role" in present-day Latin America, as Oxhorn says, a neopopulist government cannot ignore its remaining influence. Hence while its importance has clearly declined since the era of classical populism, labour cannot be wholly excluded from the analysis.

In summary, the emergence of neopopulism brought several theoretical innovations in the interpretation of Latin American populism. Studies on neopopulism have drawn attention to the recurrent character of populism. This is a great contribution because it challenges the old studies which positioned "classical" Latin American populism as the product of a specific era with very special socio-economic conditions. The emergence of neopopulism freed scholars from interpretations that stressed factors like migration and the process of import substitution which had accelerated migration. Both sides in the debate over Peronism had argued that Peronism was a function of the special conditions of the period. Germani stressed migration while Murmis and Portantiero stressed the deteriorated conditions of labour in general. The new approach posits that populism can occur in any place and at any time. This new understanding makes possible a comparative study of several kinds of populism, for example between neopopulism and classical populism in Latin American populism, and between populist regimes in different regions of the world. In this regard, I applied prospect theory to clarify the established workers' support for Perón, especially in regard to the incident of 17 October 1945, when Perón was freed as a consequence of workers' mobilisation against his detention by the armed forces.[35] According to prospect theory, the workers were prepared to undertake such a bold action because they were in the domain of loss after Perón's removal. Murmis and Portantiero emphasise only the rationality of the old workers' support for Perón, but prospect theory allows us to explain the psychological aspect of the workers' action, something which had been ignored in earlier work (including my own).[36] The theoretical advances made in the study of neopopulism can also enrich our knowledge of classical populism. In this sense, the emergence of neopopulism opened a new horizon for further research on populism.

The Decline of Neopopulism

Yet neopopulism, both of the party-based and non-party variants, turned out to be short-lived. Levitsky explains the failure of party-based neopopulism in the following way.[37] The AD party in Venezuela, which had relatively strong inner party discipline, did not allow its leader to adopt neoliberal policies which ran clearly contrary to the party's principles. As a result, Pérez had to resign one year early. In Argentina, by contrast, the PJ party lacked inner party discipline, allowing Menem to continue neoliberal policies such as privatisation and pro-U.S. diplomacy even though they contradicted the three-part traditional *peronista* slogans of social justice, economic freedom, and political sovereignty. However, Menem's policies gradually increased social and political discontent until he was defeated in the presidential elections of 2003 by Néstor Kirchner, a rival within the same party who clung closer to the traditional party line. The fate of the PRI in Mexico was similar. As its party's structure was loose, Carlos Salinas and Ernesto Zedillo were able to pursue more or less neoliberal policies without receiving strong opposition within the party. However, at the presidential elections of 2000, the PRI was defeated for the first time since its creation in 1929. Yet Levitsky argues that the anti-PRI vote in the elections of 2000 reflected opposition to authoritarian rule rather than opposition to the government's economic programme.[38]

In the case of non-party neopopulism, both Collor de Mello in Brazil and Fujimori in Peru were brought down by scandal. Though De Mello ruled less than three years, Fujimori's government continued more than ten years, yet only six months after his third election, he was deposed by the Congress in November 2000 chiefly because of his close relationship with the corrupt leader of the Armed Forces. His own party also lost seats drastically in the national elections held in 2001 and 2006, although it continued as a minority party in the Congress. It can be said that neopopulism was defeated by *votos* (votes in Spanish), while classical populism was usually defeated by *botas* (boots; in Spanish, b and v sound the same).

However, the defeat of neopopulism did not mean the end of populism. In several countries, we see a resurgence of something that resembles classical populism. In particular, the populism of Hugo Chávez, who assumed the presidency of Venezuela in 1999, reminds us of Perón's nationalistic populism.[39] Besides, his influence is spreading over some Latin American countries, and especially their governments. For example, Evo Morales who took power in Bolivia in 2006, Daniel Ortega who returned to the presidency of Nicaragua in 2007, Rafael Correa who rose to power in Ecuador in 2007, and Fernando Lugo who assumed power in Paraguay in 2008, are all influenced greatly by Chávez thought to differing degrees.

It is evident that we are now facing a fourth period characterised by a kind of populism similar to classical populism. How can we understand its emergence in the first decade of the twenty-first century? In the next section, we make a brief sketch of populism in recent Latin America focusing on two perspectives, namely from above and from below.

A Return to Classical Populism?

In present-day (early 2009) Latin America, there are several regimes which can be considered as populist besides those listed above. For example, the

government of Cristina Fernández de Kirchner in Argentina (2007–) is
similar to that of Chávez with respect to some domestic policies. At the
same time, there are two other presidents who come from more traditional
populist parties: Allan García (2006–) at the head of APRA (Alianza Popular
Revolucionaria Americana) in Peru; and Oscar Arías (2006–) at the head
of the Frente de la Liberación Nacional in Costa Rica. But their policies
are considered rather conservative. Therefore, it is difficult to generalise
about these populist regimes. The reasons for their emergence are not the
same. But those that resemble classical populism seem to have emerged as
a reaction against the neoliberalism of the 1990s. In this sense, they are a
distinct change from the neoliberal neopopulists of the prior phase, though
there is no agreement among scholars on how they should characterised.
Levitsky, for example, includes Chávez among neopopulist presidents such
as Fujimori and Collor, because his populism does not basically depend on
a party.[40] But I feel that Chávez's policies on nationalisation, his abundant
patronage to his followers, and his redistributive measures are so similar to
the strategies of classical populism that he should be considered a classical
populist. However, his methods of appealing to people through television,
and his heavy use of mass media to make propaganda for his policies, are
very similar to neopopulism. In effect, he has combined the methods of
the classical populism (real concrete benefits to followers) with some of
the manipulative strategy of neopopulism (low-cost performance). In my
opinion, here is one important reason why his regime is more robust than
many other regimes of classical populism and neopopulism. Of course, as
the failure of neopopulism demonstrated, the methods of classical populism
are more effective in winning popular support. Other regimes in the orbit of
Chávez, such as Morales, Correa, Ortega, Lugo, and the more independent
regime of Cristina Kirchner, tend to imitate that aspect of his populism to
some extent. How can we explain the resurgence of populism similar to
classical populism?

To answer this question, we must again subdivide these regimes into
party-based populism (PJ of Argentina and the Frente Sandinista de Liberación
Nacional of Nicaragua), and non-party populism with relatively weak party
structures (Chávez, Morales, Correa, and Lugo).

In Argentina, Néstor Kirchner defeated the neopopulist Menem to take
control of the PJ party. One important factor in Kirchner's rise and victory
at elections in 2003, and the victory of his wife, Cristina in 2007, was the
support of one section of the Confereración General del Trabajo, the most
powerful labour union, as well as of some marginal groups such as the *piqueteros*

(the unemployed who protest by closing streets and bridges). Even though organised labour has been in decline, this perspective "from below" helps to explain the party-based variant of resurgent classical populism. The return of Ortega to power after a 17-year interval can be explained in the same light. His party has a certain electoral base in society consolidated through the Sandinista revolution of 1979. In addition, the failures of the previous governments in economic policy, and the financial assistance promised in Ortega's 2006 electoral campaign, contributed to Ortega's victory.

By contrast, the non-party variant seems best explained "from above". The rise of Chávez was similar to that of Fujimori in the sense that he appealed to popular dissatisfaction with politics by focusing his attack against the political classes, especially the two traditional two parties (AD and the Comité de Organización Política Independiente, basically Christian Democrats), blaming them for causing economic and social disaster. But while Fujimori did not pay much attention to grassroots organisation, Chávez in power succeeded in organising his mass following as a political and social base for his rule. In 2000, he organised the Bolivarian Circles which have played an important role in promoting Chávez's health, education, and other social programmes. According to the government, "by 2003, 2.2 million Venezuelans were registered in some 200,000 circles".[41] But this organisation has worked precisely because Chávez has given more benefits to the people in the style of classical populism, unlike Fujimori.

The importance of this grassroots organisation was demonstrated in April 2002 when Chávez was removed by a military coup. According to Roberts, the Bolivarian Circles "played an important role in mobilising the urban poor to protest the detention of Chávez".[42] The episode resembled Perón's release from detention by mass action in October 1945. Possibly, as in the 1945 incident, the detention of the leader put his followers in the domain of loss according to prospect theory, and triggered a furious mobilisation. Possibly too, the people's victory in this case, as with Perón, helped to create a strong psychological link between leader and followers. Possibly too, just as Peronism became more robust after the October 1945 incident, Chávez's position was consolidated after the April 2002 incident. Besides the material relationship between leader and followers based on concrete benefits, there is also an emotional or sentimental identity.[43]

Besides the grassroots organisation, Chávez is trying to establish his own solid party organisation since his electoral victory in December 1998, when he won as a candidate of an electoral front called the Movimiento Quinta República. After his re-election in December 2006, Chávez recognised the need for his own party. In March 2008, he created the Partido Socialista Unido de Venezuela with anti-imperialist and anti-capitalist slogans.[44] Although it is not yet clear what kind of role this party is expected to play in the near future, the name of the party and its anti-capitalist slogans seem to indicate that he wants to inspire socialism among his followers to create an ideologically solid party.

With the exception of Venezuela, the other populist governments with weak party-base obviously cannot be explained by the perspective "from above". Yet one important reason why Morales and Correa were elected was that they had received strong support from civil society, especially social organisations working for indigenous people.[45] This feature is a new aspect of this new type of populism similar to classical populism. However, for this kind of populism to survive, there must be some grassroots organisation and some emotional linkage between leader and followers. In Bolivia, Morales has the advantage of being the first president of Indian origin in his country, and thus has some sentimental linkage with the ethnic movement to sustain his fragile government, but will also need stronger grassroots organisation to survive for long. The demise of manipulative neopopulism shows the importance of popular support from below.

Although several current regimes in Latin America are similar to classical populism, they do not uphold the same doctrines as their predecessors more than half a century ago. They adopt some of the doctrines but also need to adjust to the present world situation. For example, the Argentine governments of Néstor and Cristina Kirchner departed from Menem's pro-U.S. diplomacy and returned to a more independent stance towards the United States, yet they cannot be as aggressively independent as Perón was. I cannot agree with Jorge Castañeda who argues that in today's Latin America, populism "perseveres in its cult of the past", unlike the old left parties that have adjusted to current realities.[46] At the same time it is worth mentioning that some populist regimes similar to classical populism want to advance on social reform, inspired by Chávez who advocates a "socialism of the 21st century". The Bolivian and Ecuadorian governments have spoken of socialism, though without clarifying what they mean in practice.[47] In the past, no classical populist regime defined its goal as socialism. This resurgent classical populism has a high possibility to realise many social reforms that the past classical populism neglected. Some progress has been made in Venezuela and Bolivia to improve the conditions and rights of the indigenous peoples. What kind of reforms these regimes achieve will affect how they are interpreted within the framework of Latin American populism. As Latin American populism is not dead, work of interpretation lives on.

Concluding Remarks

Latin America is a treasure-house of populism of many kinds. This chapter has covered only a small part, and made only a brief review of the evolution of Latin American populism and the theoretical insights gleaned from its study. Yet within that constraint it should be clear that there is an interplay between the evolution of populism and changes in theorising about it. This interplay is largely a product of the politicisation of the academic world. The interpretation of populism is highly influenced by the current political situation. Even so, the insights gained from the early controversy over Peronism provide a useful perspective for analysing Latin American populism through its various phases. The early analysis of Peronism took a perspective "from above" and stressed its manipulative character. This argument was later replaced by a perspective "from below", stressing the real benefits that Peronism offered to its supporters. This change in interpretation also reflected a real change in Peronism which acquired its autonomous and popular character after Perón's fall in 1955. The rise of neopopulism seemed to be a return to the perspective "from above", though not completely. As the tenure of neopopulism was rather short-lived, in recent years, the perspective "from below" has regained ground along with the resurgence of classical populism with an emphasis on concrete economic and social policies. Yet the perspective "from above" should not be ignored, especially with respect to those movements that have weak or non-existent party organisation, such as the early phase of Chávez's rather unique regime. To analyse populism we need to look at both the perspective "from above" and "from below", which vary in emphasis from time to time, and from regime to regime.

The controversy over neopopulism destroyed the once influential idea that populism was a product of the special conditions of the 1930s and 1940s. Now it is readily accepted that populism of many kinds can appear regardless of time and place. Comparative study of populisms is thus possible. Comparison of classical populism and neopopulism yields important insights. Mobilising prospect theory to look anew at Peronism was illuminating. Comparing Latin American and Asian experiences of populism will further broaden the research field. And I hope that the two perspectives "from above" and "from below" will be useful in such an attempt.

Notes

[1] Nicolás Lynch, "Neopopulismo: un concepto vacío", *Socialismo y Participación* 86 (Dec. 1999): 63, 67, 71.

[2] Michael L. Conniff, *Latin American Populism in Comparative Perspective* (Albuquerque: University of New Mexico Press, 1982), p. ix.

[3] For example, Roberto Fellari, "Los neopopulismos latinoamericanos como reivindicación de la política", *Cuadernos Americanos* 126 (2008): 11–27. While we define neopopulism as a kind of populism that adopts neoliberal policies, Fellari uses the term for a kind of populism that opposes neoliberalism and is a continuity of so-called classical populism.

[4] Torcuato Di Tella, "Populism and Reform in Latin America", in *Obstacles to Change in Latin America*, ed. Claudio Veliz (Oxford: Oxford University Press, 1965), p. 47.

[5] Gino Germani, *Sociedad y política en una época de transición: De la sociedad tradicional a la sociedad de masa* (Buenos Aires: Editorial Paidós, 1966); "Hacia una teoría del fascismo. Las interpretaciones cambiantes del totalitalismo", *Revista Mexicana de Sociología* 30, 1 (Jan.–March 1968).

[6] Gino Germani, "Democracia representativa y clases populares", in *Populismo y contradicciones de clase en Latinoamérica*, ed. Gino Germani, Torcuato S. di Tella, and Octavio Ianni (Edicciones Era, Mexico, 1973), p. 31.

[7] Germani, "Democracia representativa y clases populares", p. 30, italics in original.

[8] Mariano Plotkin, "The Changing Perceptions of Peronism: A Review Essay", in *Peronism and Argentina*, ed. James P. Brennan (Wilmington, Delaware: Scholarly Resources Books, 1998).

[9] Miguel Murmis and Juan Carlos Portantiero, *Estudios sobre los orígenes del Peronismo* (Buenos Aires: Siglo Veinteuno Argentina Editores, 1971).

[10] Murmis and Portantiero, *Estudios sobre los orígenes del Peronismo*, p. 124.

[11] Gino Germani, "El surgimiento del Peronismo: el rol de los obreros y los migrantes internos", *Desarrollo Económico* 13, 51 (Oct.–Dec.1973). The author of this article participated in the debate with my book, *El Movimiento Obrero Argentino 1930–1945: Sus proyecciones en los orígenes del Peronismo* (Buenos Aires: Siglo Veinte, 1983).

[12] Joel Horowitz, *Argentine Unions, the State and the Rise of Perón, 1930–1945* (Berkeley: University of California Press, 1990), p. 3.

[13] Torcuato Di Tella, *Perón y los Sindicatos, El inicio de una relación conflictiva* (Buenos Aires: Grupo Editorial Planeta, 2003), p. 11.

[14] Paul Drake, "Populism in South America", *Latin American Research Review* 42, 1 (1982): 192.

[15] Steven Levitsky, *Transforming Labor-Based Parties in Latin America: Argentine Peronism in Comparative Perspective* (Cambridge: Cambridge University Press, 2003), p. 227.

[16] Kurt Weyland, "Neopopulism and Neoliberalism in Latin America: Unexpected Affinities", *Studies in Comparative International Development* 31, 3 (Fall 1996): 10.

[17] Kenneth M. Roberts, "Neoliberalism and the Transformation of Populism in Latin America: The Peruvian Case", *World Politics* 48, 1 (Oct. 1995): 112.

[18] Weyland, "Neopopulism and Neoliberalism", p. 10, emphasis added.

19 Kurt Weyland, *The Politics of Market Reform in Fragile Democracies: Argentina, Brazil, Peru, and Venezuela* (Princeton: Princeton University Press, 2002), p. 63.

20 Cited in Weyland, *Politics of Market Reform*, p. 40.

21 Weyland, *Politics of Market Reform*, pp. 37–48.

22 Ibid., p. 63.

23 Roberts, "Neoliberalism and the Transformation", p. 113.

24 Ibid., p. 112.

25 Ibid., pp. 97–8.

26 Ibid., p. 112.

27 Ibid., p. 91.

28 Levitsky, *Transforming Labor-Based Parties*, p. 202.

29 Philip D. Oxhorn, "The Social Foundations of Latin America's Recurrent Populism: Problems of Popular Sector Class Formation and Collective Action", *Journal of Historical Sociology* 11, 2 (June 1998): 235.

30 Philip D. Oxhorn, "Is the Century of Corporatism Over?", in *What Kind of Democracy? What Kind of Market?*, ed. Philip D. Oxhorn and Graciela Ducatenzeiler (University Park, Pennsylvania: Pennsylvania State University Press, 1998).

31 Weyland, "Neopopulism and Neoliberalism", p. 10; Roberts, "Neoliberalism and the Transformation", p. 97.

32 Oxhorn, "Is the Century of Corporatism Over?", pp. 199–200.

33 María Victoria Murrillo, "From Populism to Neoliberalism: Labor Unions and Market Reforms in Latin America", *World Politics* 52, 2 (Jan. 2000).

34 Hiroshi Matsushita, "Un análisis de las reformas obreras en la primera presidencia de Menem: la perspectiva de opción estratégica", in *El Sindicalismo en Tiempos de Menem*, ed. Santiago Senén González and Fabián Bosoer (Buenos Aires: Editorial Corregidor, 1999).

35 Matsushita, "Un análisis de las reformas obreras".

36 Germani, "El surgimiento del Peronismo".

37 Levitsky, *Transforming Labor-Based Parties*, ch. 9.

38 Ibid., p. 243.

39 Some similarities have been pointed out by scholars, for example: Nelly Aenas, "El gobierno de Hugo Chávez, populismo de otrora y de ahora", *Nueva Sociedad* 200 (Nov.–Dec. 2005): 39–42. Chávez himself denied Perón's influence on his policies in an interview with an Argentine writer; see Mempo Giardenelli, "Me siento distante de Juan Perón", *Socialismo y participación* 86 (Dec. 1999): 168–73.

40 Levitsky, *Transforming Labor-Based Parties*, p. 227n16.

41 Kenneth M. Roberts, "Populism, Political Conflict, and Grass-Roots Organizations In Latin America", *Comparative Politics* 38, 2 (Jan. 2006): 142–3.

42 Roberts, "Populism, Political Conflict, and Grass-Roots Organizations", p. 142.

43 Fernando Coronil, "Estado y nación contra el golpe contra Hugo Chávez", *Anuario de Estudios Americanos* 62, 1 (Jan.–June 2005): 105.

44   Luis Bilbao, "Puntal para la revolución latinoamericana", *Crítica de nuestro tiempo* 42, 37 (2008): 3–4.

45   I refrain from trying to analyse Lugo's rise owing to a lack of information about Paraguay.

46   Jorge G. Castañeda, "Latin America's Left Turn", *Foreign Affairs* 85 (2006): 34–5.

47   Fellari, "Los neopopulismos latinoamericanos", p. 11.

PART I

Populism in Southeast Asia

CHAPTER 3

Estrada and the Populist Temptation in the Philippines

Joel Rocamora

Is "populist" a four letter word? It would seem so the way it is used in media and academic discourse. It is indiscriminately attached to political leaders whom the writer disapproves of. Anyone who is "popular" soon becomes "populist". It has become a pejorative term for attacking politicians whose politics you don't like. More often than not, anyone who espouses progressive politics is labelled "populist". Calling any politician who criticises liberal democracy and advocates nationalist and redistributive politics "populist" mobilises the term for the ideological goals of those who oppose nationalist and redistributive politics.

Used properly, however, it can be mobilised to signify a particular set of relations between political leaders and their followers, and as a response to the prevailing political economy. There is general agreement in the literature differentiating between "classical populism" and "neoliberal populism" (see Chapter 2). Mainly applied to Latin American regimes in the 1950s, the term "classical populism" refers to the organisation of unions and social movements into political parties to support regimes which, in Kenneth Roberts' description, "expanded the role of the state by subsidising and protecting basic industries, restricting foreign investment, regulating labour markets and providing a broad range of social benefits".[1]

The characteristic import substitution industrialisation (ISI) policies of that period gave way to export oriented industrialisation (EOI) policies by the 1970s and neoliberal policies a decade later. Neoliberal populism was a response to accelerating impoverishment and political alienation of large segments of the population, especially in urban areas, under neoliberal policy regimes. This was qualitatively different from classical populism in that the mobilisation of people was not mediated through unions, social movements, and political parties. As Roberts argued, neopopulist leaders relied on new communications technologies and personalistic appeal. [2] Neoliberal populism contributed to the demobilising effect of neoliberal economic policies.

What might be called the supply side of classical and neoliberal populism are leaders with the organisational and communicative skills required. Not all leaders during those periods can be considered populists. The demand side are specific social and political conditions generated by the political economy of ISI and EOI. Pasuk and Baker (see Chapter 4) make a point that "Thaksin's populism was more complex than his policy offering; that it developed over time in response to social demand; that it has strong affinities with political trends elsewhere in the world owing to a common political economy.... This demand was a function of social forces created by Thailand's pattern of development in the era of outward-orientation and neoliberalism."[3]

Where populist unions, social movements, and parties were integral parts of ISI policy regimes, the decline of unions, social movements, and parties under neoliberal populism form part of the more pervasive demobilisation of the population. Neoliberal populists "mobilise" urban and rural populations around occasional elections and mass campaigns without providing more regular participation within organisations. Neoliberal economic policies marginalise large segments of the rural and urban population, creating the conditions for populism. The economic policies of neoliberal populism are limited to "poverty alleviation" and welfare provision separate from the main thrust of neoliberal economic policies.

In this chapter, I analyse the political career of President Joseph Estrada, elected president of the Philippines in May 1998 and overthrown in a "people power" mobilisation in January 2001. Estrada's career illustrates one specific form of neoliberal populism distinct from that, for example, of Thaksin in Thailand and Mahathir in Malaysia. To understand Estrada's career, it is necessary to concentrate on political culture. My main proposition is that populists succeed when they are able to bridge the discursive gulf between the Westernised elite and poor people. Populism is possible only when the elite politician finds a shared cultural frame, common ways of deriving meaning with the poor majority. There does not have to be one cultural frame, minimally there has to be compatible cultural frames.

Explaining Erap[4]

Estrada is most often referred to by his nickname "Erap". While many Filipino political leaders are often referred to by their nicknames with unfortunate results (a Supreme Court Chief Justice was known as "Dingdong"), Estrada's nickname is a perfect illustration of his political persona. Erap is a reversal of the letters in *pare*, a term used in lower class male friendships to signify a close connection. *Pare* in turn comes from *kumpare* which denotes ritual kinship. The name "Erap" is loaded with meaning. It locates Estrada in the class structure, and equally important, labels him as a macho male in a sexist culture. It communicates accessibility and being "approachable".

After a long career as a movie actor, Erap began his political career as mayor of the Metro Manila city of San Juan in 1969.[5] During the martial law years (1972–86), Erap supported the dictator Ferdinand Marcos. He made a supreme act of loyalty by saying goodbye to Marcos in 1986 as he was about to leave into exile. Despite being identified as a Marcos loyalist, Erap won election to the Senate in 1987, one of only two winning opposition candidates. He ran and won as vice president in 1992, again as an oppositionist during the Fidel Ramos administration. In 1998, he won election as president with a large majority.

Erap became nationally known for his work in the movies. Because people saw Erap primarily in terms of his movie persona, as an "action star", he did not have to work at shaping a separate "public official persona". Not much was required beyond being a "no nonsense *aksyon agad* (immediate action) hero" to become a good San Juan mayor. He did not do much as senator, nor as vice president since as head of the Presidential Anti-Crime Commission (PACC) he could act out his movie roles in practice. Philippine elections provide perfect occasions for campaigning on the basis of popularity divorced from a record of public service.

Erap's political career was unusual mainly in that he managed to get so far without the standard instruments of a Philippine political career: a political clan, legal training or equivalent education, support by key centres of power, the Church, business, and the U.S. government. His first run was for mayor of his hometown, San Juan, in 1967. He surprised everybody by becoming a good mayor, improving services and keeping his constituents happy. He lost the position 20 years later only when the Aquino government fired all local government officials during a period when Aquino had decree making powers. He sharpened his macho image by barricading himself in the mayor's office, to no avail, but with massive public support.

His campaign for election to the Senate in 1987 again burnished his image, running against all odds as a Marcos loyalist when every other politician avoided the designation like the plague. In macho culture, and of course in his movies, *walang iwanan* (don't run from a fight even when you're the underdog) is a defining value. He could not excel in a Senate whose culture required superior debating skills; his biggest enemy probably was boredom. But again he surprised everyone, and gained the support of key left intellectuals, who were later to prove useful in his run for the presidency, when he supported the Senate's refusal to extend the lease on U.S. military bases, a milestone in Philippine political history.

His victory for the vice presidency in 1992 was courtesy of an electoral system that allows a president and vice president from different parties. In a closely fought election, Ramos won the presidency with only 24 per cent of the vote. Normally the vice presidency is derided as a "spare tire", but it became a platform for a run at the presidency when Ramos made Erap head of the Presidential Anti-Crime Commission. Erap milked the role to its swashbuckling limits, going on raids and shoot-outs, always with TV coverage. When he ran for president in 1998, he was the hands-down favourite despite being an opposition candidate.

Estrada won by a landslide, garnering 40 per cent of the vote in a field of eleven candidates. The next three candidates combined polled fewer votes than Estrada alone. He won despite the endorsement of his opponents by two former presidents, and active campaigning against him by the Catholic church. His chief opponent, house speaker Jose De Venecia, was endorsed by the incumbent, and by most local political clans. Estrada won because of support from poorer voters. "The SWS[6] exit polls in May 1998 revealed that almost half of the poorest E population and 40% of the D class across different regions nationwide elected him to office. Their votes, in turn, made up 25% and 63% of the total respectively."[7]

Estrada's campaign brilliantly combined traditional sources of power with populist appeal. Patricio Abinales commented, "The coalition that formed around his presidential campaign was also much broader than that of Ramos. It brought together top Marcos cronies Eduardo Cojuangco, Jr. and Lucio Tan, alongside politicians, academics, and former radicals of the communist movement. And these extreme flanks were much more powerful now — the cronies with their still unexpropriated billions, the radicals with a depth of organising experience from the communist movement."[8] With crony money, Estrada won over key local political leaders. His radical friends organised JEEP (Joseph Ejercito Estrada for President), a network that combined local leftist organisers along with business people laying a bet on an Erap victory.

More than anything else, it was Erap's movie persona that played well in the campaign. Cynthia Bautista summed it up:

> Illusion and reality meshed in the campaign as the masses equated Estrada
> with the poor but always golden-hearted characters he portrayed throughout

his movie career — as a jeepney driver, stevedore, tricycle driver and ice-cream vendor among others. More importantly, his cinematic roles as a local Robin Hood in the movie, "*Asiong Salonga*", and as heroes of poor people's uprisings (e.g., "*Kumander Alibasbas*") made him a larger-than-life savior in the eyes of the poor.[9]

Erap took advantage of his movies in the campaign, using mobile cinema in urban and rural poor communities, showing a 45-minute documentary on his life, and one of his old movies.

Movie Power

Erap was born into an upper middle class family, his father a doctor. He grew up in a middle class district, but preferred the company of his *barkada* (tight friendship groups) from the neighbouring urban poor area. He went to Ateneo, an elite university, but failed, got kicked out, moved to an inferior university, and failed again. He went into movies which, at that time, were considered a bit disreputable. This was the material that Erap shaped into a successful political persona. With bravado and biting humour he transposed his failure to earn the credentials for the class he was born into. He transferred the life he knew among the urban poor *barkada* to the silver screen, and later to politics. Since the poor are the most numerous movie goers and voters, this was a brilliant, winning formula.

Erap's standard movie role mimicked his own life — someone from the edges of the elite who prefers the company of the poor. The hero sees some example of oppression, observes it, and then fights against it, even against his own class. Because the poor are indeed oppressed, their lives provided innumerable opportunities for movie heroism. The culture of the urban poor male *barkada* provided justification for Erap's sexual appetites and ingrained sexism. His success in movies and in politics licensed Erap's disdain for the upper middle class values he could not live by. His lower class audience, with no access to this world, nonetheless resented the upper classes, and enjoyed watching Erap poking fun at it. Erap tapped a rich vein in Philippine Roman Catholic culture, that of the intermediary between the everyday and the afterworld, between the mundane and the spiritually unreachable.

Erap's movie role as a hero, a defender of the poor and the oppressed, was only part of the image. Equally important was his image as someone exposing elite oppression and hypocrisy. In her elegant prose Sheila Coronel provides an excellent description of Erap's "unique contribution to Philippine public life". Referring to a colloquial expression used by one of Erap's friends, "*weather-weather lang yan*", essentially, "It is now our turn to feast on the public trough", Sheila says,

> It was a statement that was both refreshingly honest and horribly cynical, simultaneously subversive (because it mocks elite pretensions to a *delicadeza* they never actually practice) and sensible (because if all past presidents had appointed their friends, why shouldn't Estrada?). It sums up Erap's unique contribution to Philippine public life: he translates the prerogatives of power into the language of the streets, making them seem acceptable and normal. After all, he challenges everyone, who among the most righteous have not favored their friends? Or for that matter, who among them have not cheated on their wives?... By speaking plainly, Estrada exposes the hypocrisy of political discourse, thereby depriving his critics of the moral high ground.[10]

The ability to "tell it like it is" is perceived as a mark of authenticity by people sick of the hypocrisy of politicians. Erap has also worked at shaping a political persona consistent with his movie persona. His campaign slogan does not say *Si Erap ay mahirap* (Erap is poor) in the way that other politicians including past presidents Magsaysay and Macapagal did. Instead he says *Erap para sa mahirap* (Erap is for the poor), in the process locating himself outside of the poor. But he also does not identify himself with the rich, nor with politicians. He has shaped his role as someone negotiating for the poor among the rich and the politicians.

The subtle power of Erap's movie persona becomes clearer by comparison with another movie star who tried to transfer his movie personality into politics. Fernando Poe, Jr., FPJ to his fans, ran against Arroyo in the presidential elections of 2004. He lost but subsequent events showed that Arroyo cheated and FPJ may have won. His margin of victory, however, if indeed he actually won, was not large. If it had been, it would have been difficult for Arroyo to cheat. FPJ's campaign suffered from serious organisational problems. FPJ himself was unwilling to do the sometimes undignified antics of politicians on the campaign trail. He also reportedly refused to make the kinds of promises to politicians needed to get their support.

People equate FPJ and Erap especially because they were close personal friends. If Erap won elections because of his movie popularity, FPJ should also win. But FPJ's movie persona is radically different from that of Erap. Erap is quintessentially "human"; flawed but willing to admit his flaws and even boast about them. So it is easy for his fans to identify with him. The FPJ of his movies is the opposite. The *Aguila*, the *Panday* is "supra-human". He is a demigod, an archetype. He appears from out nowhere, and returns just as suddenly to god knows where. When he fights, he fights alone. People watch, but from hastily closed windows. I cannot imagine Erap agreeing to become a "saviour". FPJ was reportedly persuaded to run for president by politicians because they convinced him that he is the only one who could "save" the country.

What sets Erap apart from other traditional politicians who have also mastered the art of deferring to popular culture is that Erap actually lives his reel performance outside the movie house. He does not make a distinction between reel and real. Other elements of the Estrada political persona are consistent with a reel/real composition. Thus his position *in between* the poor and the rich is given "taking action" content by what some people call his "Robin Hood style of politics" — taking from the rich to give to the poor. His "tough guy on the street" stance is given expression in discourse and action. Explaining the suspension of peace talks with the Moro Islamic Liberation Front, he used a popular advertising line, *hindi beni-beybi and rebelyon, pinipisa* (you do not pamper a rebellion, you squash it). His tendency to take quick, off-the-cuff decisions, often later reversed, is consistent with the image. Tough guys don't deliberate and consult; they act.

Erap's self-presentation resonates with the poor majority because it articulates their desire to be part of a larger political community. Erap signifies a subversion of the political field that has long been confined to the politically "knowledgeable and endowed". Erap's self-presentation is tacitly a critique of elite culture: a self-made man who comes from an upper middle class family, a college drop-out from an elite university who works as a janitor, later as a movie actor (in the Philippines, not a respectable occupation until recently), and converses with elite snobs in "carabao English". This self-presentation coupled with his "unconventional" lifestyle (heavy drinking, womanising, gambling) defy the self-presentation, the conventions of the privileged few who dominate Philippine economy and politics. In Eva-Lotta Hedman's words:

> Estrada's lack of what Filipinos call *delicadeza* (discretion) and his evident enjoyment of all that polite society abhors — the *bakya* and the *baduy*, even the (*medjo*) *bastos* (the common, tacky, and (semi) vulgar) — unleashes into national political discourse the return of the repressed, whose mere presence, let alone aspirations, in everyday life is otherwise so carefully (although never seamlessly) contained through social hierarchies and geographies. In this vein, the fear of the subaltern (*masa*), previously identified with the threat of communist-led revolution, now haunts bourgeois sensibilities with the spectre of populism.[11]

Estrada's use of political symbols and its effects are intertextual. While the success of the *Erap para sa mahirap* slogan constitutes a subversion and inversion of dominant political discourse and facilitates a sense of popular participation in politics, it also personalises politics in such a way that participation becomes mainly symbolic. Citizen stakes in politics are dissolved and transferred wholesale to one person, in this case Estrada. Erap may bring the popular *medjo bastos* into political discourse, but he does not bring citizens into formal processes of political participation. In contrast to populists who mobilise people, Estrada is a demobilising populist.

Downfall

During the first year of the Estrada presidency, analyses by the Institute for Popular Democracy[12] focused on trying to understand the sources of Erap's popularity in the political culture of the lower classes, his main base of support. After a year of drift and inaction during which Erap's popularity seemed unassailable, we began to wonder what it would take for Erap to lose his popularity. What line of cultural attack would the opposition have to take? We looked for elements of popular political culture that, when disturbed, would lead to loss of popularity.

As usual, theory lagged behind reality. Estrada's popularity plunged before we could figure out how to attack it. In March 1999, Estrada's net satisfaction rating (the balance between those satisfied and dissatisfied) was a high 67 per cent. By October, it had plunged to 28 per cent.

Estrada attributed the drop to opposition to Concord (his proposal to amend the constitution), rising oil prices, and an adversarial press. Reacting with his usual macho bravado, he said he would sacrifice popularity for the "good of the country". Besides, he was confident that the drop in popularity was "temporary" and he would rebound quickly. When a Social Weather Stations survey showed that his "net satisfaction rating" had dropped further to 5 per cent,[13] Estrada realised that bravado was not enough.

Estrada made a determined effort to reverse this downward spiral in his *Ulat sa Bayan* (Report to the Nation) on 8 January 2000. He retreated on Concord, fired his "advisers", replaced them with more respectable figures, and reshuffled and reorganised his economic management team. By any measure, it was the single most important step the president had taken to respond to widespread criticism. But the impact of these moves did not last long. A series of exposés came one after the other until, by November 2000, Erap became the first Philippine president to be impeached by the House of Representatives. The Senate trial glued everyone to their TV screens until a tactical error by Estrada supporters in the Senate led to the massive mobilisation that brought Estrada down in January 2001.

Economy

What were the elements that contributed to this ignominious end for Erap? It is important to look into the economy at this time because it formed the backdrop for an epic political struggle. Erap took over the presidency barely a year after the onset of the Asian financial crisis of 1997. The crisis meant that the economic pie available for division among elite claimants was considerably less than during the Ramos period (1992–98) when the economy was growing. This was not just a matter of how much revenue the administration had to play with. With the economy heading into recession and opportunities for profit receding, the exercise of the government's other economic powers also produced less occasions for rent seeking.

The government's economic policies made things worse. The Estrada government was bent on continuing to toe the IMF line despite increasing criticism of the IMF in Asia and in the U.S. As complex as the debate on how to deal with the Asian crisis was, there were two interrelated issues. One was whether to continue to orient economic policy towards the return of foreign investors or to pay more attention to restoring economic growth. The other was whether to keep interest rates high to provide arbitrage opportunities for foreign investors, and budget deficits and inflation low to restore foreign investor confidence.

For all of its rhetoric about pushing down interest rates and raising the budget deficit limits, the Estrada administration hewed closely to the IMF austerity formula. The Concord amendments would have removed constitutional restrictions on foreign investment in key sectors of the economy. Despite this, the foreign business communities turned against Erap. Business groups led by the Makati Business Club called for Erap to resign. A series of surveys showed that anti-Estrada sentiment was almost unanimous in the business community. The IMF announcement that it would postpone the release of the last tranche of its loan added international pressure. In quick succession, the World Bank and the Asian Development Bank also postponed disbursement of already committed loans. Within a week of each other both Standard and Poor and Moodys downgraded the Philippines' credit rating to negative.

Another factor was that the regime was simply inept. The most detailed descriptions of Erap's "management style", if we can call it that, is provided by two members of his Cabinet, Karina Constantino David, chairperson of the Housing and Urban Development Coordinating Council, and Aprodicio Laquian, Erap's chief-of-staff. Both are former professors at the University of the Philippines. David wrote:

> Erap involved himself too much in micro-management and showed an impatience for policy discussions. He would get excited by projects, but not by programs. In certain moments of inspired decisiveness, he preferred to tap his reservoir of common sense, rather than to rely on serious studies. He would demand instant results, forgetting that there were processes and procedures that could not be dispensed with. Because of the president's extremely short attention span for policy issues, the weekly Cabinet meetings not only became less frequent they also degenerated into updates and reporting sessions. Members of the Cabinet could have profited from collective discussions of directions and plans.[14]

Erap's casual, macho, devil-may-care attitude towards decision-making did not survive the transition from movie action hero to Malacanang. People understood, if only instinctively, that gunning after crooks on a movie screen and running a small city government is different from leading a complex, national bureaucracy and political system. Erap showed little capacity for understanding, or even the patience to seriously learn about, the complex issues that his Cabinet had to deal with. He seldom met with the Cabinet. Worse, he tended to pit Cabinet members against one another. The resulting, highly public bickering among top administration officials pushed Erap to retreat into social circles he trusted and knew best — family and friends.

Ellen Tordesillas' description of what she called Erap's "Midnight Cabinet" is instructive:

> The meetings take place at night and last until dawn. There, views are traded, strategies prepared, and deals struck. By the time the men at the table stand up and stagger out the door, much has been accomplished that may affect the way things are done in this country.... Pres. Estrada, of course, presides over these meetings. But more often than not, those gathered around him during these caucuses are far from being Cabinet secretaries. Rather, they are his personal friends, some of them buddies of long-standing such as Ilocos Sur Rep. Luis "Chavit" Singson and Caloocan Congressman Luis "Baby" Asistio, say Malacanang insiders, are among the president's most constant late-night companions.[15]

Estrada's chief-of-staff Laquian takes the analysis further, explaining why this circle was deliberately kept out of public attention.

> The closest friends of Erap were his nocturnal drinking and joke-swapping buddies, his gambling pals, some police and military officials who had been

his battling comrades at PACC, and financial backers from the Chinoy business community. Most of these people would not have qualified for governmental posts. Many would not have been interested. Quite a few would have considered public office a grave disadvantage — they preferred to be in the shadows where they were free to carry on their questionable activities well away from the glare of media attention.[16]

Erap's friendship with a number of shady Filipino-Chinese business interests fed into still prevalent anti-Chinese sentiments. This was especially true in segments of the business class, especially those associated with the reform bourgeoisie in organisations such as the Makati Business Club. Popular culture divides the business community into "Chinoy" (Filipino Chinese) and "Kastilaloy" (Spanish-American mestizo). If the "Kastilaloy" are organised in the Makati Business Club, "Chinoy" are in the Filipino-Chinese Chamber of Commerce and Industry.

Much of this is, of course, overstated and stereotypical. What is true is that the Chinese business community has historically had to operate under discriminatory conditions imposed on a pariah community. One of its defensive responses has been for segments of the community to develop relations with politicians. While other business people do the same thing, pariah status has meant that these relations have had an element of furtiveness. What made things worst for Erap was that his predilection for casinos and nightclubs meant that several of his friends from this social world were not only gamblers but those engaged in various semi-legal and illegal business activities.

Erap made administrative changes which opened more opportunities for corruption by Malacanang Palace. Contracts for sums exceeding 50 million pesos now had to have palace approval; the contract-rich National Food Authority, Securities and Exchange Commission, and government controlled financial corporations were placed directly under Malacanang. Insiders pointed out that the influence of Erap's shady friends appeared to increase the longer he was in office. Laquian noted, "Later, ... we noticed, with increasing concern, the rising influence on the resident, of some of his opportunistic cohorts, rapacious assistants, self-promoting advisers, rent-seeking consultants, conniving cronies, and assorted sycophants who catered to the president's all-too-human frailties."[17] While corruption is endemic in Philippine politics, corruption associated with shady characters multiplied the public impact. Emmanuel De Dios noted,

> Amounts attributed to Erap were not particularly large, more striking was the sheer number and variety of dealers and fixers including ...

not only members of the immediate official family but also mistresses, bastard children, denizens of show business, gambling partners, business partners both established and obscure, not to mention the underworld. A bounty-hunting system appeared to be in place, where enfranchised deal-cutters competed over who would be first to interpose themselves between approving authorities and private contractors. The effect was something akin to a feeding frenzy, as members of this privileged swarm sought to secure niches for themselves.[18]

The disarray in the executive branch spilled over into the legislative branch. The president is so powerful in the Philippine political system that leadership and the main thrusts of the legislative process are usually determined by the president. Estrada, however, did not use this power well. More importantly, he failed to mobilise the ruling party, LAMMP, to push his legislative agenda. A year and a half into Estrada's term, LAMMP did not have a programme or even a party constitution and by-laws. As a result, Congress had little to show from a year and a half of work. The FY2000 national budget had not yet been passed in mid-January 2000.

Anti-Poverty Policies

I think Erap really wanted to do something for the poor, to give reality to his campaign slogan. You cannot consistently play a role over a whole lifetime without some of it rubbing off on you. Laquian noted,

> Erap sincerely felt for the poor but he did not seem to know how to deal with the core issues of poverty. He really had no understanding of how it was to be truly hopelessly poor. Because of this lack of understanding, he was unable to appreciate the need for a coherent program of development. He did not know enough of the complex factors linked to poverty to pursue a workable development strategy. His charisma and his pro-poor emotions were enough to attract the poor, raise their hopes, and get their votes. However, as events showed in the end, he failed to deliver the goods.[19]

Two of Erap's pro-poor initiatives illustrate Laquian's point well. Probably repeating a successful programme when he was a small city mayor, Erap set up a Presidential Action Centre to serve the poor with packages of rice and sardines in the presidential palace itself. The programme was quickly closed down when so many poor people showed up and two people were trampled and died in the crush. Another programme provided services and other interventions to the hundred poorest families, in the hundred poorest towns in the country. While the programme was easy to promote, its impact was minimal, serving only 16,000 families, roughly 96,000 individuals in a country of 76 million.

The assessment of Archie Balisacan, the country's main anti-poverty expert, is damning.

> While it [the Estrada administration] was able to reduce the proportion of the population deemed poor, the rate of reduction (less than one percentage point per year) was so slow that there are more poor now than in 1997. On an annual basis, the rate of reduction was slower than that achieved in 1985–1997, especially in 1995–1997. Among the major Asian countries, the Estrada administration's track record in terms of poverty reduction was quite pathetic.[20]

Apart from his limited policy perspectives, Erap's attitude towards the poor left much to be desired. Again Laquian captures the gap between aspiration and delivery:

> … despite his avowed love for the poor, Erap regarded what he saw as their weaknesses with disdain. During our Malacanang days, we often heard Erap complain bitterly about the Filipinos tendency to be meek, humble and uncomplaining. He saw this as being *walang beklog* (having no balls). *Ang mga Pilipino masyadong mababait at masunurin* (Filipinos are meek and very obedient). *Kaya tingnan mo, sikat na sikat tayo bilang OCW* (That is why we do so well as domestics and Overseas Contract Workers).[21]

Laquian also observed that Erap treated his subordinates, aides, secretaries, waiters, servants in a bullying and disrespectful way.[22]

Erap para sa mahirap is one of the more successful slogans in the history of Philippine elections. I've always insisted that poor people do not really expect their political leaders, including Erap, to suddenly make life better for them. They know enough history to allow themselves that dream. But when, after a year and a half, he cannot even show that he has at least tried to give real content to the slogan, people do begin to wonder. The administration's record on agrarian reform, on urban poor housing, and on anti-poverty programmes was, if anything, worse than that of Ramos who never claimed to be *para sa mahirap*.

Disenchantment

Estrada's gross mismanagement of the government exacerbated the unhappiness of the upper and middle classes. These segments of the political public were already unhappy with Erap because they disapproved of his lifestyle even before the elections. Many were willing to set aside their moral judgments in exchange for performance. Since it is difficult to live with the thought of six years of unmitigated political disaster, many people wanted to believe that things might not be as bad as they feared. They built their hopes on reformers and technocrats in the Cabinet, and on the momentum of reform.

These hopes were all too soon dashed. Reformers proved unable or unwilling to push their ideas past Erap's disinterest — his unwillingness or inability to understand often complex policy issues. Or more simply they did not drink scotch or have the stomach to hang out and wait for the few minutes of opportunity to get the president to sign documents while he and his friends were drinking and gambling. Evidence of mismanagement quickly piled up. What made things worse for Erap was that public sentiment quickly moved from judgments about his administration's performance to judgments about him.

Erap did several things that returned the basis of judgment to the moral sphere. In many cases, to Erap's frustration, he did not do anything illegal or "wrong" from an administrative vantage point. His stance towards the Marcoses and their cronies such as Danding Cojuangco was instructive. Erap did not understand that the location of the Marcos issue is in the guts and cannot be processed in conventional, rational political discourse. Because politically Erap had established a connection, no matter how undefined, with the Marcoses, public disgust over a super opulent two day birthday bash by Imelda Marcos spilled over to Erap even though he did not turn up at the parties.

Erap's casual, off-hand style of decision-making contributed to a sense that something was amiss in the moral order. Again, it was the accumulation of political impressions rather than individual issues that generated a negative image of the Estrada administration. Erap's appointment of Jose Luis Yulo to replace a respected civil society leader as housing tsar turned into a public relations disaster when it was revealed that Yulo had a pending arrest order for bounced checks. When you add to this the controversy over smuggled cars parcelled out to high administration officials, Erap's promotion of various kinds of gambling, and the government movie rating body's supposed failure to curb explicit sex scenes in local movies, then you have a president vulnerable to attack on moral grounds.

This sense of moral unease also changed people's perspectives on Erap's moral foibles. Where people used to ignore Erap's lifestyle choices or even enjoy him as a foil to elite hypocrisy, there was a growing tendency to disapprove of its more recent manifestations. When a young woman claimed that she was Erap's daughter, many were turned off by Erap's reply that maybe it was true because "many women want babies with me". People who did not find a problem with Erap's drinking in general had difficulty imagining, and approving of, Erap making major government decisions while drunk, whether in fact he did or not.

When it was reported that Erap and his family owned 17 mansions worth about two billion pesos, reaction was muted, perhaps because it was difficult to comprehend the scale. People reacted only when pictures of the most expensive of the mansions were splashed all over print and broadcast media, showing a swimming area complete with a wave-making machine, and white sand flown in from a Visayas beach. People were generally blasé about Erap's sex life, but thought it too much that bedrooms in Erap's various houses were designed to look alike so that when he woke up in the morning, Erap would not feel disoriented no matter which mistress' house he slept in.

Most attempts to explain why Erap lost popularity have focused on his performance; on his failure to give reality to his *Erap para sa mahirap* slogan; on his leadership style; on the discordance between his "Midnight Cabinet", his drinking buddies, and his real Cabinet; on corruption; and on the Concord constitutional amendments. These undoubtedly had an impact. But we have to understand other meanings of "performance" than those having to do with government organisation, policy, and policy outcomes. Erap "performs" for many audiences, with differing and often conflicting discourses, different languages (English, Tagalog, Taglish), even different media (radio vs. TV vs. newspapers).

Erap is a professional performer. He has been able to, as it were, "step out of the movie screen" and carry his hero persona into politics. His main political base, the urban and rural poor, the D and E crowd, is used to him as a performer. The middle and upper classes, the A and B crowd, have a radically different understanding of "performance" that is related to "job description", to modern "performance criteria". But these are not hermetically sealed categories; they represent poles of a continuum. Our mistake was to think that the D and E crowd does not think at all of more modern "performance criteria".

In the movies, the "suspension of disbelief" on part of the audience is key. To enjoy a movie, the audience has to believe that what is happening on the screen is "real" enough to relate to the characters and what happens to them. The actor is supposed to be aware, to know the line separating reel and real, to understand that movie "acting" is pretending. The problem with Erap was that he did not seem to know the difference between "acting" in his movies and "acting as president". Living out his movie roles was fine for getting elected, for running a small government unit such as San Juan where most things can be done on a personalised basis.

The presidency is a much bigger, more public stage. Movies are supposed to be edited, but there are limits to "editing" the president's actions, and their impact. Erap as movie actor can largely determine his performance, especially in Philippine movies where scripts are often non-existent. In the presidency, the Cabinet, the president's advisers and friends, and his family all contribute to shaping the post-movie Erap.

The movie audience sits in the dark; people cannot talk to one other. Movie viewing is an individual, not a social experience. In national politics, the president is under constant media glare, and his opponents are always looking for opportunities to expose him. Politics competes with sex as a focus of rumour.

Partly because I shared the D and E crowd's enjoyment of Erap's deliberate, derisive pricking of elite hypocrisy, I did not see that the retort of anti-Erap elite factions, a steady drumbeat of criticism, would have an effect on Erap's lower class base. I also did not see that the presidency, its very public power and Erap's way of exercising that power, would erode Erap's movie action star persona. Erap's lower class base adopted him enthusiastically to give expression to their unhappiness with their lot in life and with the elite. This was a deliberate, normative, highly personalised choice; enough to get Erap elected. But apparently it did not mean that people were incapable of changing the norms with which they make judgments.

The very public character of the presidency, made even more public by elite criticism and by the media's generally anti-Erap stance, steadily eroded one by one the elements of Erap's "culture hero" persona. It became increasingly difficult to perceive Erap as not part of the elite when his daughter had a highly publicised grand wedding to a scion of the very elite Lopez clan, and when he was *ninong* (godfather) at the weddings of the children of taipans, Lucio Tan and John Gokongwei. When the media came out with pictures of Erap's many mansions costing hundreds of millions of pesos, he began to be perceived as conspicuously, scandalously rich.

Erap's political persona as an "intermediary" depended on his being perceived as equidistant from the poor and the rich. By hobnobbing with the identifiably rich such as Danding Cojuangco, Lucio Tan, and the Lopezes, he moved closer to the other end of the class spectrum. How can poor people continue to imagine Erap as "Robin Hood" when on issues pitting the rich and the poor, whether about labour or selling land to foreigners, he invariably took the side of the rich? If anything, left groups had an easy time painting Erap as the "Sheriff of Nottingham", taking from the poor to give to the rich.

One of the apparent effects of Erap's tremendous popularity at the start of his term was that it gave him a sense of invincibility. This aura combined with macho swagger to produce a president who, at times, seemed as if he did not care about the impact of his shoot-from-the-hip statements on public opinion. Or maybe Erap thought that "invincibility" meant people could not see what he was doing, that his base in the rural and urban poor would continue to enjoy their *medjo bastos* president. What Erap did not understand is that people have a sense of the limits of the antics of the elite. *Tama na, sobra na* (enough is enough) is one of the more powerful sentiments of popular political culture.

Context

Estrada is the perfect embodiment of a neoliberal populist. Having explained the specifics of his career, it remains for us to examine the phenomenon of populism in the Philippines in general. We will do that by locating populism within the characteristic organising structures of Philippine politics as they have evolved over time. The most obvious connection is that populism is a particular variant of the personalism which pervades Philippine politics. Personalism is a continuity in Philippine political history. In several important ways, populism is a throwback to the pre-colonial political culture of local strong men.

As John Sidel notes, strong men pervade Southeast Asian political culture:

> ... local strongmen come to exercise social control by delivering key components for the "strategies of survival" of the local population. All people combine available symbols with opportunities to solve mundane needs for food, housing and the like to create their strategies for survival — blueprints for action and belief in a world that hovers on the brink of a Hobbesian state of nature. Such strategies provide not only a basis for personal survival but also a link for the individual from the realm of personal identity and self-serving action (a political economy) to the sphere of group identity and collective action (a communal moral economy).... These strategies of survival, sewn from the symbols, rewards and sanctions are the road maps used to guide one through the maze of

daily life, ensuring one's existence and, in rare instances, pointing the
way toward upward mobility.[23]

The main difference is that the contemporary populist does not deliver
the material requirements of survival. It is doubtful that the poor voted for
Estrada because they actually thought he would do something concrete for
them. Many of course did — witness the crush in Malacanang of poor people
looking for jobs. But the Philippine poor are smart enough to be cynical.
They know that very few politicians have actually done anything for them.
They love Erap not because they expect direct rewards from someone who
as president is beyond the reach of their pleas for help, but because he identifies with them. He identifies with them because he looks comfortable and
at home eating with his hands in an urban poor home. More importantly,
by flouting the social conventions of the rich, he gives expression to the
poor's resentments.

For most of the past century, the characteristic form of Filipino political
organisation is what has been described as "patron-client" relations. The
dominant description of clientelism was made by Carl Lande.

> ... the Philippine polity... is structured less by organized interest groups
> or by individuals who in politics think of themselves as members of
> categories, i.e., of distinctive social classes or occupations, than by a net-
> work of mutual aid relationships between pairs of individuals ("dyadic"
> ties, in anthropological terminology) ... these ties are vertical ones, i.e.,
> bonds between prosperous patrons and their poor and dependent clients.[24]

Analysts since Lande have pointed to the way patron-client relations
are anchored on socio-economic relations of inequality, and at times the use
of coercion to maintain relations. Both populism and clientelism reinforce
existing relations of power. The characteristic relationship is personalised.
Patrons, like populists are the only links of the poor to the political system.
Both discourage the self-organisation of the poor, and the establishment of
regularised, organised access to the government. Ana Maria Karaos explains
the differences:

> There are a number of important differences between the clientelism of
> traditional politics and the relationship between Estrada and his urban
> poor allies. The first relates to the way the leader views the existing power
> structure. Populist leaders create and maintain their populist appeal by
> challenging — at least in rhetoric if not in their actions — the existing
> power structure and typically portray themselves as the enemy of the
> elite. Estrada not only cast himself as an enemy of the rich, he even

criticized the leaders of the Catholic Church for being elitist. Populist leaders make an effort to blur the class distinction between themselves and their followers. They build their legitimacy on this identification with the masses.[25]

The traditional patron does not identify with "clients" except through a personalised relationship. In contrast to the populist who recognises the gap between the poor and the elite and gives expression to the victimisation of the poor, the patron undermines class identity by tying the "client" to a one-on-one relationship. The patron ensures the reproduction of the system by acting as an intermediary between the rich and the poor. He succeeds as patron only if he is capable of providing subsistence needs of his "clients". The neoliberal populist, as Hedman puts it, organises the simulation of patronage through spectacle.[26]

Patron-client relations gave way to political machines especially in urban areas. Where the characteristic patron-client relationship involves exchanges of "private goods" — food, cash for funerals or school — between the patron and the client individual or family, political machines give priority to organised communities that can deliver blocs of votes for which they will be rewarded with "projects". It is within this matrix that populist political relations develop. As Karaos points out, however,

> ... it must be made clear that we are not claiming the existence of a populist movement or even the emergence of some form of populist politics.... The existence of relatively autonomous, often self-organized, community organizations that in due time acquire the skills in mobilizing and engaging with government authorities provides the backbone for collective mobilizations in the populist mold. We have also seen the rise of a number of highly skilled leaders, which I have labelled as political entrepreneurs, who operate through networks built on connections with NGOs, political movements and with government representative bodies. How quickly these networks are formed and mobilized for politicians' political projects has been demonstrated by the May 1 riots in 2001.[27]

It is again Karaos who points out that,

Marxist analyses of the relationship between the growth of cities and capitalism have pointed to the rise of specific urban contradictions brought on by the dynamic of capitalist growth (Harvey, 1973; Armstrong and McGee, 1985). Similarly, neo-Marxist perspectives on urban social movements have noted heightening social conflicts in cities over control

of the means of consumption — rather than the means of production —
as an offshoot of the process of capital accumulation (Castells, 1983).
While these authors have generally made this assertion in the context
of advanced capitalist societies, the observation carries some validity
for developing countries. In Third World cities, the most intense social
conflicts have occurred over issues of land rights, housing, eviction, and
access to water and basic services — all of which are consumption issues.
Collective identities underlying social mobilization of the poor in Third
World cities have typically revolved around these issues rather than class-
based issues of jobs, labor rights and union organizing.[28]

Populist leaders like Estrada, in effect, simply ride on the basic organisations of the urban poor and on local political leaders. Djorina Velasco
argues, "These 'primary' organisations are struggling to make life in the
community more liveable through what we might call 'subsistence mobilizations'. These forms of collective action are not aimed at changing the political culture, but at fulfilling basic, material needs. 'Larger' political issues
are outside their purview."[29] Because "subsistence mobilizations" to ensure
service delivery make use of existing patronage networks but do not contest
or attempt to change the nature and conditions of these patronage relations,
they actually reinforce patronage.

Why Populism?

The reason we have come to this dangerous pass can only be understood
by going right to the heart of the Philippine political system. It is a system
built on networks of local political notables organised in ascending order
up to the national level. For most of the last century, these networks nego-
tiated control of patronage among themselves. They retained enough influence on voters to give elections a semblance of democratic reality while
retaining control over the allocation of power.

Population growth brought a rapidly expanding electorate. Urbanisation and commercialisation eroded traditional patron-client ties of deference.
The inability of corrupt and incompetent governments to do anything about
scandalous poverty undermined trust. Politicians controlled less and less of
the vote. Their political parties never developed enough to give people electoral choices. Media — action stars, news anchors, comedians and basketball
heroes — took over from politicians in guiding electoral choice.

Manila was at the centre of this phenomenon, as Hedman noted:

> ... by the 1960s the National Capital Region replaced the northern and
> southern frontiers as the principal destination of internal migration in the

Philippines. The socio-economic terrain also included both an increasing segment of urban poor and, in absolute terms, a growing urban middle class. These developments, scholars have argued, signaled an overall decline in the "integrative capacity of political machines" because of mounting costs of "particularistic rewards" and weakening client leverage due to the "specialization in clientelistic structures".[30]

Karaos tracked how this form of urbanisation nurtured populism:

> The increasing concentration of poor people and voters in cities is likely to further fuel the populist dynamic. As the urban mass vote becomes more decisive in winning national elections, we are bound to see the waning power of provincial warlords and political bosses and the increasing power of urban political machines and ward leaders. At the same time, we are likely to see politicians relying more on popularity enhancers, PR strategists, and the mainstream media to cultivate direct mass appeal. The increasing density of cities and the concentration of population in large urban centers will lead national politicians to focus more on urban constituencies.[31]

Populism is a mode of mobilisation where populist leaders mobilise unorganised and sometimes organised poor. As the example of Manila urban poor shows, populist mobilisations can be a form of interest intermediation. But these mobilisations are built on patronage relations. Because they mainly serve the interest of the populist leader, they are episodic. They do not increase the political power of the poor. They fail as a mode of political representation. Estrada's populism exacerbated the Philippines' crisis of political representation.

Populism and Democratisation

Erap was removed from the presidency in January 2001; three months later, he was in jail, accused of the non-bailable crime of plunder. For the next six and a half years, he was incarcerated, first in a special cell in a hospital, later in his own well appointed villa. He remained a political force, securing the election of both his wife and son to the Senate. The political opposition to the Arroyo regime considered him their leader. He openly financed mass mobilisations against the regime and, rumour has it, military rebels.

He was finally convicted in 2007, and soon thereafter pardoned by President Arroyo. This highly controversial pardon means that Arroyo considered the political cost of keeping him incarcerated too high. Estrada's continuing political relevance is not just because he has powerful friends such as the *Iglesia ni Kristo*, a disciplined religious sect, or that he is willing to spend his accumulated billions for political action. I am not sure I agree that he continues to control some 20 per cent of the national vote as some political analysts say. What is clear is that he still has a following, built mostly on populist appeal. He remains the prime example of the relevance of populism.

Populism is the antithesis of democratic reform. It feeds on the anguish of the poor without providing anything other than temporary access to symbolic goods. Although they are not referred to as "populist", evangelical sects are cut from the same cloth as populist movements. Under fast-changing cultural conditions, disorientation and uncertainty make people susceptible to religion, to the "certainty of the unknowable". Unlike classical populism, contemporary populism does not facilitate the organisation of the poor. Far from contributing to democratisation, populism is an obstacle to democratisation.

The Erap phenomenon, in particular the aborted attack on the presidential palace on 1 May 2001, provoked a lot of anguished self-examination within the left. As one young activist put it "EDSA 3 may have been misguided. Its purpose was all wrong. But the rage was real. The rage was pure. It was the rage of the dispossessed, the disempowered blindly clawing at forces that bound them hopelessly to their despair."[32] Most of all, the left felt terrible about not being with the masses in their moment of explosive self-assertion.

The Erap phenomenon provides dramatic illustration of the failure of the left to connect with the very people who are supposed to be their social base. The vulnerability of urban poor groups organised by the left, not just to episodic populist mobilisations such as EDSA 3, but to regularised cooptation into urban circuits of patronage, means that the left has participated in its own political marginalisation. Part of the problem is a simple case of opportunism. Left urban mobilisations in the last few years have often been in response to the initiatives and financial resources of the pro-Erap opposition. As a result they have made their urban poor base accustomed to *hakot*, to being fetched by jeepneys and being provided with food.

In the process, these factions of the left encouraged the people's populist hopes. They abandoned their materialist pretensions by not exposing the naivety of reposing people's hopes on a populist hero. They betrayed the very masses they are supposed to serve by cynically transposing hopes for a better life to their own insurrectionary illusions. They did not understand that right wing populism of the Erap/FPJ type demobilises people. In the end, they put themselves further away from the masses that they hope to lead.

The left's problem is that of perspective. Very few on the left are believers in *Erap para sa mahirap* even if, the story goes, the slogan was proposed by someone on the left. Those on the left who continue to dream of "rupture", even if they do not have the capacity to provoke it, cynically hope that incompetent populists such as Erap will cause a disruption of the state that will open up insurrectionary spaces. Others who have given up on "smashing the state" hope that they can carve out spaces for reform within populist regimes. This has been the case in both the Erap and Thaksin regimes.

The left's problems form part of a larger crisis of democratic representation not just in the Philippines, not just in the South, but also the North, as described by Hilary Wainwright.

> It reflects the crisis of traditional institutions of representative democracy; it's indicative of the extent to which these institutions have become beyond popular control. But it also presents the left and social movements with a huge challenge and an urgent challenge because in many ways, time is not — ecologically, economically and in terms of the degradation of political culture and the destruction of public spaces and resources — on our side. The gap between the depth and extent of popular disaffection in Europe and the relative weakness of left parties and movements — though with important, often momentary, exceptions — is an indictment of our often parochial political imagination and all too self-referential ways of organizing.[33]

If we did not have the example of what happened under Erap, one could share the emotional satisfaction of the victory of a populist hero. But if we want a real democracy and a government capable of doing something about poverty, there's no substitute for careful, painstaking advocacy for reform, combined with building political parties of the left. More than the ultra left and the populist right, the real enemy of this political project is frustration and the comforts of cynicism.

To counter the manipulative "representation of the poor" by populists, we have to work with the poor in carving out participatory spaces for radical democracy. Much of this work has to be done at the base of the political system, at the local level. If there's little local political participation, there's more room for national level populism. The left also has to provide a national political frame. In Karaos' words, "Without an independently critical frame of analysis on which to anchor their actions, local organizations become vulnerable to the type of populist mobilization ... that can be harnessed to support a corrupt president."[34]

We have to lead in the struggle against manipulative populists such as Erap. But we also have to figure out how to become "popular" enough to win elections. To do that we have to be aware of the cultural gap between the left leadership and civil society on one side and the poor on the other. We have to admit that culturally we are on the other side of that gap. We have to accept, and to build on, our cultural "otherness".

Without this required reflexivity, we cannot even begin to manifest the respect that the poor demand. As Eric Gutierrez put it: "A critical opposition posture towards Estrada is more meaningful when the message of the mandate he received is understood and appreciated. The reasons for disliking Estrada are legion. But we have to check if we have started to dislike the will of the people as well. There is a way of criticizing Estrada that will not be disrespectful of the voice of the people."[35]

Notes

[1]   Kenneth Roberts, "Populism and Democracy in Latin America" (2000), <http://www.cartercenter.org/documents/nondatabase/Roberts.pdf>, p. 6.

[2]   Roberts, "Populism and Democracy", p. 7.

[3]   See this volume, pp. 66–7.

[4]   This section is for the most part based on an essay I co-wrote with Myrna Alejo in January 2000.

[5]   Erap won in the 1967 election but was disqualified. He took office after winning an election protest in 1969.

[6]   Social Weather Stations, a leading polling agency.

[7]   Maria Cynthia Rose Banzon Bautista, "People Power 2 — The Revenge of the Elite on the Masses?", in *Between Fires: Fifteen Perspectives on the Estrada Crisis*, ed. Amando Doronila (Manila: Anvil Publishing, 2001), p. 4. Philippine polling organisations use census housing data to classify respondents into AB, C, D, and E categories. AB is upper class, C is middle class, D and E lower class. In the 1998 election, the polling firm, Social Weather Stations (SWS) said ABC accounted for 10 per cent, D for 72 per cent, and E for 18 per cent of the voting population.

[8]   Patricio N. Abinales, "Governing the Philippines in the Early 21st Century", unpublished paper.

[9]   Bautista, "People Power 2", p. 3.

[10]   Sheila S. Coronel, "The Pare Principle", *I Magazine* 4, 4 (Oct.–Dec. 1998): 7.

[11]   Eva-Lotta Hedman, "The Spectre of Populism in Philippine Politics and Society: *artista, masa Eruption!*", *Southeast Asia Research* 9, 1 (2001): 8.

[12]   At this time, I was executive director of the institute and part of the team doing regular analysis of the Estrada regime.

[13]   *Philippine Daily Inquirer*, 31 Dec. 1999, p. 1.

14 Karina Constantino-David, "Surviving Erap", in *Between Fires: Fifteen Perspectives on the Estrada Crisis*, ed. Amando Doronila (Manila: Anvil Publishing, 2001), p. 217.

15 Ellen Tordesillas, "The Nocturnal President", *I Magazine* 4 (Oct.–Dec. 1999): 6–10. Tordesillas is a well-informed columnist for the daily *Malaya*. Her description of Erap's "Midnight Cabinet" is confirmed by other sources, most importantly Laquian, who told reporters that at four in the morning he was often the only one sober in palace discussions. He was soon fired by an angry Erap.

16 Aprodicio A. Laquian and Eleanor R. Laquian, *The Erap Tragedy: Tales From the Snakepit* (Manila: Anvil Publishing, 2002), p. 135.

17 Laquian and Laquian, *The Erap Tragedy*, p. xi.

18 Emmanuel De Dios, "Corruption and the Fall", in *Between Fires: Fifteen Perspectives on the Estrada Crisis*, ed. Amando Doronila (Manila: Anvil Publishing, 2001), p. 47.

19 Laquian and Laquian, *The Erap Tragedy*, p. 105.

20 Arsenio Balisacan, "Did the Estrada Administration Benefit the Poor?", in *Between Fires: Fifteen Perspectives on the Estrada Crisis*, ed. Amando Doronila (Manila: Anvil Publishing, 2001), pp. 110–1.

21 Laquian and Laquian, *The Erap Tragedy*, p. 111.

22 Ibid., p. 112.

23 John T. Sidel, *Capital, Coercion and Crime: Bossism in the Philippines* (California: Stanford University Press), 1999, p. 3.

24 Carl Lande, *Leaders, Factions and Parties: The Structure of Philippine Politics* (New Haven: Yale University Southeast Asia Studies, 1964), pp. 1–2.

25 Ana Marie A. Karaos, "Populist Mobilization and Manila's Urban Poor: The Case of SANAPA in the NGC East Side", in *Social Movements in the Philippines*, ed. Aya Fabros, Joel Rocamora, and Djorina Velasco (Quezon City, Manila: Institute for Popular Democracy, 2006), p. 29.

26 Hedman, "The Spectre of Populism", p. 11.

27 Karaos, "Populist Mobilization", pp. 28, 30.

28 Ibid., p. 27.

29 Djorina Velasco, "Life on the Fast Track: Mobilizing the Urban Poor for Change", in *Social Movements in the Philippines*, ed. Aya Fabros, Joel Rocamora, and Djorina Velasco (Quezon City, Manila: Institute for Popular Democracy, 2006), p. 6.

30 Hedman, "The Spectre of Populism", pp. 9–10.

31 Karaos, "Populist Mobilization", p. 28.

32 *Newsbreak*, 20 (9–15 May 2001).

33 Hilary Wainwright, "Rethinking Political Organisation in an Era of Movements, War and the Global Market", opening address at the XXII CLACSO General Assembly, Rio de Janeiro, 20 August 2006 , at <http://www.tni.org/detail_page.phtml?&lang=en&page=archives_wainwright_clacso&lang_help=en>.

34 Karaos, "Populist Mobilization", p. 30.

35 Eric Gutierrez, personal communication, 2001.

CHAPTER 4

Thaksin's Populism

Pasuk Phongpaichit and Chris Baker

Thaksin Shinawatra was the first Thai politician to be widely described as a populist. Indeed a Thai version of the term was invented specifically to label him. The term was used by some to abuse and undermine Thaksin, but it is still apposite and useful. Thaksin represented a new kind of politics in Thailand which was a challenge to the mainstream trend of liberal democracy and which had many affinities to populist regimes elsewhere, especially in Latin America. Fear that populism would enhance the power of the mass in Thai politics at the expense of established elite interests was a major factor in assembling the coalition of forces behind the coup which overthrew Thaksin in September 2006.

Thaksin's populism is often equated with his policies, especially a three-point electoral platform of 2001 (cheap health-care, agrarian debt relief, village funds). It can quite properly be argued that such policies are the everyday stuff of electoral politics and do not deserve the label of populism. The equation of Thaksin's populism with this programme also gives the impression that Thaksin's populism was present at least from the time of his rise to power.

We argue that Thaksin's populism was more complex than his policy offering; that it developed over time in response to social demand; that it has strong affinities with political trends elsewhere in the world owing to a common political economy; and that it helped provoke the urban middle class rejection of Thaksin which was background to the coup.

The first part of the chapter plots the growth of Thaksin's populism, showing that it became by stages a much more important part of Thaksin's public politics. The second part argues that a policy platform was only one aspect of Thaksin's populism, and that two others were the projection of a relationship between political leader and supporters that was dramatically new in the Thai context, and an explicit attack on the form of liberal democracy which has been the template for Thailand's constitutional development. The third part argues that Thaksin's embrace of populism was not mere opportunism but the response to social demand. To put it another way, Thaksin may indeed have been opportunistic, but there would have been no opportunity if there had not been a social demand. This demand was a function of social forces created by Thailand's pattern of development in the era of outward-orientation and neoliberalism.

The fourth section compares Thaksin with other examples of modern populism, especially in Latin America. There is often resistance to such comparison on grounds that the histories and social profiles of Latin America and Southeast Asia are so different. But the similarities between the Thaksin regime and certain examples in Latin America, especially Fujimori's Peru, are so striking that it is worth looking at the extensive analysis of Latin American populism for help in understanding Thaksin. One key message of this comparison is that populism mutates and matures. Another is that populist regimes which lack mass organisation fall easily victim to elite attack. The final section looks at the role of Thaksin's populism in the crisis of 2006.

The academic literature on populism has grown in volume and sophistication in recent years, in response to the appearance of many movements and regimes that have attracted the label in different parts of the world. The analysis associated with Ernesto Laclau has shifted the emphasis away from trying to define populism in terms of its ideology or sociology towards understanding populism as a type of practice that can appear in many different social and ideological contexts. In this approach populism is a challenge to an existing order that happens when some parts of the society claim the mantle of the people in opposition to others who wield power. Often "the people" coalesces around a leader who is able to represent many diverse demands.[1] Kenneth Roberts summarised "the essential core of populism" as "the political mobilization of mass constituencies by personalistic leaders who challenge established elites". He argued that such movements encompass many shades of ideology, and various types of organisation.[2] We use the term in this sense.

Becoming a Populist

When Thaksin formed the Thai Rak Thai (TRT) party in July 1998, there was little sign of his later populism. Thaksin was a spectacularly successful businessman from a prominent business family in Chiang Mai. On founding

the party, he explained that its principal mission was to rescue Thai businessmen from the 1997 financial crisis and to restore economic growth.[3]

He later broadened his political mission to include reforms which would
modernise Thailand, especially the bureaucracy and the political system, and
hence prevent the recurrence of financial crises in the future. The slogan
chosen for his party — "Think new, act new for every Thai" — reflected
the image he projected as a modernist and reformer. In the statement of
his political ideas at this time, there is no social agenda except for one brief
general commitment "to bring happiness to the majority of the country". The
single-minded focus is on "enabling Thailand to keep up and be competitive
with other countries".[4]

The 23 founding members of the party, and the 44 members of a kind
of shadow cabinet publicised a year later included only one figure identified
with rural or mass issues. Thaksin's speeches of this era do not make use
of the term "the people" and do not imagine any social change other than
the triumph of business over bureaucracy. For the 2001 elections, the initial
party platform focused on measures to help small and medium businesses,
and the centrepiece of the media campaign was a dramatisation of Thaksin's
own life in which he was cast as a poor boy who made good as a rich
businessman — a distillation of the lives and legends of Thailand's urban
society of Thai-Chinese migrant families, not of its rural society of frontier
rice farmers. As signals of his modernism, Thaksin appeared in public in a
suit, the uniform of business, and littered his speeches with English words
and references to the sayings of Bill Gates.

To put together a broader campaign platform, Thaksin drew on the
services of a group of former student radicals from the 1970s era. The key
contact was Phumtham Vejjayachai, who had met Thaksin in 1975–6 when
Thaksin worked as an aide to a minister who had to negotiate with leaders of
the student movement. In response to a call for policy ideas, another 1970s
student leader turned orchard farmer, Praphat Panyachatrak, contributed a
scheme of agrarian debt relief. This subsequently became the first item in a
platform designed for rural appeal.[5]

Subsequently the TRT policy team adopted ideas for a universal health
scheme which had been developed over some time within health-oriented
NGOs. The scheme was initially based on an insurance model with a low
annual premium, but was subsequently changed to a retail model with a low
price per visit.[6] This mass platform was rounded off by a scheme of village
funds essentially similar to a scheme which Kukrit Pramoj and Boonchu
Rojanasatian had launched in 1975.[7]

This three-point platform figured in the campaign material which TRT distributed, especially in rural areas, in the two months before the election. But the agrarian debt scheme and village funds were not evidence of any special tilt towards rural issues on the part of Thaksin and TRT. The policy team also contacted activists working with urban labour, and put together a programme appealing to this interest.[8] In the same way, TRT attempted to appeal to businessmen, environmental groups, the moral reform lobby, and various other sectional interests. It was trying to please everyone.

At the polls in January 2001, TRT won two seats less than an absolute majority. Thaksin's policy platform was strikingly new and will have contributed to the result, but it would be wrong to imagine, with the benefit of hindsight, that this was a populist victory. Many factors contributed to this result: the opposition Democrats were damned by their association with the IMF's disastrous crisis recovery programme; other parties and politicians were still suffering financially from the crisis; Thaksin was successful in persuading many established politicians to join his party; and the electoral system introduced under the 1997 constitution was designed to deliver fewer but larger parties than in the past.[9] Thaksin drew attention because of his platform, but even more because of his novelty as a leader and because of his wealth. Opinion polls run after the election found that many voters believed the TRT platform was simply "too good to be true".[10]

While in the international context populism is an old term with many meanings, it is important to understand that in the Thai context it was a totally new word and wholly defined by its usage with reference to Thaksin. Anek Laothamatas shows that "prior to 2001 and Thaksin's election victory, the terms *populism* and *populist* were used by almost nobody in academic circles, the media, or the society at large".[11]

Just two weeks after the election, Kasian Tejapira[12] wrote articles in *Matichon*, applying the term populism to Thaksin and TRT, and explaining to his audience what the word meant.[13] At first, however, he used a Thai transliteration, *poppiwlit*. The term was so new and unfamiliar that no translation was in common usage. In the same week, two Thai academics translated the term as *prachaniyom* during a seminar in Thammasat University. Kasian switched to this term in his article on 3 February and Anek suspects this was the first time this Thai word was used in print.[14]

From Capitalism to Populism

By background Thaksin is a successful businessman. His initial promise as a party leader was to promote Thai capital and accelerate the economy. In power, this remained his priority. During his first months in power, the international press questioned whether Thaksin's government would take an economic nationalist stance, reflecting many Thai businessmen's anti-globalisation sentiments after the ravages of the 1997 crisis. Thaksin pointed out that his own business was transnational, and that he was viewed within the country as a modern and international figure.[15] From this time, Thaksin began to advertise his government's economic stance as "dual track". This phrase was used in two ways. First, government would embrace the open economy and promote the exports and foreign investment which were well established as the engines of growth, but at the same time would nurture the domestic economy by encouraging domestic investment, identifying key growth sectors, and making more efficient use of domestic resources and expertise. Second, "dual track" also meant promoting both the modern urban economy and the grass-roots rural economy.

In practice, Thaksin's government complied closely with the neoliberal trends of the time. Although Thaksin claimed to pay off the IMF loan ahead of time and staged a showy celebration of this "Independence Day", this was mere window-dressing. His government reversed not a single one of the reforms or strictures that the IMF imposed on Thailand in the eye of the 1997 crisis. The open fiscal and monetary stance remained unchanged. Exports continued to be the main foundation of growth. Foreign investment was welcomed. Thaksin enthusiastically promoted free trade agreements, launched an ambitious plan to privatise state enterprises, and proposed a slew of "megaprojects" to upgrade the country's infrastructure by drawing on multinational capital and expertise.

Most local businessmen cheered these policies. In the government's second year, the economy revived. In the third, the stock market soared. Thaksin's family businesses benefited from accelerating profits and rising market value, as did many other domestic businessmen. The IMF's initial nervousness about Thaksin's nationalistic posturing totally disappeared. By 2002 the World Bank were enthusiastic about a "Thaksin model" and its possible application elsewhere. He had become a hero of neoliberalism.

But at the same time, the populism which had been one element in his broad-reaching electoral campaign of 2000–1 became a much more prominent part of Thaksin's politics.

Bidding for Popular Support

Thaksin's embrace of populism had two main stages, both when he found himself under attack. In December 2000, Thaksin was indicted by the National Counter Corruption Commission for failing to report his assets accurately in three statutory declarations made when he served briefly as a minister in the mid-1990s.[16] If found guilty, Thaksin faced a five-year ban on participation in politics. He fought the case with legal arguments and with attempts to suborn the judges, but also deployed two other strategies.

First, he manufactured a public presence significantly greater than that attempted by any previous Thai prime minister, primarily by using state-owned media now under his control. He launched a weekly radio show in which he talked to the nation for an hour about his activities and his thoughts on issues of the day. He dominated the daily television news, and also appeared in several special programmes, including an evening chat show in which he lamented his predecessors' handling of the economy. In the final climactic sessions of the assets case, he walked the final stretch to the court through an avenue of supporters, pressing the flesh like an American electoral candidate. In an extraordinary innovation, the final summaries by plaintiff and defence in the assets case were run live as a television special.

Second, his government implemented the three-point electoral programme with extraordinary speed. For the health scheme, a workshop was held in February, a pilot scheme launched in April, and the roll-out completed in October (except in Bangkok).[17] The agrarian debt relief scheme was made available to 2.3 million debtors by the same month,[18] while by September the scheme of village funds[19] was extended to most of the country's 75,000 villages and 5.3 million loans approved.[20] The three schemes were immediately popular.

Thaksin's personal popularity, measured by a monthly poll, rose from around 30 per cent in December 2000 before the election to a peak of 70 per cent in May 2001 as the asset case decision approached.[21]

With this change in public presence and popularity went a change of rhetoric. In direct reaction to the assets charge, Thaksin announced a new and leading feature of his political mission: "Nothing will stand in my way. I am determined to devote myself to politics in order to lead the Thai people out of poverty."[22] He and his aides portrayed the assets case as a conspiracy by Thailand's old elite to remove someone who had been elected "by the people" and was dedicated to work "for the people". Thaksin said on the eve of the verdict, "The people want me to stay and the people know what's right for Thailand. And who should I be more loyal to? The people? Or to the Court? I love people. I want to work for them."[23]

In rhetoric, over the nine months of the asset case, Thaksin went from modernist reformer championing businessmen in the face of economic crisis, to populist championing the poor against an old elite. By late 2001, academics and journalists, both Thai and foreign, used the term populist more regularly

in reference to Thaksin. But most analysts still pictured Thaksin primarily
as a business politician who had adopted populist policies as a strategy to
win popular acquiescence for reforms designed primarily in the interests of
capital. Kevin Hewison dubbed this formula a "new social contract".[24]

Going to the People

The second stage of Thaksin's development as a populist began in late March
2004. Thaksin came under increasing attack in the press and on public
platforms, especially over his management of the upsurge of violence in the
far south, but more generally over a range of issues including corruption,
government aid for his family businesses, the privatisation of state enterprises, and the government's handling of avian influenza. With an election
approaching in early 2005, Thaksin reacted quickly to secure his electoral
support in the countryside. He launched a series of tours covering every
region of the country. His motorcade swept into villages and district centres, where provincial officials and local leaders had been gathered. Flanked
by other ministers and high officials from the capital, Thaksin listened to
reports on local problems and petitions for budget assistance. In many cases,
he then gave instant approval for projects, using a vastly expanded central
fund under his own control which he had created by reforms in the budget
process. In a 7-day swing through the northeast in April 2004, he pledged
approval of projects totalling 100 billion baht.[25] In a 6-day swing through
the north in July, he pledged approval of projects totalling six billion baht.[26]
He visited the central provinces in several shorter trips, and the south in
August. In Chiang Mai he promised to rid the city of poverty within three
years. In Nakhon Pathom, he told students, "Come and tell me if you don't
have a notebook [computer] yet and I will buy one for you out of my own
pocket."[27] Thaksin also invited all Bangkok's taxi drivers to Government
House for lunch.[28]

In the month prior to the election in February 2005, Thaksin made
further tours, mainly in rural areas of the north and northeast. Election
law forbade any instant handouts in this period, but Thaksin announced
a much more elaborate programme of election promises than in 2001, including an extension of the village funds, land deeds for every landholder,
a government pond dug for anyone prepared to pay a small fuel cost, four
new cheap loan schemes, free distribution of cows, training schemes for the
poor, cheaper school fees, special payments for children forced to drop out
of school because of poverty, an educational gift bag for every new mother,
care centres for the elderly, more sports facilities in urban areas, cheaper
phone calls, an end to eviction from slums, more cheap housing, lower

taxes, more investment in the universal health scheme, a nationwide scheme of irrigation, and a deadline for the end to poverty — "Four years ahead, there will be no poor people. Won't that be neat?"[29] For this election, the modernist "Think new, act new" slogan of 2001 was replaced by the intensely populist, "The heart of TRT is the people."

After the 2005 election, Thaksin toured less but made increasing use of a practice, begun in 2001, of holding occasional "mobile Cabinet meetings" in an upcountry location. These events similarly created occasions for local people and officials to present petitions to Thaksin, and for Thaksin to pledge local budget spending, all in full view of the public media. This strategy climaxed in January 2006 when Thaksin led a troop of ministers and senior officials to spend a week in At Samat in Roi-et province, one of Thailand's poorest districts, supposedly to devise systems for eradicating poverty which could then be replicated elsewhere.

These events dramatised Thaksin bringing government to the people, and were rewarded by increased popularity. Even though very little concrete action resulted from the At Samat poverty experiment, popular support for Thaksin in this area increased dramatically from an already high level.[30] Although the motorcades, mobile Cabinet meetings, and the poverty experiment only reached a small sample of places, the events were magnified by display on television. The poverty experiment ran all day on live television as a form of "reality show". The upcountry tours provided opportunities for Thaksin to be photographed in homely situations — emerging from a village bath-house in a *pakoma* (common man's lower cloth); transported on a village tractor (*i-taen*); riding a motorbike down a dusty village street; accepting flowers from toothless old ladies.

In this period, Thaksin changed his public appearance and speech. He shed his business suit in favour of shirtsleeves with buttons open at the neck, sometimes all down to his waist, and his hair lightly tousled. He stopped littering his speeches with English to denote internationalism and modernity, and instead used dialect and earthy humour. He stopped quoting Bill Gates, and instead often mentioned his own family and sex life. The format of his weekly radio show underwent a subtle change: instead of commenting on current issues, Thaksin related the events of his week like a diary, allowing listeners *into* his life.

Thaksin's Three Messages

By the end of this period, Thaksin's populism had expanded beyond a policy platform into a distinctly new form of politics which can be portrayed as three messages to his supporters.

I Give to All of You

Thaksin's government had launched three major schemes of social provision, and promised many more. The distinctive characteristic of most of these schemes was that they were available to all. Previous governments had provided cheap or free healthcare for the poor by distributing cards. However, through corruption and inefficiency, these cards reached only a minority of the families which deserved and needed them. Using these cards carried a stigma, and often subjected the holder to poor treatment. Thaksin's health scheme was available to all as a right, and significantly extended access to health care. According to the Thailand Development Research Institute (TDRI), which was generally critical of Thaksin, the scheme lifted more people out of poverty than any other single government measure. While there remained a service differential between the 30-baht scheme and private treatment, participation in the scheme conveyed no stigma and the treatment was mostly judged to be good.[31] In polls, the health scheme regularly rated as the TRT government's most popular measure.[32] This popularity outstripped actual experience of the scheme. People who had not used the scheme liked the *idea* of it.

In the same way, the debt relief scheme was available to all indebted farmers, and the village funds extended to every village. The slew of schemes floated in the 2005 election campaign offered provisions for everyone through every stage of life — from birth through education and employment to old age.

As Pitch Pongsawat has argued, people felt empowered by the TRT schemes, partly through the very real impact of the programmes, partly through the impression that Thaksin and his party were responsive to their demands, and partly because the schemes positioned each citizen in an equal and direct relationship with the state.[33] From interviews and observation in Mahasarakham in 2005, Charles Keyes concluded, "The relationship with the rural populace was clearly symbiotic and grew over time. As villagers benefited from Thaksin's populist programs, they felt empowered because they were responsible for putting him in power…. In one interview, a middle-aged villager said that in the past people in Bangkok controlled politics, but today we villagers do."[34]

I Belong to You

Thaksin transformed himself into a public property over which people felt they had some ownership. He used the media and public appearances to convey an image of constant and dominating presence in public space. He re-crafted the presentation of himself to become much less distant from the ordinary person. He distinguished himself from previous political leaders and from other figures in the political arena including officials, academics, and journalists. He delighted in provoking criticism from such figures, and then boasting about such criticism on his radio shows, upcountry tours, and election appearances. He understood that presenting himself as an enemy of Thailand's political elite conveyed an appealing message to his mass audience.

Deft use of the media is of course commonplace in modern politics in any country. But in Thailand, Thaksin's development of a powerful public image was new and broke many local conventions. On public appearances, he was received in scenes normally reserved for rock stars, and certainly never before seen around a Thai political leader.

I Am the Mechanism Which Can Translate the Will of the People into State Action

In many of his public statements from 2004 onwards, the government was reduced to the first person singular. For example, in his last speech before the 2005 poll, Thaksin spoke as follows:

> I will make the Thai economy improve. I have already raised the GDP from 4.8 to 6.5, and now I will take it from 6.5 to 9 trillion [baht]. I will increase exports. I will expand the markets .... I will fix the economy by fixing the problem of poverty .... I ended the IMF loan. I changed the status of the country from one which chases around borrowing money to one which lends .... I will take care of kids by developing their brains.... I will change the way of giving financial support to universities .... I will build more sport stadiums and more parks .... I already gave officials a salary adjustment in 2002, and I will give another .... I will provide opportunities for people to study at university level without their parents having to open their wallets.[35]

At this and other campaign meetings, he dispensed with the usual ritual of introducing the local party candidate, and instead launched into his speech as if the election were a presidential poll. His domination of television news became so overwhelming that other ministers spent ministry budgets to buy billboard space to display their own face and achievements. In a specially televised Cabinet meeting, Thaksin presented himself as a traditional *taokae* (Chinese boss) commanding and instructing a group of passive subordinates. He told NGOs that they no longer had any role because there was no need for intermediaries between the leader and the people.

After the landslide 2005 election victory, Thaksin constantly repeated, "I have the votes of 19 million of the people."

In his speeches before the 2005 election, Thaksin offered himself as the vehicle through which the wishes of the people could be translated into action on the part of government.

> These past four years, this kind of change was not by chance or *fluke* [in English], but because of the power of your belief in me. I work hard, don't I? If I work hard, but you don't believe in me, there could be no trust. But when you believe in me, then people listen when I speak, and bureaucrats are not stubborn, because they listen to the people. This is democracy.... I have the same power as prime minister as every person who is prime minister. But I have special power more than the others because I do what I say I will do. People put faith and belief in me, don't they?[36]

Thaksin devalued the importance of parliament, neutralised the check-and-balance bodies of the 1997 constitution, micro-managed the electronic media, and said in public that law, the rule-of-law, democracy, and human rights were not important because they often got in the way of "working for the people". In his 2005 election speeches, he suggested to his audience that the bundle of liberal democracy — rule of law, freedom of criticism, human rights, oversight by parliamentary opposition, checks and balances on the executive — had done little for them in the past, and that making him into a powerful executive would deliver them greater benefit. He described criticism by press or opposition as "destructive" and exhorted his audience, "We want politics with meaning, don't we? We want politics which have something for the people, don't we? And this politics which is just destructive, can we get rid of it yet?"[37] In his public criticism of opponents, he focused especially on people associated with Thailand's history of democratic development (Thirayuth Boonmi) or with the reform pressure of the 1990s (Prawase Wasi, Anand Panyarachun). On several occasions, he encouraged people to draw parallels between himself and authoritarian military leaders in the past, especially Sarit Thanarat, whose memory had become associated with direct and decisive action.[38]

Thaksin's authoritarian tendency was clear from the beginning of his premiership. It stemmed from his enormous self-confidence, his need to conceal the massive conflict-of-interest over his family business, and perhaps his police training and experience as an old-fashioned *taokae* of a family-based business. But Thaksin's embrace of populism gave him a means to justify this authoritarianism as an alternative to the liberal model of democracy.

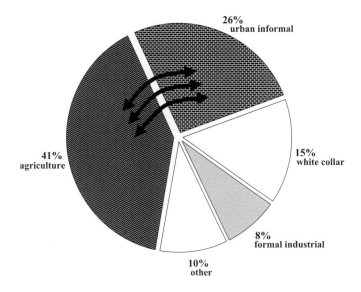

Figure 4-1 Thailand Labour Force, Early 2000s

The Social Context of Populism

Thaksin populism was a response to social demand, with roots in the social structure moulded by Thailand's strategy of outward-oriented economic development. With the development policies adopted by governments since the 1950s, Thailand became significantly more industrialised and urbanised. But Thailand's decision to develop with a relatively open economy and high reliance on external sources of capital, technology, expertise, and even labour resulted in a social structure which differs significantly from the classic pattern of the West, and that of the early Asian industrialisers such as Japan, Taiwan, and Korea. Figure 4-1 is an attempt to sketch this social structure using the 2004 Labour Force Survey, February round, and the 2002 Industrial Survey.

The formal working class is small, accounting for around 8 per cent of the workforce. By "formal" working class we mean those with relatively permanent employment in sizeable establishments. As a proxy, we use the numbers employed in manufacturing in establishments with more than ten workers, as recorded in the National Statistical Office's Industrial Survey. This is not "the working class" as a whole which would be far larger. This formal working class is small because the multinational firms that dominate manufacturing tend to employ technology which is more capital-intensive than Thai conditions would merit.[39] It is weak in bargaining power because of labour competition on a global scale, and suffers from the legacy of the Cold War when Thai governments devoted considerable care to controlling labour organisation through legal measures, political co-option, and outright suppression.[40]

The white-collar middle class is relatively large at around 15 per cent of the workforce. This figure is calculated from those with higher education and a professional, managerial or clerical job, as recorded in the Labour Force Survey. This class developed very rapidly over little more than a single generation because of the rapidly rising demand for skills to service the expanding modern economy.

The numbers remaining in agriculture have fallen, especially over the 1985–95 economic boom, yet still two-fifths of the workforce returns their major occupation as agriculture. However, for most nominally agrarian families, agriculture is no longer the sole source of income, and for many it is only a minor contributor. Because of low public investment directed towards the agricultural sector, a long-term trend of decline in international prices, and environmental destruction, returns to agriculture have declined. Agrarian households rely on transfers from the urban economy to supplement their incomes.

There is a steady seepage of people from agriculture into the urban informal sector, which has ballooned to around a quarter of the workforce. This sector includes the whole "shophouse" sub-sector of "mom-and-pop" stores, and other family and micro-scale enterprises; vendors; the self-employed; many illegal or semi-legal enterprises; and a large workforce which floats between construction, seasonal agricultural work, sweatshops, legal and illegal services industries, and other forms of casual employment.[41]

The agricultural and urban informal sectors are closely linked through flows of people and remittance. For shorthand we will refer to these two combined as the informal mass. Together they account for around two-thirds of the workforce, and roughly the same proportion of the electorate. As electoral democracy has developed in Thailand, the potential importance of this informal mass in politics has advanced in parallel. But numbers are only part of the story.

Those who depend for a living on the informal economy also tend to be involved in informal systems of social organisation and political regulation. As they are not directly affected by the taxation, budgetary spending, or regulatory action of government, they have low motivation to invest in the organisation needed to make their weight felt in national politics. At the same time they are bound by informal linkages into clientelist politics.[42] In

Thailand, they were mainly recruited into politics through the *hua khanaen* (vote bank) systems of electoral organisation, in which candidates rely on village heads and other locally influential people to deliver the people's votes.

However, the politics of the informal mass has changed markedly over the past two decades. Over the 1980s, the controls through which the military suppressed grassroots political organisation through intimidation and force during the Cold War were eased. From the late 1980s onwards, civil society movements raised political consciousness over issues concerning rights, environment, livelihood, and equity. Then in 1997, the financial crisis hit very hard on the informal mass. The two million who were immediately made unemployed by the crisis came mostly from this segment. Returns to agriculture were initially improved by the currency movements, but then sharply depressed. Numbers below the poverty line rose by three million.[43] Declining remittances from urban work knocked through into rising levels of agrarian debt. This severe and sudden impact had a politicising effect.

The two years following the crisis saw the biggest upsurge in rural protest since the early 1970s. The chief demands were for agricultural price support, agrarian debt relief, and land for the landless.[44] Thaksin and his advisers adopted exactly these demands. Agrarian debt relief was the first measure which Thaksin's ex-activist advisors inserted into his rural electoral platform; Thaksin frequently distributed land deeds during his rural tours; and government support for rice prices became a key policy through which Thaksin consolidated rural support.[45]

Thaksin connected with the emerging political demands and aspirations of the informal mass. Although he was not an obvious candidate to become a populist leader, and although he had shown no interest in "the people" before 2000, he was drawn into this position by the mechanisms of electoral politics. As his political career was threatened, first by legal process, later by growing urban opposition, he discovered a new and powerful base of support in the growing political involvement of the informal mass. He gave them a form of leadership which brought their demands and aspirations to bear in national politics. At the same time, Thaksin's programme, leadership style, and political message were shaped by the aspirations and insecurities of this support base. As Nidhi Eoseewong observed, "'Think new, act new' is just somebody taking the dreams of Thai society and making them into policy."[46]

The universalism of his policies had immediate appeal to people who lived and worked within informal rather than formal structures, and who often missed out on government schemes which were designed and delivered within a formal institutional frame. The failure of previous targeted schemes of subsidised health care are a good case in point. Similarly, his leadership style was a targeted appeal to the informal mass. He approximated the style of the local boss with a strong streak of personalism ("*I* do this for *you*"), a promise of generosity in return for loyal support, and a cavalier, tough-guy, dismissive attitude towards enemies. Finally, his promise to act as the mechanism through which popular demands would be translated into state action carried an implicit message that old-style politics, and the whole liberal-democratic bundle, had done little for the mass of the people.

Thaksin's populism thus went far beyond a transactional relationship in which he appealed for support in return for a menu of policies. He tapped the aspirations, insecurities, and sense of exclusion of this major segment of the population, and was rewarded with support which was both emotional and rational.

> Brothers and sisters, look at me! My ribs are all cracked, because when they hug me, they hug me tight, solid, humph! Today, I was hugged a bit too heavily. My arms are starting to be different lengths. Today, I was pinched all over. But I'm happy because people have the feeling that I care for them. I want to see them escape poverty. They have placed their hope in me. I know that I'm taking heavy burdens on my shoulders with the things I'm saying here. But I'm confident I can do them. Someone born in the year of the ox in the middle of the day likes working hard — has to plough the field before he can eat the straw.[47]

Latin American Parallels

Leaders with many similarities to Thaksin have appeared in many other countries in recent years. In Turkey in 2004, for example, a new prime minister whose party's base of support comprises small-scale producers and the informal sector, launched a slew of populist schemes, and stood aggressively against the country's political tradition going back to Ataturk in the 1920s.[48] However, the region where this political tradition has the longest history and the most extensive academic analysis is Latin America.[49]

Two main schools of thought emerged to explain a shift in Latin American populism in the 1980s from the classical form to neopopulism (see Chapter 1). The first concentrated on the political economy. Labour movements had declined with the rise of multinational capital and the development of an internationalised labour market, while the decay of agriculture had swelled numbers in the informal sector, creating a "disorganized mass". This mass was mobilised as a political force by a "critical juncture", such as a severe cyclical economic crisis, or the delegitimation of an old ruling elite. The second explanation, coming from the rational choice tendency in political science, argued that the rise of mass media had supplanted the need for political entrepreneurs to use "labour intensive" techniques of mass mobilisation.[50] These two arguments are not mutually exclusive, though it is difficult to see how the rational choice version can work without some political economy underpinning.

The most striking example of this era of neopopulism was Alberto Fujimori's Peru. As an ethnic Japanese former professor of agronomy, Fujimori was a total outsider to the old political elite, and enjoyed very limited support only a few months before his rise to power in 1990. He was swept to the presidency on a wave of emotional reaction against the old political elite in the aftermath of an economic crisis. He consolidated his support with a raft of welfare schemes which included universal health care, and other mainly universal schemes. He systematically undermined the parliament, media, and judiciary by bribery on a massive scale, while simultaneously telling his supporters that democratic institutions were a hindrance to his efforts on their behalf.[51]

Fujimori was far from alone. Menem in Argentina and de Mello in Brazil followed similar patterns in the early 1990s. Kurt Weyland summarised the populist leaders of Latin America in this era as follows: "They … appeal to unorganized, largely poor people in the informal sector, have an adversarial relation to many organized groups in civil society, and attack the established 'political class' as their main enemy." They rely on "a strongly top-down approach and … strengthening the apex of the state in order to effect profound economic reform and to boost the position of the personal leader". They have tended "to ally with the army, sideline or destroy existing political institutions (unions, parties), and manipulate the media".[52] They also tended to align with the U.S., acquiesce in neoliberalism, and pursue rapid economic growth to win the support of local business elites. The similarities to Thaksin are obvious.

In short, Thaksin's populism is far from unique but follows in broad outline a pattern which was dominant in Latin America a decade or so earlier. But the Latin American case has a second important learning. Populist politics are not static. Just as neoliberal neopopulism supplanted an earlier "classic" era, so neopopulism has already been supplanted by distinctly new trends in Latin America, particularly associated with the rise of Hugo Chávez in Venezuela (see Chapter 1). Populism evolves and mutates in response to ideological development, shifts in the political economy, and changes in the international environment.

Organisation and Party

In the neopopulism phase, Latin American populism moved away from mobilisation based on structured parties and social movements towards looser organisations and "electoral populism" in which the party existed only for the purpose of election campaigning. Fujimori is again a primary example. He formed a new party on each of the three occasions that he stood for election, and promptly abandoned or disbanded the party in the aftermath of his victory. The lack of any institutional form to bind Fujimori to his electoral promises gave him the freedom to woo local business and make his settlement with the U.S.[53]

Roberts argues that change in the degree of organisation by Latin American populists is not a trend over time but a function of the fierceness of opposition. Populist leaders who face no serious response from an old elite can afford to operate without any organised base of support, but those that provoke opposition need defences.

> Populist leaders are often polarizing figures who generate fervent loyalties and intense opposition, particularly among elites who feel threatened by populist reforms, rhetoric, redistributive measures, or mobilizational tactics. The more radical the discourse and behavior of populist leaders, the more intense the opposition, and the more likely that socio-political conflict will be channelled into extra-electoral arenas. These conflicts create incentives for populist figures to organize and empower their followers for political combat. Followers not only vote, but they may be called upon to mobilize for rallies and demonstrations, participate in strikes and occupations, or even take up arms to defend their leader in times of peril.[54]

Fujimori's lack of organised support eventually became "a congenital defect of *Fujimorismo*". When the extent of the organised corruption which underpinned the regime became public in 2000, the government collapsed and Fujimori had to flee into exile.[55] As Matsushita Hiroshi notes (Chapter 1), Hugo Chávez also began his political career without organised support but later rectified this in order to sustain his time in power.

Thaksin's TRT party closely resembled the loose form of electoral populism in Latin America. It differed little from other Thai parties except in the scale of its funding.[56] Its prime function was to orchestrate election campaigns. It held an annual conference, and occasional regional meetings, principally as rituals to celebrate the party leader. The party claimed to have signed up eight million members before the 2001 election, and extended that to 14 million by the 2005 poll.[57] But these members paid no party dues, engaged in no party activities, and had no part in selecting the party executive. There was no formal channel for party members to influence policy. Thaksin's aides used market research techniques to help formulate policies. The party membership list served principally as a database for election campaigning.

TRT organised for the 2001 election by the classic tactic of persuading factions of sitting MPs to join the party on the expectation that TRT would form the next government and be in a position to reward them.[58] Thaksin thus attached the existing clientelist networks, which extended down from the MPs into the localities, to his new party. He continued this strategy after the election by persuading two surviving parties to merge into TRT. At the 2005 poll, the influence of TRT as a party, Thaksin as a leader, and the clientelist networks of individual MPs are impossible to disentangle. The MPs were bound to the party by constitutional barriers against splitting away, and by the continued expectation that TRT would again win. TRT as a party thus continued to draw on their clientelist networks.

Prior to the 2001 election, Thaksin and his aides toyed with schemes to ally civil society groups to his party. In particular, Thaksin appeared in public with the Assembly of the Poor, the most prominent activist coalition of the 1990s. He promised to act on their agenda of complaints, and won their endorsement for his election campaign.[59] Similarly, TRT met with representatives of organised labour, resulting in a nine-point policy document, and endorsement of TRT's election campaign by labour organisations.[60] But Thaksin reneged on both these promises. When the party's labour policy was submitted to parliament in the month after the election, four of the nine points had already disappeared, including those considered the most important — ratifying the ILO conventions on freedom of association and collective bargaining, and establishing an occupational health and safety institute. Organised labour's support for Thaksin dwindled, and turned to outright opposition over privatisation in 2003. The Assembly of the Poor's major demand was decommissioning the Pak Mun dam which disrupted the ecology of a major river and the livelihoods of people depending on it. Thaksin visited the dam, and called for research on the issue, but then personally made a summary decision to retain the dam before the studies were even completed. The Assembly of the Poor turned hostile.[61]

Subsequently Thaksin avoided arrangements with civil society groups which might place him under some obligation to deliver against his promises. Once in power, with a virtual monopoly control over the electronic media, he relied on his ability to dominate public space to secure public support.

However, as opposition increased from 2004, Thaksin not only intensified his efforts to win public support by populist strategies, but also began to consider strengthening the party as an organisation. In campaign speeches before the 2005 poll, he promised that TRT would soon introduce a system to allow local party members to select the TRT candidate on the model of the U.S. primaries.[62] In July 2005, the TRT party moved into massive new offices in two buildings (of 8 and 14 storeys) previously occupied by a state bank, and Thaksin announced his aim to "institutionalise" the party.[63] Nothing concrete had emerged, however, before the 2006 coup.

Instead, he tried to mobilise support through informal means. His lieutenant for this task was Newin Chidchob. Before the 2005 poll, Newin was sent to the south in an apparent attempt to disrupt the Democrat Party's support base through wholesale vote-buying delivered through the bureaucratic apparatus. The scheme was exposed and had to be abandoned. As opposition to Thaksin accumulated over 2005 and early 2006, Newin was involved in organising support among Bangkok taxi drivers and among farmers groups from the northeast. The taxi drivers were occasionally assembled for shows of support for Thaksin in the capital. In 2006, groups of northeastern farmers travelled to Bangkok and set up camp in a city park to serve as a counter to the demonstrations organised by Sondhi Limthongkul and the People's Alliance for Democracy, and to demonstrate against newspapers which opposed Thaksin.[64] Thaksin's aides threatened to bring a million farmers to the city.

As with Fujimori, the lack of any strong organisational base proved to be a "congenital defect". Thaksin and TRT crumbled when confronted by opposition from the palace, the military, and a hostile middle class.

Populism and Reaction

On 19 September 2006, Thaksin was overthrown by a military coup. As Hewison argues, the coup was very much a royalist event.[65] Yet it depended also on urban middle class support in the public space of the media and public platforms. The army's planning for the coup appears to have begun after an attempt by a Thaksin ally to buy up the Matichon press group in September 2005 turned the press and intellectuals openly hostile, and after the Shinawatra family's tax-free sale of Shin Corp in January 2006 provoked a gut reaction in the tax-paying middle class.

Royalist opposition to Thaksin was evident from the beginning of his first government in 2001 and thus predates the development of his populism, though royalist opposition undoubtedly increased as the implications of Thaksin's populist leadership became clearer.

The evolution of Thaksin's populism and the growth of middle-class opposition were interrelated in a kind of dialectic: as Thaksin lost urban middle-class support, he intensified his populist appeal to the informal mass; as Thaksin's populism became more strident, the middle class felt more alienated.[66] Thaksin's threat to bring millions of rural supporters into the capital was the logical conclusion to this spiral, and a key trigger for staging the coup. Beneath this interplay lay the massive gap in incomes between city and village, and a long-standing middle class fear of empowerment of the rural mass. Among the four reasons which the junta gave for staging the coup was that Thaksin had "caused an unprecedented rift in society", meaning the rift that ran between the Bangkok middle class on one extreme, and Thaksin's largely rural support base on the other. The threat which the middle class perceived in Thaksin's populism was partly fear that they would be obliged to pay for his redistributive schemes,[67] but more fear that they would no longer have a privileged position to influence the state agenda. Sondhi Limthongkul, who set out to channel middle class aspirations, stated explicitly that Thaksin had to be overthrown in order to restore political influence to the middle class. In talks given in the US following the coup, Sondhi was reported as follows:

> He [Sondhi] argued that there cannot be electoral democracy in Thailand such as is found in the West because most people outside the middle class lack sufficient knowledge to understand how power can be abused. The rural people only vote, he claimed, for those who pay them either directly through party organizers (*hua khanaen*) or indirectly through the populist programs. He compared the populist programs of Thaksin to those of Peron in Argentina. Khun Sondhi said that in the future he himself will work only with the middle class who have sufficient education to truly understand how populist politicians can abuse power.[68]

A more detailed rejection appeared in a book *Thaksina-prachaniyom* (Thaksin-style populism) completed in mid-2006 in parallel with the countdown to the coup. Anek Laothamatas is a prominent political scientist who entered politics in the late 1990s, became an MP under the Democrat Party in 2001, and switched to lead the Mahachon Party which was annihilated at the 2005 poll. Anek argued that the rural electorate supported Thaksin because his populist policies were in their self-interest, but these "irresponsible" policies had made people dependent on handout welfare, politicised the bureaucracy, and would result in fiscal crises of the sort endemic to Latin American populist regimes. Anek suggested alternative policy offerings, including a version of TRT's policies cleansed of their intrinsic irresponsibility and dishonesty, and an adaptation of the third-way welfarism of Anthony Giddens. But ultimately Anek seemed to doubt that these policy offerings would sway the Thai electorate, and instead offered a political solution.

Anek argued that populism would outlast Thaksin because it was founded on the surviving vertical linkages in rural society. Thailand's rural voters were not free agents but bound by patron-client ties. Where they had once been clients of a local boss, they had now been transformed into clients of a national boss and his party.[69] In this social setting a "pure democracy" was bound to lead to de Tocqueville's "tyranny of the majority" and irresponsible populism. Anek's answer was that, "A better democracy is a balanced compromise between three elements: the representatives of the lower classes who are the majority in the country, the middle class, and the upper class."[70] In this democracy, the only time when everybody would have equal rights would be when they dropped their ballot paper in the box. After that "the importance of each person will depend on knowledge, ability, experience, and status", so that the wishes of the majority would not be able to replace "what is correct according to ethics and academic principles".[71]

The "tyranny of the majority" would be avoided by ensuring that the opinions of two groups had special weight. The first, Anek called *ekaburut* and translated as "monarchy", but glossed that this was not simply equivalent to royalty, but comprised "a small number of upper class people who are leaders or governors of the country at the highest level, who are prominent by their office and by themselves, and who command the trust of the majority". The second group, Anek called *apichon* and translated as "aristocrats". This included "the middle and upper classes, especially the leaders with wisdom and experience in politics and administration", including senior bureaucrats, top intellectuals, and senior journalists.[72] He cited examples of samurai and medieval knights as *apichon* who "had won acceptance of state and people through leadership on the battlefield",[73] suggesting that *apichon* is a metaphor for the military. Anek claimed that such a "mixed system" had in fact been in operation in Thailand "ever since October 1973".[74] A major duty of this leadership would be to educate the lower classes so that they "upgraded their needs and demands" to be less self-interested, and more aware of the interests of society and nation.

For the longer term, it would be necessary to transform rural society through education, welfare, and employment "to make rural people stronger and more self-reliant so they do not remain clients of state policy". This would "benefit the middle class and those in the city as the rural people would no longer be the foundation for populist-style democracy".[75] Both Anek and Sondhi argued that Thaksin's populism mobilised popular support for change, and that more power had to be given to the elite and middle class to prevent this.

Partly in reaction to Thaksin's populism and partly as a result of royalist fear-mongering, large parts of the Bangkok middle class not only supported the 2006 coup, but cheered demonstrations which brought down two elected Thaksin-successor governments in 2008, and welcomed calls for a "new politics" which would prevent an electoral majority dictating government policy.

Conclusion

Thaksin Shinawatra was an unlikely candidate to become a populist leader. Prior to his arraignment for false asset disclosure in December 2000, he had shown little interest in rural society and made no reference to "the people" in his rhetoric. However, when he made a bid for popular support, he became the instrument of popular aspirations. He was swept along by social forces shaped by Thailand's strategy of outward-oriented development and subjection to neoliberalism. The content of his populism began with a simple raft of redistributive policies which responded to the needs and aspirations of the informal mass that constituted around two-thirds of the workforce and the electorate. Thaksin subsequently went much further by responding not only to this constituency's demand for political goods, but also for a leader they felt they could own. People supported Thaksin because he gave them cheap health care and accessible credit, but also because he gave them a feeling of empowerment. Thaksin appealed to people by setting himself up as the enemy of the "old politics" represented by the bureaucracy and the Democrat Party; by adopting the familiar style of the local boss inflated to the national scale; and by arguing that his personal leadership would deliver more than the old liberal-democratic model which had failed to prevent massive inequality in economy and society. Thaksin's populism was thus not just a policy platform, but matches the three key points of Roberts' definition, namely mass mobilisation, personalised leadership, and a challenge to established elites.

In the old model of "development", based on the historical experience of the West, industrialisation creates a domestic capitalism, urban working class, and white-collar middle class; these new social forces sweep away old social and political elites, and support liberal democracy as the best means to resolve the conflicts among themselves. This model was replicated in the post-Second World War transformation of Japan, Korea, and Taiwan but has since become irrelevant. Since the collapse of the Cold War, the West has lost interest in nurturing domestic capitalism in developing countries and sees the outside world solely as a field of expansion for western capitalism. Countries like Thailand find the barriers against independent industrialisaation are now too high, and choose instead to adopt outward-oriented development strategies and become dependent links in the global production chains of multinational capital. This strategy results in a very different social evolution. The domestic capitalist class is weak and embattled; the formal working class is small and politically marginal; the white-collar working class is conscious of its dependence on global forces; and a high proportion of the population remains in declining agriculture or in a swelling urban informal sector. Thaksin's populist politics echoed themes visible elsewhere in Southeast Asia, in Latin America, and in Eastern Europe because the political economy underpinnings and neoliberal framework are similar.

Latin America offers the most interesting parallels because of the long history of populism in the region, and the consequent subtlety of its academic analysis and debate on the topic. Thaksin's populism had strong affinities with a phase of Latin American populism in the 1980s and 1990s, in which the most striking example was Fujimori's Peru. These populist regimes tapped the support of the informal mass by offering universalist schemes of welfare and redistribution, and by posing as enemies of an old political elite. These regimes was careful to direct their fire against the *political* and *social* elite, while simultaneously cooperating with U.S. neoliberalism in external policies, and supporting domestic business. Fujimori undermined the parliamentary system, media, and judiciary with corrupt money flows, while promoting an alternative model of personal, authoritarian rule. In order to avoid incurring obligations to their support constituency and to retain their freedom of action to negotiate with other social forces, populist leaders of this era dispensed with mass party structures and close links with civil society organisation, and relied instead on modern media and mass communication to mobilise electoral support. The cost of this strategy was insecurity, especially in the face of elite counter-attack. Most of these regimes lasted between two and five years. Fujimori was the exception, surviving for a decade, but ultimately falling just as precipitately.

This phase of populism in Latin America has since been superseded. The new wave of leaders, exemplified by Chávez, Lula da Silva, and Morales, has seen a return to more explicit leftist ideology, mobilisation of ethnic divisions, and new types of mass organisation. We are not implying that Thailand's populism strain will move in the same direction, only that the Latin American story shows that populism evolves in response to social change, the external environment, and local history.

Thaksin's tilt towards populism marks a major change in both the material and cultural aspects of Thai politics. Rafts of policy promises and catchy populist slogans are now fixtures of Thai electoral politics. While the term "populist" has been deployed by Thaksin's supporters as a pejorative and a rallying cry, it has also been adopted by his supporters and heirs as a badge. In 2008, a party formed mainly by ex-TRT members adopted as its slogan, "Populism for a Happy Life".

Thaksin's populist leadership challenged the monarchy's claim to be the sole focus of political loyalty. It threatened the ability of key sections of the middle class to influence politics — businessmen through money, bureaucrats through position and tradition, and media and intellectuals through command of public space. It promised to replace Thailand's plural, managed democracy with something akin to a personalised one-party regime. Thaksin's populism was thus a key factor in assembling the support which persuaded the military to undertake a manoeuvre which had generally been counter-productive for its own interests over the prior quarter-century. It also provoked a rupture in Thailand's democratic history. Many former enthusiasts for democracy openly supported the coup. Against this background, the junta oversaw the preparation of a new constitution that reduced the power of parliament while increasing that of the bureaucracy, military, and judiciary. After parliament was restored in 2008, Sondhi Limthongkun proposed reducing directly elected members to only 30 per cent of the lower house. The fears raised by Thaksin's populism led Thailand's old institutions, along with large sections of the intelligentsia and middle class, to fear electoral democracy itself.

Notes

An earlier version of this chapter appeared in *Journal of Contemporary Asia* 38, 1 (Feb. 2008). As that issue was a special number on the Thai coup of September 2006, this earlier version put stress on the significance of Thaksin's populism in the context of the coup. In this revised version, we have reduced that emphasis but the bulk of the text and the main arguments remain unchanged.

[1]   Ernesto Laclau, *On Populist Reason* (London and New York: Verso, 2005); Francisco Panizza, ed., *Populism and the Mirror of Democracy* (London and New York: Verso, 2005).

[2]   Kenneth M. Roberts, "Populism, Political Conflict, and Grass-Roots Organisation in Latin America", *Comparative Politics* 38, 2 (Jan. 2006). According to another definition, populism is any movement that "mobilises those who feel themselves to be disadvantaged by socioeconomic and political dislocation, as well as a

leadership style that draws on a sense of disaffection from the established political system and elites"; see C. Sabatini and and E. Farnsworth, "A 'Left Turn' in Latin America? The Urgent Need for Labor Law Reform", *Journal of Democracy* 17, 4 (2006): 63n2.

3   *The Nation*, 15 July 1998.

4   Walaya (Phumtham Vejjayachai), *Thaksin Chinnawat: ta du dao thao tit din* [Thaksin Shinawatra: Eyes on the Stars, Feet on the Ground] (Bangkok: Matichon, 2001), p. 211.

5   *The Nation*, 28 Mar. 2000; 23 Mar. 2001.

6   Viroj NaRanong and Anchana NaRanong, "Universal Health Care Coverage: Impacts of the 30-Baht Health-Care Scheme on the Poor in Thailand", *TDRI Quarterly Review* 21, 3 (2006): 3–10.

7   *Bangkok Post*, 17 Aug. 2000.

8   Andrew Brown and Kevin Hewison, "'Economics is the Deciding Factor': Labour Politics in Thaksin's Thailand", *Pacific Affairs* 78, 3 (2005).

9   See especially: James Ockey, "Change and Continuity in the Thai Political System", *Asian Survey* 43, 4 (2003); Duncan McCargo and Ukrist Pathamanand, *The Thaksinization of Thailand* (Copenhagen: NIAS Press, 2005), ch. 3; Michael H. Nelson, "Thailand's House Elections of 6 January 2001: Thaksin's Landslide Victory and Lucky Escape", in *Thailand's New Politics: KPI Yearbook 2001*, ed. M.H. Nelson (Bangkok: White Lotus, 2002).

10   *Bangkok Post*, 12 Feb. 2001.

11   Anek Laothamatas, *Thaksina-prachaniyom* [Thaksin-style Populism] (Bangkok: Matichon, 2006), p. 78.

12   Kasian Tejapira, "Pisat poppiwlisam" [The Spectre of Populism], *Matichon Raiwan*, 20 Jan. 2001; "Thunniyom phuk-kat upatham vs. wara prachaniyom" [Patrimonial Monopoly Capitalism vs. Populism], *Matichon Raiwan*, 3 Feb. 2001.

13   The first use of the term "populist" to describe Thaksin in English appeared two days earlier in the *Far Eastern Economic Review*, but in an off-hand way, expressing the view that the TRT election platform was not meant to be taken seriously: "In reality, stripped of its populist sheen, Thaksin's government will be one of big money and big-business interests, reflecting its leader's pedigree"; see Shawn Crispin and Rodney Tasker, "Thailand Incorporated", *Far Eastern Economic Review*, 18 Jan. 2001. The *Review* did not regularly apply the adjective to Thaksin until one year later.

14   Anek, *Thaksina-prachaniyom*, p. 79.

15   *Bangkok Post*, 26 July 2001; Pasuk Phongpaichit and Chris Baker, *Thaksin: The Business of Politics in Thailand* (Chiang Mai: Silkworm Books, 2004), pp. 120–2.

16   Large volumes of shares in the Shinawatra companies had been filed under the names of the family's housekeeper, maid, driver, and security guard, making them figure among the stock market's largest shareholders.

17   Viroj and Anchana, "Universal Health Care Coverage".

18   *Bangkok Post*, 18 Oct. 2001.

19   "Village" here is an official territorial unit used in both urban and rural areas. The funds were available to both urban and rural communities.

20   Worawan Chandoevwit, "Thailand's Grass Roots Policies", *TDRI Quarterly Review* 18, 2 (2003): 3–8.

21   *The Nation*, 7 Jan. 2002.

22   *The Nation*, 23 Dec. 2000.

23   *Time*, Asia edition, 13 Aug. 2001, p. 19.

24   Kevin Hewison, "Crafting Thailand's New Social Contract", *Pacific Review* 17, 4 (2004). The first drafts of this argument by Hewison appeared in early 2002, as did our similar analysis of the double-headed nature of Thaksin's populism, see Pasuk Phongpaichit and Chris Baker, "'The Only Good Populist is a Rich Populist': Thaksin Shinawatra and Thailand's Democracy", City University of Hong Kong, Southeast Asia Research Centre Working Papers 36, October 2002.

25   *The Nation*, 28 Apr. 2004.

26   Ibid., 23 July 2004.

27   Ibid., 14 May 2004.

28   Ibid., 16 May 2004.

29   Thaksin Shinawatra, "Thaksin's Election Speech: Translation of Thaksin's Speech, Sanam Luang, 4 February 2005", <http://pioneer.netserv.chula.ac.th/~ppasuk/papers.htm>; see also *The Nation*, 18 and 19 Oct. 2004; *Bangkok Post*, 7 Nov. 2004.

30   This can be seen by comparison of the vote for TRT in the February 2005 and April 2006 polls, before and after the At Samat event. Votes cast for TRT increased by 11.5 per cent in Roi-et (and by 13.2 per cent and 17.9 per cent in the neighbouring provinces of Yasothon and Kalasin which were also peripherally involved in the event), while falling 8.6 per cent nationwide. Our calculation using unofficial results for the 2006 poll (there are no official results as the poll was rescinded).

31   Viroj and Anchana, "Universal Health Care Coverage".

32   For example, *The Nation*, 26 Sept. 2004.

33   Pitch Pongsawat, "Senthang prachathippatai lae kan prap tua khong rat thai nai rabop thaksin" [The Path of Democracy and the Modification of the State under Thaksinism], *Fa dieo kan* [The Same Sky], 2, 1 (2004).

34   Personal communication, February 2007.

35   Thaksin, "Thaksin's Election Speech".

36   Ibid.

37   Ibid.

38   For example, *Matichon Raiwan*, 30 Sept. 2003.

39   Thai industrialisation is also very much part of global production chains, with many manufactured goods assembled using imported parts and inputs produced elsewhere.

40   Andrew Brown, *Labour, Politics and the State in Industrializing Thailand* (London and New York: RoutledgeCurzon, 2004).

41   Tamaki Endo, "Promotional Policies for the Urban Informal Sector in Thailand: Analysing from the Perspective of Policies for the Urban Poor", Kyoto University Economic Society, PhD Candidates' Monograph Series, no. 200212006.

42   Mushtaq H. Khan, "Markets, States and Democracy: Patron-Client Networks and the Case for Democracy in Developing Countries", *Democratization* 12, 5 (2005); Anek, *Thaksina-prachaniyom*.

43   World Bank, *Thailand Social Monitor: Poverty and Public Policy* (Bangkok: World Bank, 2001).

44   Pasuk Phongpaichit and Chris Baker, *Thailand's Crisis* (Chiang Mai: Silkworm Books, 2000), ch. 5.

45   From 2003, the Thaksin government set rice procurement prices above the market price. The coup government estimated this policy had cost 101.76 billion baht (*The Nation*, 14 Oct. 2006).

46   *Matichon Raiwan*, 26 May 2003.

47   Thaksin, "Thaksin's Election Speech".

48   T.P. Carroll, "Turkey's Justice Development Party: A Model for Democratic Islam", *Middle East Intelligence Bulletin* 6 (2004).

49   Kenneth M. Roberts, "Neoliberalism and the Transformation of Populism in Latin America: The Peruvian Case", *World Politics* 48, 1 (1995); Kurt Weyland, "Neopopulism and Neoliberalism in Latin America: Unexpected Affinities", *Studies in Comparative International Development* 31, 3 (1996); M.L. Conniff, *Populism in Latin America* (Tuscaloosa: University of Alabama Press, 1999).

50   Roberts, "Populism, Political Conflict, and Grass-Roots Organisation".

51   Roberts, "Neoliberalism and the Transformation of Populism"; S. Ellner, "The Contrasting Variants of the Populism of Hugo Chavez and Alberto Fujimori", *Journal of Latin American Studies* 35, 1 (2003); J. McMillan and P. Zoido, "How to Subvert Democracy: Montesinos in Peru", Centre for Democracy, Development, and the Rule of Law, Stanford Institute of International Studies, CDDRL Working Papers, No. 3 (11 Aug. 2004).

52   Weyland, "Neopopulism and Neoliberalism", p. 10.

53   Ellner, "The Contrasting Variants"; Roberts, "Populism, Political Conflict, and Grass-Roots Organisation".

54   Roberts, "Populism, Political Conflict, and Grass-Roots Organisation".

55   McMillan and Zoido, "How to Subvert Democracy".

56   McCargo and Ukrist, *Thaksinization*, ch. 3.

57   *The Nation*, 18 Dec. 2000; 21 Feb. 2005.

58   Ockey, "Change and Continuity".

59   *Bangkok Post*, 19 Dec. 2000.

60   Brown and Hewison, "'Economics is the Deciding Factor'".

61   *Bangkok Post*, 8 and 9 Jan. 2003.

62   Thaksin, "Thaksin's Speech".

63   *The Nation*, 15 July 2005.

64   Kasian Tejapira, "Toppling Thaksin", *New Left Review* 39 (2006): 8–10.

65 Kevin Hewison, "A Book, the King, and the 2006 Coup", *Journal of Contemporary Asia* 38, 1 (Feb. 2008).

66 As a crude index of the middle-class interest in populism, these are the total mentions of populism or populist in *The Nation*, using their web cache of past issues. 2001: 66; 2002: 150; 2003: 265; 2004: 280; 2005: 206; 2006: 307.

67 A graphic created by an anonymous academic and circulated in March 2006 purported to show a "Thaksin model" in which taxes levied on the middle class (25 per cent of the population) paid for populist policies lavished on the poor (70 per cent) to keep Thaksin in power to boost the wealth of the rich (5 per cent). It concluded, "The middle class has to support the whole country." The graphic appeared in several newspapers including *The Nation*, 20 Mar. 2006.

68 Keyes, "Sondhi Limthongkul in Seattle".

69 Anek, *Thaksina-prachaniyom*, pp. 123–4.

70 Ibid., p. 177.

71 Anek, *Thaksina-prachaniyom*, pp. 178–9. Anek initially argues that people are rational to support Thaksin's populism, and should not be pictured as stupid and fooled (pp. 164–5). But later he compares populism to a mantra which can stupefy (*sakot*) people and to a whirlpool which can suck them down (pp. 166, 186); he dismisses TRT's election victory as illegitimate because of the use of money (pp. 179, 182); and argues that people need education to "upgrade their needs" (pp. 167, 185, 189–91).

72 Anek, *Thaksina-prachaniyom*, pp. 178, 179, 181.

73 Ibid., p. 181.

74 Ibid., p. 183.

75 Ibid., p. 198.

CHAPTER 5

Democracy and Populism in Thailand

Yoshifumi Tamada

Thaksin Shinawatra was the first national leader in Thailand who was widely regarded as a populist. Thaksin came to power after a victory in the 2001 elections, and was ousted by a military coup on 19 September 2006.[1] During his premiership, Thai politics changed drastically.[2] Thaksin's antagonists "argued that Thaksin's populism mobilised popular support for change, and that more power had to be given to the elite and middle class to prevent this" (see pp. 86–7).

Populism "is a notoriously vague term".[3] Taggart points out that, "Often populist style is confused with a style that simply seeks to be popular — to appeal to a wide range of people. This is not simply an incomplete but also an inaccurate use of the term."[4] As a leader, Thaksin undoubtedly sought to be popular and he is often regarded as a populist leader.

Probably it matters little for political players in Thailand whether Thaksin was a populist or not. It does for researchers, however. The purpose of this essay is to insist that Thaksin was branded as a populist for political reasons although Thaksin was not a populist. As he was too popular and full of electoral legitimacy, the anti-Thaksin forces coined *prachaniyom*, a Thai word for populism and used the word in an accusatory tone. The term populism has been used mainly as a weapon to denounce a certain type of politics — not only seeking popularity but also buying votes. This was a way of rejecting or diluting democratic legitimacy of elected leaders and finally justifying a coup.

Is Thaksin a Populist?

What is Populism?

Is Thaksin a populist or not? The answer can be yes or no depending upon the definition of the term populism.

Here, I follow Canovan: "Populism in modern democratic societies is best seen as an appeal to 'the people' against both the established structure of power and the dominant ideas and values of the society."[5]

Canovan's definition highlights four important features: power structure, an appeal to "the people", political style, and a characteristic mood. First, populist movements "involve some kind of revolt against the established structure of power in the name of the people". Canovan argues that "The crucial difference" between populist movements and other anti-system mobilisation "is that while both are anti-system, populism challenges not only established power-holders but also elite values. Populist animus is directed not just at the political and economic establishments but also at opinion-formers in the academy and the media."[6]

Second, "Populism is not just a reaction *against* power structures but an appeal *to* a recognised authority. Populists claim legitimacy on the ground that they speak for *the people*: that is to say, they claim to represent the democratic sovereign, not a sectional interest such as an economic class."[7] What types of people do populists speak for? Canovan identifies three types. One is "the *united people* ... as against the parties or factions that divide it". Second is "*our people*, often in the sense of our ethnic kith and kin". Third is "'the common people' or '*ordinary people*' against the privileged, highly educated, cosmopolitan elite".[8]

Third, "Populist appeals to the people are characteristically couched in a style that is 'democratic' in the sense of being aimed at ordinary people". "[S]imple, direct language is not enough to mark a politician as populist unless he or she is prepared also to offer political analyses and proposed solutions that are also simple and direct."[9]

Fourth, populism has a characteristic mood. "Populist politics is not ordinary routine politics. It has the revivalist flavour of a movement, powered by the enthusiasm that draws normally unpolitical people into the political arena.... Associated with this mood is the tendency for heightened emotions to be focused on a charismatic leader. Personalized leadership is a natural corollary of the reaction against politics-as-usual."[10]

A Political Version

Criticism of the Thaksin administration started in 2001 when Thaksin came to power. Thaksin enjoyed democratic legitimacy because he gained and retained power through elections. Thaksin's party (Thai Rak Thai party, TRT) promised appealing policies and won election in 2001. Thaksin implemented these policies through the first four years of his premiership. The electorate approved the policies, and TRT achieved an overwhelming victory

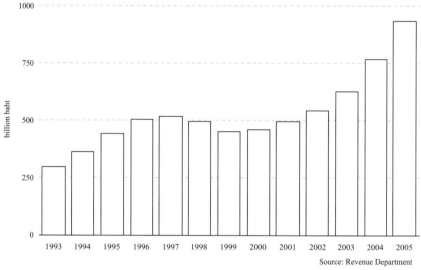

Source: Revenue Department

Figure 5-1   Total Taxes Collected, 1993–2005

in the 2005 general election. The policies were so popular that opposition parties had to imitate them.

It was difficult for other parties to compete with TRT in the same game of catch-all policies. It was almost impossible to denounce the TRT government as undemocratic, because the party won sweeping victories in the general elections. Thus a convenient word was coined to criticise the Thaksin administration: *prachaniyom.* According to Anek, the term began to circulate in the context of criticism of Thaksin after he came into power in 2001.[11] The word gained currency rapidly precisely because it was repeatedly used to criticise Thaksin and TRT. Thus, from the outset, the word carried negative connotations.

Thai liberals did not like Thaksin's redistributive policies and worried about damages imposed by the populist policies upon public finance. Scholars often referred to cases in Latin American countries and tried to emphasise the risk of financial catastrophe and economic collapse brought by lax fiscal policies. Such can happen in theory, but no one had seen it happen in real life before the coup.[12] Suehiro points out that Thaksin disliked debt both private and public and searched for debt-free public finance. Moreover, in promoting the grassroots economy, Thaksin preferred low interest loans to transfer payments.[13]

However, it seems to me that it mattered little whether or not Thaksin's policies were causing or would cause a collapse of the economy. Whether or not his policies were populist also did not matter to his denunciators. Therefore, these critics rarely referred to the fact that government revenue doubled during five years under Thaksin. The generous redistributive policies were fiscally supported during the Thaksin administration (see Figure 5-1).[14] Moreover, as long as Thaksin, a leading businessman in Thailand with a strong stake in maintaining a sound macro-economy, was a prime minister, there was little reason for concern about economic collapse. Nevertheless, since populism was a weapon to attack Thaksin, little attention was paid to evidence for rebuttal.

An Academic Version

Pasuk and Baker (this volume, Chapter 4) give us an excellent analysis of Thaksin's populism. They turn the commonplace assumption upside down correctly. "Thaksin's populism is often equated with his policies, especially the three-point electoral platform of 2001 (cheap health care, agrarian debt relief, village funds). It can quite properly be argued that such policies are the everyday stuff of electoral politics and do not deserve the label of populism" (p. 66). They argue that Thaksin's populism was not just a policy platform but approximated Roberts' model of mass mobilisation, personalised leadership and a challenge to established elites. They conclude, "Thaksin's populist leadership challenged the monarchy's claim to be the sole focus of political loyalty. It threatened the ability of key sections of the middle class to influence politics — businessmen through money, bureaucrats through position and tradition, and media and intellectuals through command of public space. It promised to replace Thailand's plural, managed democracy with something akin to a personalised one-party regime" (p. 89).

Although I agree with their analysis the most part, I cannot agree with them regarding the challenge to the established elite. Who are elites? Did Thaksin challenge them really? They point that the royalists disliked Thaksin from the beginning and the middle class opposed him from 2004 on. However, A's opposition against B is one thing and B's challenge against A is another. Regarding the monarchy, it is possible that the monarchy feels threatened by Thaksin as Connors writes, "In claiming to channel the voice of people, [Thaksin] was also challenging in very concrete terms the royal liberal conception of shared sovereignty between the monarch and people."[15] However, it was not Thaksin who stipulated in the 1997 constitution that sovereignty belongs to the people. The electoral system introduced by the constitution enabled the prime minister to claim a popular mandate as described later. Anek provides further revealing information about their misgivings, as follows:

We should apprehend that the populist policies [of the Thaksin admin-
istration] may undermine policies under the patronage of the monarchy.
If government leaders would pursue populist policies without great care,
they might come into conflict with the royal patronage for pre-eminence.
The author has heard a resident in Northeast Thailand say frankly, "His
Majesty the King has been on the throne for sixty years and has always
helped the poor. Regarding medical treatment, however, the royal assistance cannot match Thaksin's 30-baht-a-visit health care scheme."[16]

Thus, Thaksin clashed with the monarchy from the royalist perspective.

It is worth noting that the function that the monarchy had fulfilled for
the people in the rural area in the past was affected to a considerable extent
during the era of Thaksin's populism. This is why two kinds of populist —
royal populist and electoral populist — clashed with each other. As a result,
the military seized power for the purpose of reinforcing and saving the royal
populist.[17]

However, we should still ask whether Thaksin challenged the monarchy? It is impossible for anyone to challenge the institution publicly in
Thailand. It would be extremely difficult to mobilise the people to challenge
kingship. It is quite apparent that no one had any intention to challenge the
monarchy when they voted for TRT at elections. When Pasuk and Baker
write, "[Thaksin] understood that presenting himself as an enemy of Thailand's political elite conveyed an appealing message to his mass audience"
(p. 75), the monarchy must not be included in the "political elite". Therefore,
it is not probable that Thaksin was a populist who challenged the monarchy.

Regarding the middle class, can we regard it as an established elite?
Pasuk and Baker place emphasis on the middle class.

> The evolution of Thaksin's populism and the growth of middle-class
> opposition were interrelated in a kind of dialectic: as Thaksin lost urban
> middle-class support, he intensified his populist appeal to the informal
> mass; as Thaksin's threat to bring millions of rural supporters into the
> capital was the logical conclusion to this spiral, and a key trigger for staging
> the coup. Beneath this interplay lay the massive gap in incomes between
> city and village, and a long-standing middle-class fear of empowerment of
> the rural mass. The threat which the middle class perceived in Thaksin's
> populism was partly fear that they would be obliged to pay for his
> redistributive schemes, but more fear that they would no longer have a
> privileged position to influence the state agenda. Sondhi Limthongkul,
> who set out to channel middle-class aspirations, stated explicitly that
> Thaksin had to be overthrown in order to restore political influence to
> the middle class. (p. 85)

As stated later, Thaksin and TRT were very popular in Bangkok at the 2005 general elections although the urban middle class might feel threatened by them. The urban people began to oppose Thaksin after Sonthi Limthongkun started his talk show. They were mobilised by Sonthi to challenge Thaksin. Moreover, it was not necessary for powerful Thaksin to challenge the opposition parties, bureaucracy, business community because he could cope with them without mobilising the people. It was quite unnecessary and fruitless for Thaksin to antagonise the upper and middle class in order to solicit the lower class support.

Populism and Mobilisation

To Divide and Mobilise the People

One of the four reasons that the Council for Democratic Reform (CDR, official title of the coup junta) gave as justification for the September 2006 coup was a rift in the society between the pro-Thaksin side and the anti-Thaksin side. As Pasuk and Baker note, it was a "rift that ran between the Bangkok middle class on one extreme, and Thaksin's largely rural support base on the other" (p. 85). Although it was true that there was a rift, the boundary was defined by the anti-Thaksin forces with the intention to draft the urban middle class people into the anti-Thaksin camp.

Sonthi Limthongkun, a leader of PAD (People's Alliance for Democracy), incited animosity against Thaksin and his supporters among the people through simple and clear agitation. First, he used an ambiguous but catchy term, the "Thaksin regime", coined by intellectuals[18] to create an easy target for criticism. Not only Thaksin but also his entourage and supporters were lumped together and regarded as being as bad as Thaksin, who was corrupt and irreverent. In Sonthi's universe, there are only two types of people: ordinary people who are ignorant and easily bought out; and PAD supporters. Thirayut Bunmi, a famous student leader in the 1970s, summoned the press and disclosed his idea about the present political situation on 4 March 2006, saying "The election on 2 April, the parliament, and the government are merely farcical and nominal." He continued by stating, "I am alarmed by Thaksin's efforts to secure support from the urban poor. Looking at the cases of foreign countries, for example Chile and the Philippines, the mobilisation of this class will cause trouble. In the Philippines, the urban poor turned into armed insurgents."[19] There have been many would-be liberalist intellectuals like Thirayut who have revealed their true character as elitist and anti-egalitarian in the last few years.

According to this camp, people who turned their back on PAD were either dullards or Thaksin's slaves. It was a choice between the two. Those who tried to act or speak from a third or neutral position were stigmatised as Thaksin's slavish following. People who did not sympathise with PAD were forced into silence. Criticisms of the TRT government filled a high proportion of newspapers columns. Only a small number of brave intellectuals expressed views critical of PAD or supportive of TRT. This is why a columnist, Kilen Pralongchoeng, of *Thai Rat* had to write, "I must be condemned as hired by the millionaire to write this", when he referred to the merits of the Thaksin administration.[20]

It is quite clear that Sonthi deployed populist tactics. He challenged the established power-holders, Thaksin and the TRT administration, and tried to mobilise urban middle class people. Since most ordinary people were supporters of the TRT administration, Sonthi tried to secure the support of the middle class. He urged the urban people to revolt against a corrupt administration supported by the poor.

The political scientist Chai-anan Samudavanija stated at a seminar on 7 March 2006,

> Although it took 40 years for the Communist Party of Thailand to divide the people in two, it took only five years for Thaksin to do that. People in the October 14 generation who once had joined the Communist Party and now are assisting the Thaksin administration know well that the [urban] middle class is capricious and cannot constitute a stable support base in contrast to the rural people who don't fail to return their grateful acknowledgment to humble favour.[21]

It is very doubtful whether all urban people were anti-Thaksin. However, talking of the division as an accomplished fact is tantamount to encouraging the division. Moreover, urban people had no choice but to take the anti-Thaksin side, due to the clear specification that rural people were on the Thaksin side. The tactic of forcing people to choose between pro-Thaksin and anti-Thaksin worked out well.

Pye and Schaffar argue, "It has become common to define the anti-Thaksin protests as a middle-class movement. This term is used loosely and lumped together with 'the urban elite', implying that Thaksin was supported by the poor in the countryside and opposed by the relatively rich in the city."[22] In this struggle for the urban middle class, the rhetoric of "populism" worked well. Anti-Thaksin leaders insisted that Thaksin bought support of the poor through redistributive policies. Branding Thaksin as a populist, they tried to dilute the electoral legitimacy of the Thaksin administration on the one hand, and to secure the support of the middle class, who thought that they were not bought although they enjoyed a similar "populist" public service, on the other hand.[23]

The middle class has acquired political importance since the May incident in 1992. Although the class is in a numerical minority, the class commands discursive power and has clout as a result of being able to influence the general trend of public opinion.[24] The class can be used to make up for the deficit of democratic legitimacy of the anti-Thaksin movement.

The Minority and a Coup

Although anti-Thaksin forces managed to mobilise the urban people against Thaksin to a considerable extent, this mobilised force was in a minority not only because the urban population is the minority among the national population but also because not all urban people necessarily opposed the Thaksin administration.

Although TRT was often regarded as a party for the poor, its election pledges set out a dual track policy called Thaksinomics. TRT tried to win the support of both the poor and the well-off. Because the party implemented its pledges after it came to power, it scored a sweeping victory in the 2005 general elections (see Tables 5-1 and 5-2).

There are two significant facts. First, the number of TRT MPs in Bangkok increased from 29 in 2001 to 32 in 2005 (see Table 5-1). Second,

Table 5-1 TRT Seats in Territorial Constituencies, 2001 and 2005

	Bangkok		Central		North		Northeast		South		Total	
	2001	2005	2001	2005	2001	2005	2001	2005	2001	2005	2001	2005
Thai Rak Thai Party	29	32	47	80	54	71	69	126	1	1	200	310
Democrat Party	8	4	19	7	16	5	6	2	48	52	97	65
Chat Thai Party	–	1	21	10	3	–	11	6	–	1	35	23
New Aspiration Party	–	–	3	–	1	–	19	–	5	–	28	–
Chat Phatthana Party	–	–	4	–	2	–	16	–	–	–	22	–
Seritham Party	–	–	–	–	–	–	14	–	–	–	14	–
Ratsadon Party	–	–	–	–	–	–	1	–	–	–	2	–
Thin Thai Party	–	–	–	–	–	–	1	–	–	–	1	–
Social Action Party	–	–	–	–	–	–	1	–	–	–	1	–
Mahachon Party	–	–	–	–	–	–	–	2	–	–	–	2
Total	37	37	95	97	76	76	138	136	54	54	400	400

Table 5-2 Votes for TRT and Democrat Party under the Party-list System in Bangkok, 2001 and 2005

	2001	*2005*
TRT	1,131,050	1,668,102
Democrat Party	717,990	972,290
DP as a per cent of TRT	63	58

although both TRT and its major rival the Democrat Party increased their votes in the proportional representative system in Bangkok between 2001 and 2005, TRT increased more than the Democrat Party. The ratio of the Democrat's votes to the TRT's votes decreased from 63 per cent in 2001 to 58 per cent in 2005 (see Table 5-2). TRT became more popular among the Bangkok electorate.

It is true that the popularity of Thaksin and TRT decreased after PAD tried to lure away TRT supporters in Bangkok. Although PAD asserted that most people in Bangkok felt an aversion toward Thaksin and demanded his resignation in 2006, opinion surveys do not bear this out. The ABAC Poll, one of the most famous research agencies in contemporary Thailand, conducted a survey on the pros and cons of Thaksin's resignation in the metropolitan area several times in 2006. According to the ABAC poll conducted on 5 March 2006, immediately after a group of people had asked the king to dismiss Thaksin, 48.2 per cent of the respondents thought he should resign while 35.5 per cent thought he did not have to resign. But this sentiment did not last (see Figure 5-2). In surveys over the next five months, the proportion hoping he would resign fell from 48.2 to 24.8 per cent, while those hoping he would remain in office climbed from 35.5 to 43.0 per cent.[25] It is certain that even in the metropolitan area, where it is widely believed there were many anti-Thaksin people, the PAD's downplaying of democratic procedure was not supported by the majority of the population, even just before the coup in September. It is needless to say that the majority of the rural population did not want Thaksin to resign at that time. The fact that the anti-Thaksin forces could not win in an election was a decisive reason why they had to resort to a coup in September 2006.

Regarding the nature of the coup, the third announcement of the CDR is revealing. It stated:

1. The current constitution, drafted in 1997, is now abrogated.
2. The House of Representatives, the Senate, the Cabinet and the Constitution Court are dissolved.

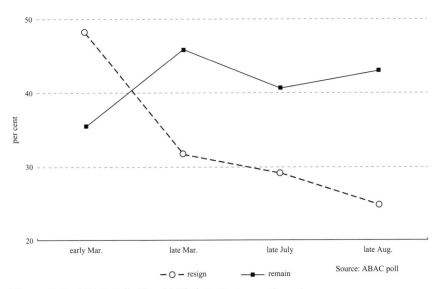

Figure 5-2 ABAC Poll: Should Thaksin Resign or Remain

3.   The privy councillors will remain at their duties.
4.   The courts of justice, except the Constitution Court, will retain their full power.[26]

Any institution not abolished or dissolved by such an announcement remained in existence. Why then did the coup council announce it was retaining the privy councillors and the courts? It would be rational to think that the privy councillors and the courts had special importance for the coup leaders, probably as indispensable allies in their fight against Thaksin. Although the privy councillors were seldom involved directly in politics, subordinates or close aides of the president of the Privy Council occupied important positions in the Cabinet, the appointed legislature and the Constitution Drafting Assembly after the coup. At the same time, the courts tried cases conducive to the removal of Thaksin and his supporters and enjoyed a larger role in politics under the 2007 constitution.

Popularity and Presidentialisation

It is very interesting to note that when Anek critically analyses Thaksin's populist policies, what really matters is not the redistributive policies themselves but the popularity and legitimacy deriving from the policies. Popularity is useful to strengthen legitimacy and leadership.

Thaksin's leadership derived from the electoral victories of his party. TRT was strong in the elections. There were three main reasons for its victory: buying of the incumbent MPs[27] and incorporation of other parties; attractive campaign pledges;[28] and the incompetence of rival parties to fight against TRT.

The electoral victory of TRT owed much to election reform under the 1997 constitution. The system of multiple-member electoral districts was changed into a mixed electoral system of single-seat constituencies and proportional representation. The single-member system worked in favour of a large-scale political party, and the proportional representation system made campaign pledges and the image of the party leader significant (see below). TRT took the lead in adapting to this new system and recorded a landslide victory. Owing to the electoral victory, Thaksin was able to administer the government quite stably.

The election reform had another very significant effect. The 1997 constitution aimed to have Cabinet members selected from party-list MPs in the proportional representation election system. The party leaders who

Table 5-3 Election Results on Party List, 2001, 2005, and 2006

	2001		2005		2006	
	number	*per cent*	*number*	*per cent*	*number*	*per cent*
Thai Rak Thai	11,634,495	38.9	18,993,073	58.7	16,420,755	56.5
New Aspiration	2,008,948					
Chat Phatthana	1,755,476					
Seritham	807,902					
Sub-total	16,206,821	54.2				
Democrat	7,610,789	25.4	7,210,742	22.3		
Chat Thai	1,523,807	5.1	2,061,559	6.4		
Others	3,287,785	11.0	2,782,849	8.6	1,935,647	6.7
Votes of all parties (A)	28,629,202		31,048,223		18,356,402	
Blank votes (B)	530,599		357,515		9,051,706	31.1
Valid votes (A + B)	29,159,801		31,405,738		27,408,108	
Invalid votes	745,829		935,586		1,680,101	
Total votes	29,909,271	100	32,341,330	100	29,088,209	100

Note: The numbers of valid votes, invalid votes and total votes in 2001 and 2005 do not correspond but they are presented here as in the original.

Source: Election Commission of Thailand.[29]

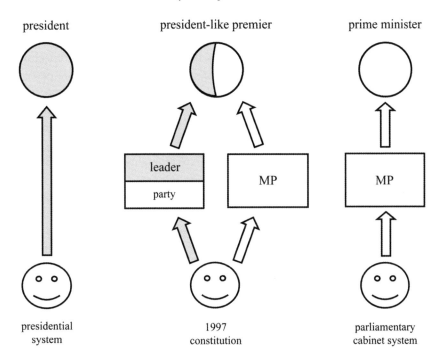

Figure 5-3 Comparison between President and Prime Minister

were candidates for the premiership were ranked at the top of each party's list. Thus when the electorate chose a party, they in fact chose a prime minister. In addition, the electoral district for the proportional representation system was the whole nation. Thus the leader of a party that got the largest number of votes in the proportional representation system in the nationwide constituency was in a position to take pride in that number. In a parliamentary Cabinet system, the legitimacy of the prime minister derives from the Lower House which selects the prime minister. In contrast, in a presidential system the legitimacy of the president derives from election by the people. There is a significant difference between the two systems. The prime minister under the 1997 constitution closely resembled a president, and enjoyed dual legitimacy: from the parliament and from the electorate (see Figure 5-3). This gave the prime minister firm democratic legitimacy. Thaksin was proud of his huge numerical vote of 12 million, 19 million, and 16 million in successive party-list polls (see Table 5-3).

Thaksin exerted strong leadership owing to the numerical majority TRT commanded in the parliament. The president-like legitimacy reinforced his leadership and legitimacy further. This could be regarded as a case of presidentialisation of politics, which has been observed in many countries in recent decades.[30] Andrew Walker reports from a northern village, "Electoral support for the various government initiatives was enhanced by the perception that they had been implemented very quickly and in a manner that largely bypassed local bureaucracy. The rapid pace of the Thaksin government's financial assistance was a key point of contrast with previous governments."[31] Walker concludes that "Thaksin government's effectiveness and Thaksin's strong and decisive leadership" were highly appreciated in the rural area he studied.[32]

However, many intellectuals reacted in an exaggerated fashion against the presidency in Thailand. President-like leadership, still less president-like legitimacy, were not permissible at all for them because they seemed to harm the authority of the king. Thaksin's arrogant manner also irritated them very much. Chai-anan Samudavanija, a leading advocate of the royalist camp, spoke at a seminar on 24 May 2006 as follows.

> There have been few national leaders who gained power owing to electoral victory in Thailand. Field Marshall Sarit Thanarat did not enjoy [democratic] legitimacy deriving from political parties.... Important is the fact that the Thai Rak Thai party has made efforts to muster support not for the party itself but for the leader. This support should be considered from a broader viewpoint. If we do not stop it, the monarchy will become only a symbolic figure and fulfil only a ceremonial role.... There is a significant difference between Sarit and Thaksin. Sarit did not have democratic legitimacy because he rejected electoral democracy. Sarit established closer rapport between the monarchy and the people [in order to get legitimacy from the monarchy]. This was why the people supported Sarit. In contrast, it is apparent that various policies of the present government led by Thaksin do not conform to the royal will.[33]

Democracy and Populism

Ji Ungpakorn argues, "The 19th September coup was ... a coup by anti-Taksin elites who hated Taksin's Populist policies because they were giving Taksin too much power."[34] Why did PAD turn its back on electoral democracy and arrange the coup so shamelessly that they were damned as "*P*eople's *A*lliance for coup *D*'état"?[35] I think that we can find an answer in the curious coexistence of two democracies: electoral democracy and Thai-style democracy.[36] On 29 June 2006, Thaksin called a meeting of senior bureaucrats and declared that he would protect democracy at the price of his life against those who were attempting to topple the democratic regime.[37] Michai Ruchuphan, a senior lawyer close to the president of the Privy Council, fought back against Thaksin, writing on his personal website, "Thaksin used the short term 'democracy' intentionally without a modifier [in the speech on 29 June]. However, as far as we have learned, the democratic regime in Thailand is a 'democratic regime with the king as head of the state', different from the democratic regime in foreign countries. Wherever there is reference to democracy in the Constitution, it is stipulated clearly as a 'democratic regime with the king as head of the state'."[38] In fact, Thaksin referred to "democracy" 31 times in the hour-long speech, and used the full expression of "democratic regime with the king as head of the state" once. It seemed that what mattered was not the expression but its content.

How is the "democratic regime with the king as head of the state" different from an ordinary democratic regime?[39] According to the outstanding historian Nidhi Eoseewong,

> In Thailand the dominant opinion has been that kingdom (*ratchaanajak*) and nation-state cannot go together. This is because there have been persistent efforts to read kingdom for royal patrimonial state [*rat ratchasombat*, translated literally as 'a state as private property of the royal family'] since the 1947 coup…. Since then every leader seizing power via coup has depended on the monarchy for political legitimacy…. If we live in a patrimonial state, it is impossible for us to justify power by the mass votes of 14 million or 18 million we got in the general elections precisely because legitimacy derives from endorsement and satisfaction of the father-like monarch.[40]

Despite the displeasure of the elite, Thai politics has been democratised since the 1970s.[41] As politics become more democratic, elections become more significant. Guardians of "the democratic regime with the king as head of the state" must increase their efforts to denigrate electoral politics. Adopting a moral view of politics, they paint elections as buying and selling of votes, with the intention of diluting the democratic legitimacy of those who win such elections. As Thaksin was exceptionally popular among the electorate, a new weapon, populism, was used to condemn him. His overwhelming popularity and the sweeping victory of TRT in elections were explained in terms of populism. As various redistributive policies, which are common in democratic countries but which were implemented for the first time in Thai history by Thaksin, were innovative gimmicks, populist criticism against him seemed plausible to some extent. For the denouncers, populism meant purchase of votes, legitimacy, and power.

Criticism was directed not only at the buyers but also at the bought, at the sellers. Phichit Likhitkitjasombun argues that the anti-Thaksin forces "believe that morality should come before election.... [They] can accept democracy and election. But the electorate must elect only politicians who they can accept. The people who don't elect such acceptable candidates should be regarded as the ignorant."[42] Phichit explained the elitist way of thinking as follows, "Since the poor and farmers are inferior to the urban population in education and information, they sell their votes for small sums of money.... As the electorates are ignorant, blinded by greed, and vote-selling", the electoral victory of TRT resulted in little legitimacy.[43] It becomes clear that populism is a term of abuse directed at popular leaders and the populace.

This is confirmed by events since Abhisit Vejjajiva of the Democrat party assumed the premiership with the help of PAD, the military and the Constitution Court in December 2008. The Democrat government has embarked extensively on mega-populist policies which are far more generous and redistributive than those of the Thaksin administration. Although several people worry about the financial burden, the forces which once cursed Thaksin's redistributive policies as vote-buying remain silent for the most part. We may point out two reasons. First, the anti-Thaksin forces wish an alterantive political leader to become more popular than Thaksin. Second, the increasing popularity of the government will not lead to the undue popularity and leadership of Abhisit personally. As long as the Democrat government lacks electoral legitimacy and political stability, and Abhisit is obedient to the establishment, the established elite will never feel threatened. Thus, while Abhisit is more populist than Thaksin on redistributive policies, Abhisit is rarely condemned as a populist leader who tries to buy votes and seek popularity. This is a good evidence to show that what really matters is not the populist policies per se but the popularity and leadership deriving from the policies.

Although anti-Thaksin forces felt that Thaksin threatened them, it was not Thaksin but political democratisation and economic globalisation that threatened them. Neoliberalism, along with the conclusion of Free Trade Agreements and the privatisation of public companies, was the order of the day. Thaksin was a product of democratisation and globalisation in that he owed his political power to democratisation and his wealth to globalisation. Although he could ride on the waves of democratisation and globalisation well, he was neither an initiator nor a mover of the waves. Even though a coup expelled Thaksin from politics, the waves of democratisation and globalisation toss the forces that try to resist these waves. As Nidhi writes, "The era of Thai-style democracy or elite politics is coming to an end."[44]

Notes

[1] Ukrist Pathmanand, "A Different Coup d'Etat?", *Journal of Contemporary Asia* 38, 1 (Feb. 2008).

[2] Pasuk Phongpaichit and Chris Baker, *Thaksin: The Business of Politics in Thailand* (Chiang Mai: Silkworm Books, 2004); Duncan McCargo and Ukrist Pathmanand, *The Thaksinization of Thailand* (Copenhagen: NIAS, 2005).

[3] Margaret Canovan, "Trust the People! Populism and the Two Faces of Democracy", *Political Studies* 47 (1999).

[4] Paul Taggart, *Populism* (Buckingham: Open University Press, 2000), p. 5.

[5] Canovan "Trust the People!", p. 3; see also Otake Hideo, *Nihon gata populism* [Japanese-style populism] (Tokyo: Chuou-Kouron-Shinsha, 2003).

[6] Canovan "Trust the People!", p. 3.

[7] Ibid., p. 4.

[8] Ibid., p. 5.

[9] Ibid., pp. 5–6.

[10] Ibid., p. 7.

[11] Anek Laothammathat, *Thaksina-prachaniyom* [The Thaksin Way of Populism] (Bangkok: Matichon, 2006), pp. 23, 76–80.

[12] It was only after the 2006 coup that some evidence of a heavy financial burden was disclosed.

[13] Suehiro Akira, "Socio-Economic Policies and Reforms of the Budget System: The Kingdom of Thailand's Modernization Framework under the Thaksin Administration", in *Thailand in Motion: Political and Administrative Changes, 1991–2006*, ed. Tamada Yoshifumi and Funatsu Tsuruyo (in Japanese) (Chiba, Japan: Institute of Developing Economies, JETRO, 2008), pp. 244–5.

[14] Suehiro, "Socio-Economic Policies", pp. 245–6.

[15] Michael K. Connors, "Article of Faith: The Failure of Royal Liberalism in Thailand", *Journal of Contemporary Asia* 38, 1 (Feb. 2008): 148.

[16] Anek, *Thaksina-prachaniyom* , pp. 100–1.

[17] Supphalak Kanjanakhundi, "Wikhro rabop sonthi" [Analysing the Sonthi Regime], in Fa Dieo Kan, *Ratthaprahan 19 kanya: Ratthaprahan phua rabop prachathipatai an mi phramahakasat song pen pramuk* [The 19 September Coup: Coup for Democracy with the King as Head of State] (Bangkok: Fa Dieo Kan, 2007), p. 273.

[18] *Fa dieo kan* 2, 1 (Jan.–Mar. 2004), issue on *Rabop Thaksin* [the Thaksin Regime].

[19] *Matichon* (online edition), 5 Mar. 2006.

[20] *Thai Rat* (online edition), 18 Aug. 2006.

[21] *Thai Post* (online edition), 8 Mar. 2006.

[22] Oliver Pye and Wolfram Schaffar, "The 2006 Anti-Thaksin Movement in Thailand: An Analysis", *Journal of Contemporary Asia* 38, 1 (Feb. 2008): 39.

[23] Regarding the middle class, Nidhi critically states, "Nothing is more intolerable to the Thai middle class than the vulgarity of politicians who were voted into office by members of the lower class. This is because it reminds them that the

political power they once enjoyed is slipping out of their hand as the electoral system has come to replace the half-electoral, half-bureaucratic polity system." See Nidhi Eoseewong, "Charter Amendment: The Vagaries and Vulgarities", *Bangkok Post* (online edition), 9 Apr. 2008.

24   Tamada Yoshifumi, "Democracy and the Middle Class in Thailand: The Uprising of May 1992", in *The Rise of Middle Classes in Southeast Asia*, ed. Shiraishi Takashi and Pasuk Phongpaichit (Kyoto: Kyoto University Press, 2008), pp. 72–4.

25   ABAC Poll. Another survey, conduct by Thurakit Bandit Poll in Bangkok on 10 and 11 September 2006, revealed that 31.9 per cent of the respondents wanted Thaksin to quit political life while 68.1 per cent hoped him to remain on the political scene; see *Matichon* (online edition), 15 Sep. 2006.

26   *Bangkok Post* (online edition), 20 Sep. 2006.

27   This was more effective for TRT's electoral victories than its election pledges. In this respect, it was important that Thaksin was by far the richest among Thai MPs and could spend money lavishly.

28   Somchai, "The Thai Rak Thai Party", pp. 117–20.

29   Election Commission of Thailand, *Khomun sathiti lae phon kan luaktang samachik sapha phu thaen ratsadon B.E. 2544* [Statistics and Results of the Parliamentary Election, 2001] (Bangkok: ECT, 2001), pp. 21, 282–3; Election Commission of Thailand, *Khomun sathiti lae phon kanluaktang samachik sapha phu thae nratsadon B.E. 2548* [Statistics and Results of the Parliamentary Election, 2005] (Bangkok: ECT, 2005), pp. 23, 253; Election Commission of Thailand, "Raingan phon kanluaktang samachik sapha phu thaen ratsadon yang mai pen thang kan 2 mesayon 2549" [Unofficial Report on the Results of the Parliamentary Election, 2 April 2006], at <http://www.ect.go.th/thai/report_mp49.htm> [accessed 18 Apr. 2006].

30   Presidentialisation has three faces, namely "the executive face, the party face, and the electoral face" "[T]he presidentialization of politics can be understood as the development of (a) increasing leadership power resources and autonomy within the party and the political executive respectively, and (b) increasingly leadership-centred electoral processes." See Thomas Poguntke and Paul Webb, ed., *The Presidentialization of Politics. A Comparative Study of Modern Democracies* (Oxford: Oxford University Press, 2005), p. 5.

31   Andrew Walker, "The Rural Constitution and the Everyday Politics of Elections in Northern Thailand", *Journal of Contemporary Asia* 38, 1 (Feb. 2008): 98.

32   Walker, "The Rural Constitution", p. 100.

33   *Matichon* (online edition), 25 May 2006.

34   Giles Ji Ungpakorn, *A Coup for the Rich: Thailand's Political Crisis* (Bangkok: Workers Democracy Publishing, 2007), p. 29.

35   Supphalak Kanjanakhundi , "People's Alliance for Coup D'état (PAD) proudly presents Thailand's 25th PM: Samak Sundaravej", at <http://www.prachatai.com/english/news.php?id=508> (posted on 1 Feb. 2008, original Thai version posted on 30 Jan. 2008), emphasis added.

36   Thongchai Winichakul, "Toppling Democracy", *Journal of Contemporary Asia* 38, 1 (Feb. 2008); Connors, "Article of Faith".

37   Thaksin Shinawatra, "Khamklao khong phantamruattho Thaksin Chinnawat nayokratthamontri nai okat pen prathan kanprachum huana suan ratchakan phua chiaeng naeothang kan patibat ngan nai chuang ratthaban raksakan na tuek santimaitri thamniap ratthaban wan phruhatsabodi thi 29 mithunayon 2549 wela 14:30 nalika" [Speech of prime minister Thaksin ... 29 June 2003], at <http://www.thaigov.go.th/news/speech/49/june49/sp29jun49-1.htm> [accessed 1 July 2006].

38   Michai Ruchuphan, "Khwamrapphitchop khong nayokratthamontri" [Responsibility of the Prime Minister], at <http://www.meechaithailand.com/index2.html> [accessed 1 July 2006].

39   Piyabut Saengkanokkakun, "Prachathipatai baep 'thai thai' khu arai" [What is Thai-style Democracy?], at <http://www.onopen.com/2007/editor-spaces/1545> (posted on 26 Feb. 2007).

40   Nidhi Eoseewong, "Pracharat vs. Ratchaanajak" [Nation-state vs. Kingdom], *Matichon* (online edition), 6 June 2005, reprinted in *Watthanatham khon yang Thaksin* [Culture of a Man like Thaksin] (Bangkok: Matichon, 2006), pp. 143–4.

41   Tamada Yoshifumi, *Myths and Realities: The Democratization of Thai Politics* (Kyoto: Kyoto University Press, 2008).

42   Phichit Likhitkitjasombun, "Mayakhati 'panyachon ti song na'" [Miasma of the Two-Faced Intellectuals], *Krungthep Thurakit* (online edition), 28 Nov. 2006; see also "Prachathipatai ru rabop aphisitchon" [Democracy or Aristocracy], *Krungthep Thurakit* (online edition), 6 July 2006; and "'Khunnatham' kap kanluaktang nai rabop prachathipatai" [Morality and Democratic Elections], *Krungthep Thurakit* (online edition), 31 Aug. 2006.

43   Phichit, "Mayakhati".

44   Nidhi Eoseewong, "Ratthaprahan lae kanluaktang" [Coup and Election], *Matichon* (online edition), 26 Mar. 2007.

CHAPTER 6

Thaksin Shinawatra and Mass Media

Nualnoi Treerat

Several studies on recent populist movements in Latin America has emphasised the impact of changing media technology, especially the spread of mass television. Leaders who wish to build a base of support among "the people" no longer need to work through civil society organisations but can make a direct appeal through mass media.[1] While earlier populists often concentrated on an urban target for practical reasons, television provides access to a larger rural mass. To gain acceptance among this group, populist leaders often appropriate elements of folk and popular culture to demonstrate their nearness to the masses, and are sometimes in turn embraced by popular culture.[2] When new populist figures are starting out, mass media often focus on them because they are newsworthy, and thus the media promote their rise. Once in power, however, populist leaders generally try to control the media because they understand its importance for sustaining their term. Although television may have a wide reach, the information it presents is rather thin. As a medium, it is better at conveying impressions, emotions, and unconscious expressions of feeling than abstract information or analysis. Viewers have a strong impression that they "know" the people they see on the screen, and can trust them, but may not absorb much in the way of message. Populist leaders who have risen with the help of mass media often concentrate more on a visual image and simple messages rather than any more complex programme. The media can also play a role in undermining populists after they achieve power.

Thaksin Shinawatra was the first Thai political leader to be called a populist. He was certainly not the first to understand the importance of media, but he was the first to make concerted use of television. Ultimately, mass media played a key role not only in his rise but also in his fall.

Table 6-1 Consumption of Mass Media in Thailand, 2001

	Nationwide	Bangkok	Other urban	Rural
Population, 12 years and above	50.2	8.7	3.8	37.8
Percentage				
Television (daily)	86	93	91	84
Radio (daily)	36	47	48	33
Newspaper (daily)	21	44	43	14
Magazines (fortnightly)	13	25	22	9

Source: AC Nielsen Media Index (2001).

This chapter is a brief survey of Thaksin's use of media. The first section describes the media environment in Thailand. The second section covers Thaksin's attempts to control and exploit mass media to portray himself as a new kind of leader. The third section shows how mass media played a key role in undercutting his immense popularity.

Thailand's Mass Media

Over the late 1980s and 1990s, television transmission and television ownership expanded throughout rural Thailand. By 2001, television had become easily the most powerful mass medium, watched regularly by 86 per cent of the population compared to 36 per cent for radio and 20 per cent for newspapers (see Table 6-1).

Historically, there has been a marked contrast between print and electronic media in Thailand. Print media have been privately owned and have been strongly associated with the rise of democratic politics. Electronic media have been generally under the control of the state. Only recently has this pattern begun to break down.

Print journalism emerged in the 1920s and was strongly associated with nationalist protests for political reform. During Thailand's long era of military rule, newspapers spearheaded demands for democracy, and journalists were often jailed and sometimes murdered. Between the 1970s and 1990s, with rapid economic growth and the extension of democratic institutions, the newspaper industry expanded rapidly. However, the 1997 financial crisis resulted in a big shake-out. Large numbers of journalists lost their jobs. Many newspapers had to close down while others were bought out and merged into larger business conglomerates. As a result, there was an extreme concentration of ownership. In 1997, four groups controlled 92 per cent of the Thai-language press. Subsequently their share has declined to 80 per cent but is still overwhelming. On average the press derives around 65 per cent of its total income from advertising and the remainder from newspaper sales.[3]

Radio was first launched by private enterprise but subsequently incorporated by the state as a tool of "nation-building". The state has reserved control over radio frequencies, and has distributed them to various state agencies, especially the armed forces and the government's Public Relations Department. These agencies subcontract the management of radio stations to private companies. By the late 1990s, there were 520 stations. The state agencies keep close control by leasing the stations on short-term contracts, often of one year only. Since 1992 there has been a strong demand for the system to become more liberalised, but the state agencies have strongly and successfully resisted this demand. In December 2001, the first community radio station went on air in Kanchanaburi province, and half a year later 150 stations were ready to start broadcasting. The Public Relations Department threatened to close down any station that did not hold a license, despite the fact that the licensing body supposed to be established under the 1997 constitution had not yet come into existence. Government had to agree to allow these stations to operate until a regulatory framework could be established.[4]

The first television channel began broadcasting in 1955. As with radio, the governments of the military era kept close control over the medium and used it for state communication and propaganda. The same model of ownership and management developed. Three channels were allotted to government agencies, and two to the armed forces. In two cases, the entire management of the channel was allotted to a concessionaire on a long-term lease (around 30 years), while in other cases some of the programming was contracted out on a short term basis. After the political crisis of 1992, there was a strong demand for liberalisation of the electronic media. As a consequence, a sixth channel was licensed to a private company, ITV. After this company fell into financial difficulty in the 1997 crisis, it was bought by Thaksin Shinawatra's family holding company shortly before the 2001 elections.[5] Two cable channels were launched in the 1990s, and subsequently merged into one operator, UBC. Their audience is mainly in the Bangkok area. There are several hundred licensed small-scale subscription-based cable operators, mainly in the provinces. With the advent of satellite transmission, several enterprises download the signals and distribute them through cable. Because the media industry has obstructed attempts to modernise the regulatory framework, the government does not have the legal means to control such operators. Both community radio and cable television have been able to develop some free space to operate because of this regulatory confusion.

Owing to the concession structure, television has become highly profitable. The two main concessionaires (Channels 3 and 7) command 53 per cent of all viewership. Their output is strongly biased towards entertainment with very little documentary or educational programming, and very little attention to public issues.[6]

New media such as internet, satellite TV, community radio and cable TV developed rapidly from the late 1990s onwards. By 2007, it was estimated that cable and satellite TV reached around 2.5 million households, 15 per cent of the total, and some two thousand community radio stations were on air. The increasing popularity of new media has created more space for freedom of expression, especially on political matters, as these media are difficult to control and censor.

Thaksin Using Media

The media were of little importance in Thaksin's rise to power. He acquired the only private free-to-air TV station in 2000, and was accused by its staff of manipulating its content to aid his election campaign, but ITV had only a small share of TV viewership at the time. In the media as a whole, Thaksin enjoyed no more prominence than what any serious electoral contender would draw. His electoral campaign relied on rather professional execution of conventional means of campaigning (posters, press ads, stickers, rallies), rather than any innovative use of media.

Once in power, however, he made more concerted and more effective use of media than any predecessor in Thailand, in three ways: suppression of opposition; inflation of his own image; and presentation of the work of government. In many ways, Thaksin changed from conventional politician to populist politician in the media.

Suppression of Opposition

Over the 1990s, analysis and criticism of political events and public figures had become well established in the electronic media. Virtually every government made some attempt to control criticism, but with very limited results. However, in the aftermath of the 1997 crisis, all media companies were sensitive about profitability, and many media employees were sensitive about their jobs. This gave political leaders much greater leverage to intimidate the media into becoming less critical.

At the start of Thaksin's premiership, there was a series of incidents involving the electronic media. Some prominent political analysts had their programmes cancelled. Some journalists and editors on news programmes were sacked or reassigned. Usually there was no obvious direct intervention from the executive. Rather there was always a rational excuse. A contract had been infringed. Or an employee had performed below standard. The number of such incidents was relatively small, but the message passed was very clear. The result was a significant increase in self-censorship by the electronic media providers.[7]

The press was equally vulnerable. A very high proportion of press advertising revenue was earned either from government agencies or from companies closely associated with the Thaksin government. The telecommunications empire owned by Thaksin's family was one of the biggest single advertisers in the press. Again, intimidation was relatively simple. Advertising was conspicuously denied to papers that were hostile to the government and sometimes ad placements were withdrawn to show displeasure at a specific article. After a short time, such measures were unnecessary as the press companies mostly cooperated for survival. The Thai Journalists' Association claimed some newspapers were especially wary of criticising certain government figures who were known to control the purchase of advertising by large government-owned agencies.

Journalists were also subject to inducements. Payments to reporters for attending press conferences or events are conventional in Thailand, and these payments (ostensibly for "expenses") can easily be inflated to buy good will. In some instances such gifts are more substantial items such as company shares, jewellery, and even cars. While he was foreign minister in 1995, Thaksin distributed mobile phones (then still rather special) to reporters covering the foreign affairs beat. After a complaint to the press association, the phones were all returned. During Thaksin's time in office, there were no similar instances of bribery, but reporters at Government House were treated with good facilities (such as free internet connections) that they were loath to put at risk.

The Thaksin era also saw the first concerted use of defamation laws to intimidate the media. The most high profile case was launched against Supinya Klangnarong, secretary-general of an NGO, the Campaign for Popular Media Reform, and *Thai Post*, a minor Thai daily. Shin Corporation, Thaksin's family company, charged that Supinya's remarks on the corporation's benefits from the Thaksin government's policies were defamatory. They claimed damages of 400 million baht (around US$10 million at the time), an amount clearly intended to intimidate not only Supinya but other critics of Thaksin, his family business, and his government. Two other similar but less high-profile cases were launched against a university lecturer and another journalist. Ultimately Supinya won the case, but she admitted personally that the case had discouraged her from further criticism, and probably the same was true for other critics during the two years while the case was in process.

The Supinya case tempted other politicians to attempt the same strategy for silencing criticism. In July 2005, for example, Picnic Corporation, a cooking gas company controlled by the family of a deputy minister of commerce who had to resign over a scandal in the company, filed cases against two newspapers in the Matichon group, claiming damages of 5 and 10 billion baht respectively.

Thaksin Talking to the People

Shortly after assuming office, Thaksin established a weekly radio broadcast programme entitled "Premier Thaksin Talks with the People". The programme was broadcast on Saturday morning and networked countrywide. Initially the broadcast ran for around 30 minutes but later it expanded to almost an hour. Thaksin connected to the radio station by phone, so the sound conveyed the feel of taking a personal call from the premier. Thaksin made a strong point of delivering the programme live each week, often phoning from upcountry or overseas, and only on a few occasions had to pre-record because he was on an aircraft or otherwise impossible to contact at the time slot.

Thaksin explained that the aim of the programme was to explain to people what he and the government were doing and why. He talked in an avuncular fashion about his activities over the previous week, and important events coming up. He explained his government's policies and took issue with his critics. A transcript of the talk was placed on a government website within a couple of days. These transcripts were collected into a series of book which sold well while Thaksin was at the height of his popularity. Each week, the programme would generate four or five news stories, especially useful to editors on Mondays when there was often little hard news generated over the weekend. Newscasts on television and radio would repeatedly broadcast key passages from the talks. "Premier Thaksin Talks with the People" was a means for Thaksin and the government to set the news agenda for the country.

This radio programme played an important role in establishing Thaksin as a new kind of Thai politician with a different relationship to "the people".

When he first rose to power, his image was very much as a modern business-man, and hence as someone very remote from the ordinary man. The radio programme, with its clever illusion of the premier talking "by phone" to each listener, made Thaksin appear much more familiar. In the early years of the programme, the content of the programme was often organised by subject, but later he adopted more of a diary format, which gave the listener an illusion of eavesdropping on the premier's daily life and times.

Yanisphak Kanjanawisit made a detailed analysis of the content of the radio programme.[8]

The messages fell into five categories: explaining the government's work for national development; detailing the difficulties that the government faced in its work and its attempts to reform the bureaucracy for greater efficiency; reassuring people that what the premier and government had done was all transparent, legal and honest;[9] instructing citizens on how they should think and behave with respect to the government; and disputing with critics, often violently and dismissively.

The messages conveyed three reasons why the government was working legitimately and deserved popular support: first, the government worked quickly and efficiently; second, it had good understanding of the people's needs; third, the government and especially Thaksin himself were very knowledgeable and thus had the expertise to solve problems. Thaksin often mentioned books — usually popular books on business management — and sometimes summarised their content.

Yanisphak concluded that the radio show built an image of Thaksin as someone intent upon solving the people's problems with honesty and integrity. This image lent legitimacy to the premier, his party, and govern-ment. The programme also spread Thaksin's convictions about the impor-tance of capitalist development, the need for populist policies, and the importance of popular sovereignty.

Another study by Jiraporn Jarerndaj found that the programme allowed Thaksin to attempt a monopoly of "truth".[10] For example, over the disturbances in Thailand's far south, Thaksin detailed what the government was doing, assured listeners that his policies were correct, and claimed there was no need to attend to other opinions. "In my position as prime minister, I have given orders already, so matters will improve."

The broadcasts presented a rather precise image of Thaksin himself. He was a straightforward, practical man oriented towards action and problem solving rather than discourse and debate. He was highly knowledgeable in a diverse range of subjects, but especially on business and matters related to money. He had a unique talent for understanding the needs of the people, because of his deep interest in the people's welfare. By contrast, his critics and opponents (including the parliamentary opposition) were both ignorant and uninterested in the people's true needs. Thaksin's main interests were in the economy, administrative reform, and the promotion of business.

Political Fantasia

In 2004, as Thaksin neared the end of his first term and an election loomed in early 2005, Thaksin embarked on a campaign of "getting close to the people". With the help of the media, he inflated his presence in the national consciousness, and also completed the translation of his image from "businessman" to "man of the people".

From April to August 2004, Thaksin embarked on a series of trips to all the regions of Thailand. These trips were branded *tur nok khamin*, "canary tours", conveying an image of a bird flying around the country. He travelled in a convoy of cars accompanied by other members of his Cabinet and senior officials of key ministries. The convoy made halts, usually in sub-district towns, where local officials and civic associations had gathered, along with a large crowd. The local officials would then report on local development projects and local problems, and make petitions for budget allocations. Occasionally local people also got a chance to air grievances, but usually these occasions were dominated by officialdom. Thaksin would occasionally give instant approval of budgets, deploying his discretionary power over a large central fund concocted by budget reform. More often, he would show support for projects, and assign officials and ministers in his entourage to follow up. The convoy would then speed away.

This project had many resonances. To begin with, it dramatised Thaksin bringing government to the people, and thus bridging the long chains of command and the huge cultural gap that separated the ordinary subject from the national leader. It also dramatised Thaksin as the ultimate source of patronage, arching over the local officials and the local politicians who the local people usually had to petition for help and patronage. Most of all these tours dramatised Thaksin as a "man of the people" who stepped down from the heights of government into the dusty street of the remote locality. The convoy was followed by a large media caravan. The succession of meetings between premier and local officialdom figured at the head of each day's television news. The premier's chats with local people provided photo opportunities for the front pages of the press. Although these encounters were often very fleeting, they acquired longer life as memorably different images of the role of a Thai leader.

In January 2006, Thaksin undertook a campaign designed to build on the success of the early tours. At this time he did not face an election but his popularity had begun to slip under fierce attack from his critics. Thaksin led a team of ministers and senior officials to spend a week in one of Thailand's poorest districts (At Samat in Roi-et province). He said, "I want to teach bureaucrats how to solve the problem of poverty". At each centre of the district, the community members gathered, and Thaksin interviewed them rather like a doctor asking a patient to describe his symptoms. Thaksin then prescribed solutions, mostly by advising people on getting access to credit or training. As in the earlier "canary tours", he also entertained requests for budget help, and commissioned various projects of small-scale local infra-structure. At times he also handed out money from his own pocket. The prime minister said that people could say anything they liked to him; he would respond and work for them. The five-day event was aired live on a cable TV station transmitted by a satellite owned by one of Thaksin's family companies. The event was branded as a "reality show". Thaksin said that those who would benefit from the project would be the poor and no other groups, and the benefits were assured. Although the event took place in only a single district, local officials from other places could watch, learn, and reproduce the methods and solutions.

This project surpassed the "canary tours" in taking government to the people. The premier devoted a full working week of his own time and many other people's time to this one enterprise. The single-minded emphasis on eliminating poverty built a very strong identification between Thaksin and this desire to aid the lowest stratum of the society.

The At Samat reality show was criticised by academics and other poli-ticians. Banharn Silpa-archa, former prime minister in 1995–96, said that Thaksin might be sincere in his anti-poverty efforts but that it was not a simple matter. When he was the prime minister, Banharn had visited four villages in Suphanburi and asked the people there about their problems but was unable to solve them in a year. A communications academic, Darunee Hirunrak, suggested the project was part of the government's marketing strategy rather than a realistic attempt to confront the problem of poverty. A political scientist, Sukhum Nualsakul, thought it was worthwhile because it gave the rich in the TV audience a chance to see how the poor lived. In other words, the project created a great deal of debate.

The Media in Thaksin's Fall

At the time he ascended to power, Thaksin's personal popularity was un-remarkable. By the end of his first term, he probably had a larger public presence and a bigger personal following than any previous Thai prime minister. The orchestration of the media to present an image of Thaksin as a new kind of leader who was closer to the people and more effective in his management of the country undoubtedly played a large role in building that popularity. In February 2005, Thaksin swept to a landslide victory, cornering 61 per cent of the vote, and 377 of the 500 seats in parliament. The media was generally supportive. The state-owned electronic media had been purged of critical content. Press entrepreneurs were wary of government reprisals, but also appreciative of the economic recovery, and generally reluctant to rock the boat. Yet over 2005–6, Thaksin became the butt of heavy criticism, often marshalled through the media. How did this happen?

The Matichon Purchase

Criticism of Thaksin by academics had grown steadily, particularly since Thaksin's "war on drugs" in 2003, and the deterioration of the security situation in the south from early 2004 onwards. The dissemination of this criticism was generally limited to book publications, public statements, and forums. While some of this criticism was reported in the press, papers were careful not to be seen as antagonistic towards the government.

In August–September 2005, two press companies became the target of a hostile buyout attempt. This was widely seen as an attempt by Thaksin and his coterie to extend their grip over public space. This perception provoked an angry reaction.

On 9 August 2005, the leading English-language daily, the Bangkok Post, published a story about cracks in the runways of the new Bangkok airport under construction. Thaksin had involved himself deeply in the airport project, and it was strongly identified with him. Thaksin and government spokesmen came out to deny the existence of the cracks and accuse the Post of bias and lack of professionalism. The paper fired the chief reporter responsible, which seemed like a tacit admission of guilt, and the government filed a criminal libel suit against the paper.[11] At that point, the Grammy Company, an entertainment group owned by Paiboon Damrongchaitham, announced plans to buy the Post. Paiboon was commonly identified as a friend of Thaksin, and Grammy had expanded its business as a content provider for state-owned radio and television during Thaksin's term. A few days later, Grammy also announced plans to buy the Matichon group. Beginning with the launch of a "quality" Thai daily in the 1970s, the Matichon group had become one of the largest Thai-language press groups with a slew of magazines and a large book publishing business. Paiboon acquired

32 per cent of Matichon, and announced plans to invest a total of 2.7 billion baht to acquire a majority stake in Matichon, and a dominant share in the Post's holding company.[12]

This hostile bid united the press in opposition. All the associations of media professionals came out in opposition. A "Friends of Matichon" group appeared and threatened to organise a boycott of Grammy products. The staff of Matichon announced they would resign en masse, leaving Paiboon with only the physical assets. Within a week, Paiboon had backed away from the deal, sold back most of his Matichon stake, and abandoned the attack on the Post.

The event was a watershed in the press disposition towards Thaksin and his government. From this point forward, the tone became distinctly more critical. The analysis of Thaksin contained in the books and presentations by academics and public intellectuals now became a source of copy for mass publications.

Sondhi Limthongkul

Sondhi Limthongkul is an ambitious media entrepreneur who expanded rapidly in the economic boom of 1986–96, and went spectacularly bankrupt in 1997. He became an early supporter of Thaksin, and was rewarded with a high level of debt forgiveness by state banks and financial agencies. While all other political comment and analysis was removed from free-to-air television, Sondhi alone was licensed to produce a weekly programme. In this slot, Sondhi provided sophisticated and highly entertaining analysis of current events which subtly supported Thaksin without doing so too obviously. But in late 2005, Sondhi suddenly distanced himself from Thaksin and became fiercely critical.

According to Sondhi's explanation, Thaksin had changed and no longer deserved his earlier loyalty and adulation. According to an explanation widely circulated in the press, Thaksin had refused to support Sondhi's patron in the largest state-owned bank. According to others, Sondhi simply sensed a growing disaffection with Thaksin in parts of the urban middle class, and set out to ride that wave.

In mid-September 2005, Sondhi's programme was thrown off the airwaves. Sondhi began to broadcast the programme from the stage at public meetings, relayed more broadly through his newspaper's website. The meetings snowballed into mass demonstrations. The webcasting evolved into a satellite broadcast from Hong Kong under the name ASTV which was downloaded and disseminated by local cable television operators in Thailand.

The Thaksin government attempted to block this technique but failed, ironically because the government itself had been obstructing modernisation of the laws governing broadcasting. ASTV effectively broke the state's virtual monopoly on television broadcasting, and broke the government's ability to block criticism in electronic media.

In the late 2005, Thaksin filed several cases both criminal and civil defamation lawsuits against Sondhi and his colleagues for statements made about Thaksin abusing power and being disloyal to the king. However, the cases were dropped following the king's advice that constructive criticism was to be encouraged and that lawsuits should not be deployed to silence critics. An attempt was made to close down ASTV by legal action, but the Administrative Court ruled that ASTV could continue its broadcast.

Sondhi attacked Thaksin for corruption and mismanagement, but also raised the emotional level of his attack by insinuating that Thaksin was a threat to the monarchy. Sondhi first accused Thaksin of intruding on the royal prerogative in making appointments in the Buddhist sangha. Next he added an allegation that Thaksin had improperly held a ceremony inside the old royal palace. Sondhi adopted the king's birth colour of yellow and a slogan "Save the nation" for flags, headbands, T-shirts and other branding material. In May 2006, his *Manager* newspaper ran a story that Thaksin and his coterie, some of whom had formerly been student activists associated with the Communist Party of Thailand in the 1970s, had discussed a plot to overthrow the monarchy during a trip to Finland in 1999.

When Thaksin's family company was sold in January 2006 for US$1.7 billion without the family incurring any significant tax liability, the press and Sondhi's street movement were able to paint Thaksin as a sharp businessman and a bad citizen who had profited from his time in power.

Sondhi arguably became the single most important figure orchestrating the swelling opposition to Thaksin from late 2005 until the coup a year later. He helped to create a base of support, primarily in Bangkok, which the coup leaders claimed as a source of legitimacy for their actions. He later claimed that he received support and encouragement from the palace and the barracks. Interestingly, Sondhi is not a politician in any formal sense. Nor is he generally acknowledged as a public intellectual or leader of civil society. Rather, he is a media entrepreneur. His political role was predicated on his media assets. He had the television programme which was the site of his first act of defiance against his recent patron. He had his battered but surviving press empire (consisting of a daily paper, weekly news magazine, and other titles) which communicated with the urban print consumer. He used new broadcast technology via web, satellite, and cable to escape the state grip over electronic media and develop a much broader audience for messages relayed from public demonstrations.

Conclusion

Thaksin used mass media to develop a novel and powerful image of himself as a national leader. Through radio and television, he appeared to break down the barriers and shorten the distance that separated a national figure from the ordinary person. He became someone that people felt they knew personally. He projected an image of himself as a man of exceptional ability who worked hard "for the people", at the same time as he denigrated his rivals and critics. Significantly he built his most loyal bases of support in areas of the country which were geographically distant from the capital, and often felt culturally distanced and administratively neglected.

He also suppressed criticism, specially in the press which had a tradition of opposing over-mighty rulers. But ultimately the mass media also played a major role in his downfall. A hostile attempt to buy out two major press groups by an entrepreneur perceived as an agent and crony of Thaksin turned almost the entire press antagonistic from then onwards. More importantly, a media entrepreneur mounted a challenge to Thaksin which spread from television to street demonstrations and new forms of broadcasting that escaped state control. Where Thaksin had used media to laud himself as a new form of leader and a "man of the people", this antagonistic campaign demonised him as a corrupt businessman and a threat to the monarchy.

Studies of neo-populist movements in Europe and some other developed countries have postulated a cycles of four phases in the media's relationship with populist movements.[13] In the first ground-laying phase, the media dwells on social or political discontents, because these matters are newsworthy, and hence indirectly helps build the environment of insecurity and political disaffection in which populist ideas and agitation can take root. In the second or insurgent phase, the media focus intensely on the new leader or movement, making sure that newsworthy events are "exploited before they wear away", so that the media and the movement function as co-travellers.[14] In the third or established phase when the populist movement has come to dominate the national political scene, "The daily political agenda obliges movements to address issues that are no longer unusual or sensational",[15] the media's attention wavers, attitudes start to vary from support to hostility, and media which serve the elite tend to become antagonistic. In the fourth stage of decline, the media is again focused on the newsworthiness of "a sensational fall", and the rise of an alternative.

Some aspects of this model can be applied to Thailand. After the 1997 financial crisis, the media played an important role in enhancing the anxiety of the people, and thus was instrumental in facilitating the rise of populist Thaksin. Although the media did not play a crucial role in his first election victory, there was intense media attention during his early months in power, and Thaksin became adept at staging events to draw the media spotlight. The model has less applicability to Thaksin in the third and fourth stages because of the state's control over so much media in Thailand. Thaksin was able to prevent the media's attention wandering away from him, and prevent the mass media becoming a site of hostile criticism. On the past experience of Thai leaders, he should have been able to maintain this position for some time. But the beginning of media liberalisation had also taken place. New media technology made it difficult for the state to retain control. Thus it was possible for a maverick small media entrepreneur with satellite investment, who was alienated by Thaksin, to deploy the new technology to hasten the decline of Thaksin and his party.

Notes

1　　Taylor C. Boas, "Television and Neopopulism in Latin America: Media Effects in Brazil and Peru", *Latin American Research Review* 40, 2 (2005); Kurt C. Weyland, "Populism in the Age of Neoliberalism", in *Populism in Latin America*, ed. Michael L. Conniff (Tuscaloosa and London: University of Alabama Press, 1999), pp. 172–90.

2　　Michael L. Conniff, "Introduction" and "Epilogue: New Research Directions", in *Populism in Latin America*, ed. Conniff.

3　　Nualnoi Treerat and Thanee Chaiwat, "Newspaper Market and Regulations in Thailand", paper for the research project on "Media Reform" under the Thailand Research Fund, 2004.

4　　Asian Forum for Human Rights and Development, "Freedom of Expression and the Media: baseline studies" (2005).

5　　ITV's concession was cancelled in 2007, and the station was turned into a public broadcasting service under new legislation in 2008.

6　　Somkiat Tangkitvanich and Tanawit Suttirattanakul (2004). "Radio and Television Market Structure", paper for the research project on "Media Reform" under the Thailand Research Fund, 2004.

7　　"Country Reports on Human Rights Practices, 2004", released by the Bureau of Democracy, Human Rights, and Labor, 28 February 2005.

8　　Yanisphak Kanjanawisit, "The Process of Meaning Construction and the Roles of Discourse in 'Premier Thaksin Talks with the People Program'", MA thesis, Faculty of Communication Arts, Chulalongkorn University, 2004; see also

Duncan McCargo, "Thaksin's Political Discourse", in Duncan McCargo and Ukrist Pathmanand, *The Thaksinization of Thailand* (Copenhagen: NIAS, 2005).

[9] For example: "Bureaucrats in this government work transparently"; "The budget used in meeting overseas is always cost efficient"; "Let me tell you that in the village fund project, corruption is simply impossible".

[10] Jiraporn Jarerndaj, "The Transformation of Authority into Power through Radio Broadcast; The Prime Minister's Talks to the Thai People. A Case Study of the Violent Crisis in Three Provinces of the Southern Border of Thailand", MA thesis, Faculty of Journalism and Mass Communication, Thammasat University, 2005.

[11] There were cracks. The labour court later found in favour of the sacked reporter and ordered his reinstatement. The libel suit faded away.

[12] *Bangkok Post*, 13 September 2005; *The Nation*, 15 September 2005.

[13] Gianpietro Mazzoleni, Julian Stewart, and Bruce Horsfield, eds., *The Media and Neo-Populism: A Contemporary Comparative Analysis* (New York: Prager, 2003), especially ch. 10.

[14] Todd Gitlin, *The Whole World Is Watching: Mass Media and the Making and Unmaking of the New Left* (Berkeley: University of California Press, 1980).

[15] Mazzoleni *et al.*, *Media and Neo-Populism*, p. 223.

CHAPTER 7

The Ends of Populism: Mahathir's Departure and Thaksin's Overthrow

Boo Teik Khoo

There has been a significant ideological gap in Southeast Asia since the July 1997 financial crisis. The gap exists mainly because nationalism and developmentalism — the two principal ideological movements in post-colonial non-communist Southeast Asian nations — have been undermined by globalisation in general and the 1997 crisis in particular. Nationalism and developmentalism shared fundamental concerns. Nationalism, while nourishing projects of decolonisation, raised far-ranging expectations of what self-rule and independence should mean. Developmentalism vindicated those projects to the degree that their results met mass demands for improved living standards and social well-being. In Southeast Asia, therefore, nationalism and developmentalism may be said to have sustained strands of communitarian ideas, as was implicit in the elite proffering of "Asian values" in the heyday of the "East Asian miracle".

But globalisation, of the neoliberal "Washington consensus" variety, has considerably inhibited (even as it provoked) meaningful reassertions of economic nationalism while the East Asian financial crisis undermined projects of developmentalism. One sign of the limitations that have been imposed upon nationalism and developmentalism comes from the preponderance of academic studies devoted to the reconfigurations of power balances between states and markets[1] — at the expense of debates over the future of communities.[2] Even much of the discourse on civil society and new forms of governance is predicated upon neoliberal injunctions to limit states to regulating markets. However, just as western liberal democracy, with its emphasis on individual political rights, did not displace "Asian forms of democracy" — however fraudulent those forms frequently were — so neoliberalism, with its stress on individual economic rights, may not satisfy post-crisis "public disaffection with the social deficits of the neoliberal model".[3] Nor, after the collapse of communism, has a practicable alternative been fashioned by replicating earlier modes of labour organisation and their related forms of political mobilisation.

Populism in Southeast Asia

What alternative ideological currents then are likely to emerge?

One growing current is populism. Populism, populist movements, and populists have exhibited so many variations in their meanings and characteristics that the difficulty of defining them clearly is axiomatic.[4] If one goes by a *Newsweek International* report, a "populist rebellion against globalization is going global", spreading a

> self-destructive form of economic nationalism started along the Caracas–Moscow axis, as Presidents Vladimir Putin of Russia and Hugo Chávez of Venezuela trumpeted the classic populist promise: to steer wealth from the rich and the foreign to the poor and the homegrown.[5]

The portrayal of a Caracas–Moscow axis is crass but the reference to the "classic populist promise" betrays a neoliberal anxiety that states and regimes and, indeed, "globalization" may be captive to "politics of redistributive justice".[6]

In the wake of the 1997 crisis, various Southeast Asian political figures and social movements challenged existing regimes or incumbent leaders. Whatever their specificities, those figures and movements refurbished nationalism, invoked communitarianism, and appealed to localism or indigenism.[7] Although these ideological stances were not homogenous, they were, broadly, populist — populism being taken to include many kinds of appeals based on the "people", "grassroots", and "communities", typically opposed to big business domination, class privilege, unresponsive government, and foreign machination.[8] Writing mainly of Thai politics, for example, Kasian Tejapira made pertinent references in passing to the strong populist appeals of Erap (Joseph Estrada) in the Philippines and Gus Dur (Abdurrachman Wahid) in Indonesia.[9] One could argue, too, that Anwar Ibrahim's populist politics contained a putative antagonism to late Mahathirist policies, an antagonism that, mishandled in 1998, led to disaster for Anwar.[10] In rhetoric, policy, and programmes, it remains to be seen how emergent forms of populism will continue to respond to post-crisis discourses on market reforms, good governance, and safety nets. Indeed, Kanishka Jayasuriya and Kevin Hewison discerned the advent of an authoritarian "global populism" that, initially pitted against neoliberal institutions, would use state-initiated redistributive social policies to foster an "antipolitics of good governance". Yet, when conditions permitted, the "antipolitics" could lead to greater degrees of liberalisation and deregulation.[11]

In short, populism in Southeast Asia faced tensions and conflicts between continuing hopes of developmentalism[12] and pressures towards greater market liberalisation. Two political figures who had to manage these tensions were Mahathir Mohamad and Thaksin Shinawatra. Populism formed one major element of Mahathirist ideology and a major component of Thaksin's political platform. The career trajectories of the two leaders did not overlap much. Mahathir's populist days were largely over and he was practically leaving office when Thaksin arrived, riding a populist wave. The former subsequently retired while the latter was recently overthrown. For all that, it might be worthwhile comparing Mahathir and Thaksin, *qua* populists, to raise some issues about populism and its entanglements with leadership, democracy, and political economy in Southeast Asia.

Two Populist Profiles

To speak of Mahathir Mohamad and Thaksin Shinawatra as being populists is not to fix them firmly in a well screened gallery of ideal populists. It is to suggest that several of their ideological positions, personal traits, and policies may best be captured by a populist designation although the personal and political differences between them were significant. For instance, Mahathir had been prime minister of Malaysia for 20 years when Thaksin won his first election. By the time he was ready to leave office, Mahathir had become an authoritarian figure as the leader of a ruling party (United Malays National Organization, or UMNO) that had never ceased to head the government. Thaksin, however, was a billionaire who had just built up a mass party and sought to remake Thai politics so that it would adhere more closely to a party-based structure than a network of local politics captive to local bosses. Mahathir's claim to populism — rather a claim I made on his behalf — goes back to his earlier days as a politician. Still, echoes of his populist sentiments and style come through, particularly during crises, when he was apt to invoke many Third World resentments and grievances, or capitalize on a kind of leader's mystique although UMNO existed and operated in a highly institutionalised system of contestation and executive-directed constitutional administration. Thaksin's comparatively brief claim to being a populist emerged from certain measures of crisis management — welfare measures and policies to alleviate rural poverty — that were unique to

Thailand in the wake of July 1997. For both of them, nevertheless, populism co-existed uneasily with autocratic, oligarchic, and authoritarian forms of rule. We may now sketch their profiles.

Mahathir[13]

In common with most populists, Mahathir based his political appeal on a loose definition of "the people" that for a long time specifically referred to *rakyat Melayu* (Malay people) because of his Malay nationalism. Mahathir's deep-seated anxieties about Malay backwardness prevented him from praising Malay-ness in the way that some African populists, in Peter Worsley's view, celebrated *négritude*.[14] But when Mahathir proclaimed the "definitive position" of the Malays in the Malaysian polity, he differed only in shades from populists who discerned virtue in the common people.[15] The obverse to this people-centred worldview was a rejection of class as an explanation of social and political conflict.[16] Mahathir's disregard for class was peculiarly revealed by his attitude towards the rich and the poor. For him, the rich and the poor stood in a poverty–wealth spectrum, with their positions determined by aspiration and application.

Mahathir was a populist in another sense. His Malay-centred appeal was rural because, for a very long time, to be Malay was to be rural. Yet Mahathir was not anti-urban in the way that some agrarian populists disparaged the city for being alien and evil. In fact, he had always accepted the town as the locus of progress. But his youthful anger at the middlemen, the *padi kunca* system,[17] and the loss of Malay land owing to peasant insolvency — rural grievance in a word — carried echoes of the American agrarian populists' fight against bank debt and farm foreclosure.

To some extent, the rural tint of Mahathir's populism sprang from the historical lack of entrepreneurship within the Malay middle class. In colonial Malaya, the Malay peasantry, unlike the Chinese and Indian working classes, was spared the worst conditions of early colonial capitalism. The incipient Malay middle class was denied a fair share of colonial capital accumulation. Mahathir, being socially rooted between the Malay peasantry and middle class, overlooked the fortune of being spared the ravages and stressed the injustice of being denied the opportunities. Thus, he had no revulsion against capitalism as such, only a resentment of the colonial administrators and immigrants who deprived the Malay of his "place in the Malayan sun".

Later, Mahathir as a Third World spokesman laced his anti-Western criticisms with overtones of agrarian populism, notably the commodity producer's distrust of brokers, dealers, and speculators. And by the time of the 1997 financial crisis, Mahathir would attack the international money market — with its manipulators and currency speculators — and neoliberal capitalism.

Populism, it has been suggested, "tends to throw up great leaders in mystical contact with the masses".[18] Mahathir always set great store by leadership qualities and claimed to "know how the people feel". When, in 1981, he launched his *Leadership by Example* campaign, he sought to put in practice his conviction that the leaders of developing countries must "influence the selection of systems and values of the people".[19] When he was asked "whether true leadership consists of being the embodiment of the hopes, dreams and aspirations of your people", Mahathir replied that true leadership was "the ability to provide guidance ... something *superior* to what your people can do by themselves", including "initiatives and ideas that are not common".[20]

As for the masses, Mahathir believed he knew them thoroughly, their problems and weaknesses. He claimed he was not surprised when the ethnic violence of 13 May 1969 occurred: "living in a rural constituency, I heard the rumblings long ago".[21] When he demanded Prime Minister Tunku Abdul Rahman's resignation, it was because, among other things, he faulted the Tunku for having lost contact with the Malays: thus, "permit me to tell you what the position, the thoughts and opinions of the people are really".[22] After Mahathir was expelled from UMNO — for going above the heads of the leaders to reach the masses, so to speak — he "always felt ... that he was popular among the party rank and file and that his views had wide support with them".[23]

When he argued in *The Malay Dilemma* for the need to "complete the rehabilitation of the Malays", Mahathir believed he had the right prescription: "a carefully planned revolution [which] must be enlightened"[24] and be "executed with speed and thoroughness to produce a complete and radical change in the Malays".[25] Mahathir claimed that "revolutions can be creative and orderly if the mechanics are understood by those best able to carry them through".[26] Only a man who considered himself to be among those "best able" would predict that the people, "left to themselves", were "more likely to subvert their own future than promote their well-being".[27] Hence, as his policies, campaigns, and slogans showed, he preferred "the people" to follow his script and tutelage.

This final aspect of Mahathir's populism explains why Mahathir's most compelling persona was that of a "spokesman" — of the Malays, Malaysians, Muslims, and the masses of the Third World. He was in contact with them, so he claimed; he knew them. He had a mandate from them; he spoke for them. In short, *vox Mahathir vox populi*. If this did not automatically conjure

an image of Mahathir as a "great leader in mystical contact with the masses",
he himself hinted that it was not entirely without mystique:

> I feel good about making contact [with crowds]. My training as a doctor
> helps me to communicate. The touch of the hand, that is important. It
> is like the healing concept of the "the laying of hands". That is why I
> try and shake the hands of as many people as I can. It is not possible
> to shake everybody's hand in a large crowd, but as many as possible....
> When people wave to me, shout greetings, I feel good.... Everything
> seems worthwhile. It's the way people greet you, the way they seem to
> accept you. You feel you are not a stranger. Your service is appreciated.[28]

Thaksin[29]

Something of a comparable bond could apparently be built upon so mundane
a basis as work, as witness Thaksin's call to Thai voters on the eve of the
nation's 2005 general election:

> Brothers and sisters, look at me! My ribs are all cracked, because when
> they hug me, they hug me tight, solid, humph! Today, I was hugged a
> bit too heavily. My arms are starting to be different lengths. Today, I was
> pinched all over. But I'm happy because people have the feeling that I
> care for them. I want to see them escape poverty. They have placed their
> hope in me. I know that I'm taking heavy burdens on my shoulders with
> the things I'm saying here. But I'm confident I can do them. Someone
> born in the Year of the Ox in the middle of the day likes working hard.
> They have to plow the field before they can eat the straw. So I really
> like to work. There's no work I run away from.... On the 6th, you go to
> work for me for just one hour, just one hour, in some places in Bangkok
> there may a be traffic jam so one-hour-and-a-half. But I'll work for you
> for four full years.[30]

During the years when prime minister Thaksin played populist, he, too,
mobilised by appealing to the "Thai people". Indeed, it has been suggested,
he did so to the point of symbolically conflating the initials of Thailand and
his name with the symbol of his party, Thai Rak Thai (TRT).[31] By then,
Thaksin had emerged from an earlier occupation in the police and miscella-
neous business ventures to become a high-flying corporate figure who had
had a stint in Cabinet. In class terms, he was already a billionaire tycoon
who hired thousands of employees and sent satellites into space, someone
who would reorganise political power to suit the requirements of big business.
Yet in a time when an unprecedented economic crisis had mangled the
fortunes of the ruling elite and hollowed their ruling ideas, what could be

more logical than for TRT's political project to issue a broadly nationalist and socially encompassing appeal, and don an apparently multi-class character?[32]

As Kasian Tejapira had observed of an early enthusiasm for Thaksin's politics and "Thaksinomics",

> ... people's organizations are impressed with PM Thaksin's willingness to take on and pressure government agencies, giant state energy enterprises, and mafia groups in certain localities on their behalf. The poor are attracted by his social welfare policy and economic-stimulus spending schemes that extend benefits to the grass-roots level. Big Thai capitalist groups, debtor and creditor alike, are ecstatic with his measures to cushion their businesses with public money and credits against the effects of the long economic recession, shrinking export market, stagnant domestic consumer and stock markets, and capital outflows. NGOs and communitarian public intellectuals admire the position he has taken in some of his addresses questioning, challenging, and criticizing the mainstream economic development line and calling for a more independent, self-reliant alternative amidst economic globalization.[33]

That multi-class character was reflected, among other things, in the variegated backgrounds of the TRT founder and the members of Thaksin's subsequent Cabinets.[34] Even so, Thaksin could just about claim a socially mixed lineage that stretched from new, poor, and provincial Chinese immigrant to settled, wealthy, and metropolitan Sino-Thai entrepreneur. Understandably Thaksin's autobiography, while tracing his rise from "modest origins to outstanding commercial success through hard work, persistence, and daring",[35] would omit all kinds of lending hands and hidden ties that facilitated his elevation. In his 51 years, as his 1999 election campaign press advertisement declared, he had been variously a "rural kid", the "son of a coffee shop owner", a police officer married to a senior policeman's daughter, a government scholar, and even an "NPL bad debtor".[36] It was a credible personal trajectory for someone whose party

> focused on two of the largest segments of Thai society — small family businessmen and the rural mass. It asked these two groups what they wanted from the state, turned the results into an electoral platform, and campaigned on this platform in a way that partially circumvented old structures of local influence.[37]

In successive elections, Thaksin's rural and social programmes formed the key planks of his populist platform which was unusual for its "clear policy issues related to agriculture, health and small and medium enterprises, and a moratorium on farm debt".[38] Well might Thaksin have depended initially on others to show him the potential of having a programme that could reach the grassroots:

> At first, Thaksin had no rural programme at all. A prominent student activist from the 1970s, now turned orchard farmer, faxed him a three-page rural programme but received no response. In early 1999, however, the rural protests reached a peak. Thaksin's team now began to consult with rural leaders and non-governmental organization (NGO) workers. He took up the activist's three-page plan. He adopted some of the localist vocabulary about strengthening communities and building recovery from the grassroots. In mid-2000, Thaksin announced a rural platform, including a moratorium on rural debts, a revolving fund of one million baht for every village, and a 30-baht-per-visit scheme of health care.[39]

Yet, Thaksin was not slow to instil a defiant sense of self-help that was grounded in a seeming store of simple and direct solutions:

> There are poor people, aren't there? The poverty caravan is going to their homes. Why are you still poor? It can be overcome. Come here quick. How much debt do you have? Restructure it. Do you have land to work on? No? Go and rent from others. Fix up the land documents. And what income do you have? Why are you unemployed? No work? Go for labor training. Get a job. Why are your kids not studying? No cash? Oh! Send them to school. Let's see, if you have more income than expenditure, will you be poor? No! I don't want to see people poor. Enough. There are lots of poor already.[40]

Most of all, it was necessary to carry out electoral promises: "not only did Thaksin and TRT make promises, but, following the election, they also moved quickly to implement them, emphasizing TRT's pledges to the poor".[41] Indeed, one critical columnist grudgingly observed of Thaksin that

> He has tried to implement every key point on his election platform, and a few things besides. The quality may be questionable. But he cannot be accused of bad faith. He has created more space for protest demands and negotiation.[42]

By paying triumphal attention to the basic needs of the critical mass of the non-Bangkok electorate, he demonstrated that the Shinawatra family's geographical and social mobility (including Thaksin's own educational so-journs in the USA) had not destroyed a feel for rural and small society that could only be intuitive for someone who had once belonged to the province but who, having moved to the capital, could perhaps evoke a wider pride in his individual progress towards the very apex of the *nouveau riche*. All that, however, came with a political condition. For Thaksin, "social policies are a 'cushion', a way to soothe the lower ranks of society so they don't create problems which obstruct entrepreneur-led growth. Under pluto-populism, the plutocrats make big money, and the people don't make big trouble."[43] In these circumstances, the personae of the big man and of someone who projected himself as a man of the people need not be mutually exclusive. Crucially, though, their blend typically produced a brand of leadership that spoke earnestly of representing the masses but strove hard to control them. As Thaksin propounded:

> When the people unite together in a state, they must agree to sacrifice some parts of their freedom so that the state can make rules by which people can live together in society with justice. That is the true core of the system of representation.[44]

In practice, it meant Thaksin was prepared to show alternately a "presidential disposition"[45] — for instance, to court and contain a large grassroots organisation such as the Assembly of the Poor[46] — or bare a repressive mien while waging "a series of 'wars' on drug dealers, mafia bosses, human rights and development NGOs, grass-roots movements and Malay Muslim separatists in the South, in which success was measured in terms of body count".[47]

Comparisons

Mahathir was virtually set to depart office about the time Thaksin sought his first election. Mahathir's populism had come to an end several years before Thaksin crafted the TRT's populist platform. Moreover, while Mahathir still presided over a mass party established a half century before, Thaksin was just building a new party, that, elected at a critical conjuncture of Thai politics, went on remake its structure and rules.

Yet, Mahathir and Thaksin shared much in the way of mass politics and elite attitudes towards the economy and state institutions.

Democracy, for instance, was for both a means, and a means that had to be limited; it would not be the goal of politics to establish a liberal democracy.[48] Few things showed that so obviously as when each of them had his political career and personal future placed before the judiciary. In 1988, Mahathir would not permit the Supreme Court to decide UMNO's status and, by extension, risk his tenure as party president. Thus was born the first of several crises of the Malaysian judiciary under Mahathir's administration. In the mid-1990s, Mahathir defended the erosion of judicial independence by insisting that, by democratic principles, an unelected judiciary could not pretend to an equal status with the elected legislature, let alone the executive. Thaksin said much the same thing when he had to answer charges of corruption brought before the Constitutional Court by the National Counter Corruption Commission. That he was acquitted on an 8–7 decision could only have vindicated his view that a crucial point of democratic politics had been missed:

> It's strange that the leader who was voted by 11 million people had to bow to the ruling of the NCCC and the verdict of the Constitutional Court, two organizations composed only of appointed commissioners and judges, whom people do not have a chance to choose.[49]

Nor would either, believing himself to be superior to others in communicating with the masses — not an outlandish claim in each case — tolerate much freedom for the "Fourth Estate". After a liberal spell at the beginning of his premiership in 1981, Mahathir rendered the Malaysian media among the most timorous in Southeast Asia. Thaksin, communications tycoon though he was, tried to curb the Thai press but perhaps failed only in degree rather than intent.

Their common intolerance of institutional rivalry differed in a major way when it came to the truly major institution of monarchy. In Malaysia UMNO was the true locus of political power, but the Malay rulers were still powerful in their individual states. Mahathir, whose antipathy to monarchy had been an open secret since his youth, first fought to curtail royal powers in 1983 and then clearly succeeded in 1992. Thaksin, however, was no match for the Thai monarchy whose interventions in Thai public life were of a different order from that of the constitutional monarch of Malaysia who served by rotation every five years.[50]

Mahathir and Thaksin each claimed to possess superior ideas for running the country and the economy for the better. Naturally they differed in practical ways. Each wanted to emulate "Japan Incorporated". Thaksin actually held that, "A company is a country. A country is a company. They're the same. The management is the same."[51] But much as he promoted his Malaysia Incorporated and privatisation policies, Mahathir maintained that a country and a company were far from being the same thing. That difference in conceiving the boundaries between country and company was arguably significant but it is not clear exactly how. In each country, the commercialisation of politics and the politicisation of business proceeded under the respective administrations of Mahathir and Thaksin. With Thaksin drawing upon his entrepreneurial experience as the fount of managerialist methods, perhaps "Thailand Company" left him almost uninhibited in pursuing private transactions that proved to be the beginning of his downfall. Mahathir, who habitually drew upon his medical training and practice for social diagnosis and political prescriptions, thought of Malaysia Inc. as a framework for healing a state–capital rupture that had occurred before he became prime minister.

The economy and business were critical sites at which both spoke to the masses but dealt with the corporate elites. Mahathir and Thaksin had early on warmed to liberalisation and deregulation when globalisation brought pay-offs in the rapid growth of the "East Asian miracle". But both treated with suspicion the globalisation that helped to bring about the 1997 meltdown. For them, looking after the poor formed one end of a policy spectrum. Looking after big business, however, was the more important end, for which many justifications were mustered.

Each came to prominence in a moment of national crisis when the dominant ideology was discredited as part of a more general social crisis, the point at which populism is likely to emerge.[52] Mahathir's moment came in 1969. Defeated in the general election, he reinvented himself as a party rebel who demanded the dismantling of the ruling Alliance's power-sharing framework and *laissez faire* policy regime. Both demands, reflecting wider UMNO sentiments, were in fact met from 1970 onwards, helping to cut a self-sacrificing figure for the otherwise down-and-out Mahathir. Thaksin's rise came when the economic debacle of 1997 had discredited the ruling elite and ruined Bangkok big business, and the 1997 Constitution had instituted reforms that opened the way for TRT's reconstitution of the political structure.[53]

Yet, if crisis bred populism, crisis could just as easily erase the fine line between populism and authoritarianism: in Malaysia that had happened with UMNO's split in 1987 and with the Anwar Ibrahim crisis in 1998, while in Thailand that came with Thaksin's "wars". Their dissimilarities lay in the scale of repression and the violence. All said and done, Mahathir was not as brutal a leader as Thaksin could be, but Mahathir was also able to use proven state instruments and experience of pre-emptive containment of political conflict. The result was a large difference in body count.

Finally, the crises that dissolved the line between populism and authoritarianism often provoked new forms of populist resistance. In 1998, the persecution of Anwar Ibrahim recast him from being an ambitious Mahathir loyalist to a populist dissident rooted in the discontents of civil society. The *Reformasi* movement in Malaysia, otherwise unfulfilled in its immediate goals, created new political space and discourses by rejecting many old parameters of state rule. In the event, *Reformasi* prodded Mahathir towards retirement, and indirectly compelled his successor, Abdullah Ahmad Badawi, to recover UMNO's electoral losses in 1999 precisely by using plebeian and populist measures to placate an estranged rural electorate and a large part of an alienated civil service. Although the military overthrew Thaksin in September 2006, 15 months later the electorate rejected the military's client parties, and chose a TRT-successor party promising to continue Thaksin's policies. Whatever party rules henceforth, it seems, will have to appease the rural base with populist palliatives as did Thaksin in his ascendancy.

The Ends of Populism

For the young(er) Mahathir, populism consisted of being the spokesman of the Malays; the end of his populism meant their "complete rehabilitation" from the ill effects of colonialism and "relative backwardness". The old(er) Mahathir's populism was underestimated for different reasons. As it were, he had slipped into power without need of a personal mobilisation, until he confronted the Malay rulers. He presided over a programme of late industrialisation that was moved by nationalist and developmentalist sentiments. Malaysia's ethnic politics often befuddled other ideological currents. Mahathir, too, scarcely needed to make discrete populist promises: the New Economic Policy was nothing if not an entrenched, expansive, and endless populist programme. Mahathir often criticised foreigners in defiant populist tones. But when Prime Minister Mahathir tried to change his people and move his nation, he spoke an idiom of work ethics and industrial discipline. By the later part of his 22-year premiership, he was less and less an approachable man of the people, although he continued to obtain his support from them, and more and more an aloof patron of the captains of commerce and industry, as well as the leading light of the movers and shakers of Malaysian politics. To that degree, *Reformasi* dissidents thought it appropriate to shout their defiance of "Pharoah's tyranny".[54]

In contrast, Thaksin's populist flowering was limited, perhaps exaggerated: "Populist promises to deliver extremely cheap healthcare, village rejuvenation projects and a debt moratorium for farmers turned Mr Thaksin into an overnight hero",[55] to be sure. But, other than urging "mass entrepreneurship" he had neither the time nor inclination to launch a "thoroughgoing reform and development policy for the countryside".[56] The end of his populist promise was too transparent — crude instrumentalist overtures to a much neglected rural base. They gained him an electoral advantage, enough to challenge the traditional elites but, within the strictures of an unreformed Thai power structure, not enough to supplant them.[57] Within a short tenure, Thaksin had enlarged upon his tycoon's persona and launched his wars in so many objectionable ways as to alienate a large part of the populace. Maybe no Thai prime minister had been as popular as Thaksin. But no populist can long endure who rapidly becomes unpopular. Even so, the specific end of Thaksin's populism exposed the institutional weaknesses of Thai politics. Against the achievements of decades of popular struggles, a military coup deposed Thaksin before sustained protests could topple him while deepening democracy.

Notes

I wish to thank the Center for Southeast Asian Studies, Kyoto University, for inviting me to its March 2007 and March 2008 Seminars (at which earlier versions of this chapter were presented). Chris Baker, Pasuk Phongpaichit, and Kanishka Jayasuriya generously provided me with various articles and materials.

1   For a different argument that nationalism in Southeast Asia had waned during the boom of the 1990s but resurfaced following July 1997 while the state-versus-market debate ended with it, see Kevin Hewison, "Nationalism, Populism and Dependency: Old Ideas for a New Southeast Asia?", Southeast Asia Research Centre, City University of Hong Kong, Working Paper Series 4 (May 2001), p. 1.

2   Yet internal debates over the fate of affected communities stimulated localist discourses, particularly in Thailand. See Duncan McCargo, "Populism and Reformism in Contemporary Thailand", *Southeast Asia Research* 9, 1 (Mar. 2001): 89–107; Nidhi Eeoseewong, "Thaksinomics", in *Kyoto Review of Southeast Asia: Selected Essays*, ed. Donna J. Amoroso (Kyoto: Center for Southeast Asian Studies, 2004), pp. 26–30; and Michael Kelly Connors, "Democracy and the Main-streaming of Localism in Thailand", in *Southeast Asian Responses to Globalization: Restructuring Governance and Deepening Democracy*, ed. Francis Loh Kok Wah and Joakim Öjendal (Copenhagen: NIAS Press, and Singapore: ISEAS, 2005), pp. 259–86.

3   Which led to populist mobilisation; see Kenneth M. Roberts, "Populist Mobiliza-tion, Socio-Political Conflict, and Grass-Roots Organization in Latin America", *Comparative Politics* 38, 2 (Jan. 2006).

4   Ghita Ionescu and Ernest Gellner, *Populism: Its Meanings and National Char-acteristics* (London: Weidenfeld and Nicolson, 1970). Also see the treatment of populism as a distinctive mode of political mobilisation in newly independent countries in Peter Worsley, *The Third World* (London: Weidenfeld and Nicolson,

1974), pp. 118–74; and the theoretical study of populism as ideology in Ernesto Laclau, *Politics and Ideology in Marxist Theory* (London: Verso, 1982).

5 George Wehrfritz and Stefan Theil, "The Rise of Populism", *Newsweek International*, 29 May 2006, <http://www.msnbc.msn.com/id/12892617/site/newsweek/> [accessed 12 Feb. 2007].

6 Kaveh L Afrasiabi, "The New Global Populism", *Asia Times Online*, 23 Sept. 2006 <http://www.atimes.com/atimes/Front_Page/HI23Aa02.html> [accessed 12 Feb. 2007].

7 Communitarian sentiments were especially powerful in local struggles against dubious "development projects" of discredited elites; for example, see Vanida Tantiwitthayapithak, "The Voice of the Poor", *Kyoto Review of Southeast Asia* 1 (Mar. 2002), <http://kyotoreview.cseas.kyoto-u.ac.jp/issue/issue0/article_74.html> [accessed 1 Mar. 2007].

8 For a critique of some discourses of nationalism, populism and dependency, see Hewison, "Nationalism, Populism and Dependency".

9 Kasian Tejapira, "On the Horns of a Dilemma", *Kyoto Review of Southeast Asia*, <http://kyotoreview.cseas.kyoto-u.ac.jp/issue/issue0/article_75.html> [accessed 22 Aug. 2007].

10 Khoo Boo Teik, *Beyond Mahathir: Malaysian Politics and its Discontents* (London: Zed Books, 2003), pp. 86–96.

11 Kanishka Jayasuriya and Kevin Hewison, "The Antipolitics of Good Governance: From Global Social Policy to a Global Populism?", *Critical Asian Studies* 36, 4 (2005): 571–90.

12 Malaysia maintains Mahathir Mohamad's "Vision 2020" (of reaching developed country status in 2020) as the national goal. Thaksin Shinawatra said in 2003 Thailand could reach that status earlier.

13 Much of this section is drawn from Khoo Boo Teik, *Paradoxes of Mahathirism: An Intellectual Biography of Mahathir Mohamad* (Kuala Lumpur: Oxford University Press, 1995), pp. 198–202.

14 Worsley, *The Third World*, pp. 119–26.

15 Peter Wiles, "A Syndrome, not a Doctrine: Some Elementary Theses on Populism", in *Populism*, ed. Ionescu and Gellner, p. 166; Bill Brugger and Dean Jaensch, *Australian Politics: Theory and Practice* (Sydney: George Allen and Unwin, 1985), p. 8, takes an early note of this point in discussing Australian populism.

16 "… populism avoids class war in the Marxist sense", Wiles, "A Syndrome, not a Doctrine", p. 167.

17 A usurious seasonal credit arrangement by which a cash advance made to a *padi* farmer about six months before harvest was repayable by a fixed quantity of rice at harvest.

18 Wiles, "A Syndrome, not a Doctrine", p. 167.

19 Mahathir Mohamad, "Whither Malaysia", in *Asia and Japan*, ed. Andrew J.L. Armour (London: Athlone Press, 1985), p. 152.

20 Rehman Rashid, "Why I Took to Politics", *New Straits Times*, 5 July 1986; emphasis in original.

21   J. Victor Morais, *Mahathir: A Profile in Courage* (Petaling Jaya: Eastern Universities Press, 1982), p. 24.

22   Mahathir's letter to Tunku Abdul Rahman, dated 17 June 1969, reproduced in Karl von Vorys, *Democracy Without Consensus: Communalism and Political Stability in Malaysia* (Princeton: Princeton University Press, 1976), pp. 372–3.

23   Robin Adshead, *Mahathir of Malaysia* (London: Hibiscus Publishing, 1989), pp. 61–2.

24   Mahathir Mohamad, *The Malay Dilemma* (Singapore: Donald Moore for Asia Pacific, 1970), p. 103.

25   Mahathir, *Malay Dilemma*, p. 114.

26   Mahathir's "revolution" was really "social engineering": "urbanization, acquisition of new skills and the acceptance by the Malays of new values which are still compatible with their religion and their basically feudal outlook would constitute a revolution" (*Malay Dilemma*, p. 114).

27   Mahathir, "Whither Malaysia", p. 152.

28   But: "I don't like adoration, adulation. That is why when people try to kiss my hand, I pull away." Supriya Singh, "The Man Behind the Politician", *New Straits Times*, 14 Apr. 1982.

29   This section draws principally from Pasuk Phongpaichit and Chris Baker, *Thaksin: The Business of Politics in Thailand* (Chiang Mai: Silkworm Books, 2004), and Kasian Tejapira, "Toppling Thaksin", *New Left Review* 39 (May/June 2006).

30   Thaksin Shinawatra, leader of Thai Rak Thai Party, Speech at Sanam Luang, 4 Feb. 2005, translated by Chris Baker and Pasuk Phongpaichit, <http://pioneer. netserv.chula.ac.th/~ppasuk/thaksinspeechelection2005.pdf, p. 12> [accessed 22 Aug. 2007]. I am grateful to Chris Baker for drawing my attention to this segment of Thaksin's speech.

31   Pasuk and Baker, *Thaksin*, p. 78.

32   Laclau, *Politics and Ideology*, p. 165, explicitly rejected any characterisation of populism as being "its appeal to the people above class divisions".

33   Kasian, "On the Horns of a Dilemma".

34   Pasuk and Baker, *Thaksin*, pp. 65, 73.

35   Ibid., p. 84.

36   Pasuk and Baker, *Thaksin*, pp. 84–8. "In one of the most striking elements of the 2001 election campaign, Thaksin presented TRT policies as the outgrowth of his own experience", noted Chang Noi, "Understanding Thaksin's Pluto-Populism", *The Nation*, 18 Feb. 2002, <http://www.geocities.com/changnoi2/pluto.htm> [accessed 1 Mar. 2007].

37   Pasuk and Baker, *Thaksin*, p. 98.

38   Michael Kelly Connors, *Democracy and National Identity in Thailand*, revised edition (Copenhagen: NIAS Press, 2007), p. 171.

39   Pasuk Phongpaichit and Chris Baker, "'The Only Good Populist is a Rich Populist': Thaksin Shinawatra and Thailand's Democracy", Southeast Asia Research Centre, City University of Hong Kong, Working Paper Series 36 (Oct. 2002), p. 7.

[40] Thaksin, Speech at Sanam Luang, 4 Feb. 2005, p. 4. Thaksin may have acquired this directness in style of leadership after his ascendancy: "Since coming to power in 2001, Thaksin has adopted a tough-guy (*nakleng*) style of leadership. He acts as if he's in sole charge. He takes decisions quickly. He bullies opponents. He deliberately abuses critics in foul language. He disdains rules, institutions, procedures. It's a leadership style which works well because it's rooted in the culture. It's the style of the local boss who gives protection and gets things done. Thaksin didn't behave like this five years ago. He learnt this style because people understand it, and it helped to make him popular." See Chang Noi, "Blowing up Thaksin", *The Nation*, 6 Mar. 2006, <http://www.geocities.com/changnoi2/blowing.htm> [accessed 1 Mar. 2007].

[41] Jayasuriya and Hewison, "The Antipolitics of Good Governance", p. 583.

[42] Chang Noi, "Understanding Thaksin's Pluto-Populism".

[43] Ibid.

[44] Thaksin, cited in Pasuk and Baker, *Thaksin*, p. 135.

[45] Kasian, "Toppling Thaksin", p. 32.

[46] Bruce D. Massingham, *The Assembly of the Poor in Thailand: From Local Struggles to National Protest Movement* (Chiang Mai: Silkworm Books, 2003), pp. 209–12.

[47] Kasian, "Toppling Thaksin", p. 29. For the "war on drugs", see Pasuk and Baker, *Thaksin*, pp. 158–67.

[48] That position was not damaging when Mahathir and Thaksin faced the voters, as shown by the electoral successes of their respective parties, even in times of crises.

[49] Cited in Pasuk and Baker, *Thaksin*, p. 5

[50] Connors, *Democracy and National Identity*, pp. 172–3, reports an instance of Thaksin's being reprimanded by the Thai monarch soon after he became prime minister. In 2006, TRT's electoral victory was nullified subsequent to the monarch's intervention (Kasian, "Toppling Thaksin", pp. 36–7).

[51] Cited in Pasuk and Baker, *Thaksin*, p. iii.

[52] Laclau, *Politics and Ideology in Marxist Theory*, p. 175.

[53] For a concise analysis of the twin conjunctures of politics and economics in Thailand as the baht crisis took place in July 1997, see Kasian, "Toppling Thaksin".

[54] Or *kezaliman Mahafiraun*, as the *Reformasi* dissidents in Malaysia used to describe Mahathir's repression after Anwar was dismissed.

[55] John Aglionby, "Profile: Thaksin Shinawatra", *Guardian Unlimited*, 19 Sept. 2006, <http://www.guardian.co.uk/print/0,,329580756-103681,00.html> [accessed 12 Feb. 2007].

[56] Kasian, "Toppling Thaksin", p. 37.

[57] Wehrfrtiz and Theil, "The Rise of Populism", offers this anti-populist interpretation: "Politicians face another worry: the populist backlash can spawn a backlash of its own. In a bold experiment, Thailand's Prime Minister Thaksin Shinawatra won election in 2001 promising to energize rural communities, and spent billions on rural subsidies and extending health care to the poor. The spending prompted

a boom and made him a hero in the hinterland, but helped to trigger a rebellion among urban elites, who forced him to step down last month." Stanley A. Weiss gives quite a different analysis: "… Thaksin was as much a symptom, as a cause, of deep divisions in Thai society. Yes, the billionaire-turned-politician was a classic populist who shamelessly exploited social, economic and class inequalities to win three elections and tighten his iron-fisted rule. But these fissures existed long before Thaksin and, if ignored, guarantee that Thailand, like other polarized societies, will remain easy prey for populist authoritarians." See "Thailand's Lesson in Populism", *International Herald Tribune*, 31 Jan. 2007, <http://www.iht.com/articles/2007/01/31/opinion/edweiss.php?page=1> [accessed 8 Feb. 2007].

CHAPTER 8

Populism under Decentralisation in Post-Suharto Indonesia

Masaaki Okamoto

Most East Asian and Southeast Asian countries have recently seen the emergence of populist national leaders such as Koizumi in Japan, Roh Moo Hyun in South Korea, Chen Shui-bian in Taiwan and Thaksin in Thailand while post-Suharto Indonesia has not had any populist national leaders until now. Indonesia was hit hard by the Asian economic crisis in 1997, destabilising both Indonesian politics and society and ending the authoritarian Suharto regime that had lasted for 32 years in May 1998. The result was a more democratic and decentralised Indonesia. This political transition might have led to the rise of populist national leaders in other countries; however, in Indonesia, national leaders tend to form coalition governments that include most of major political parties and their leadership is far from populist. Of course they show themselves as populist during the election campaign but they are just populist pretenders and start the "normal" politics of patronage and corruption once in power. I argue that the fragmented nature of Indonesian political society nurtures an accommodative style of leadership, rather than a distinctive, ideological or populist stance. The first charismatic president, Sukarno (1945–66) was populist in the sense that he took a vehemently hostile attitude to the international imperialist order and behaved as the representative of small people (*wong cilik*) by positioning himself as the mouthpiece of the Indonesian people (*penyambung lidah rakyat Indonesia*). But his flirtation with communism antagonised the military and Islamic groups, and he finally stepped down from the presidency just seven years after he had disbanded parliament and introduced his new regime of guided democracy.

Meanwhile, some regional and local political leaders have engaged in the politics of entrepreneurship and populism to gain broad support from local communities. Under the decentralisation scheme that gave wider authority to the regional and local governments, there is room for the emergence of populism at the regional and local level, where the political units are far less diverse than Indonesia as a whole. During elections, leaders at the regional and local level can campaign in ways that are culturally or ideologically acceptable, and pursue populist policies after they take power in regional or local government.

In the first section of the chapter, I discuss the reasons behind the accommodative style of leadership at the national level in Indonesia. The second section presents a case-study of a new type of local leadership that has begun to emerge in local politics as a result of decentralisation reforms over the past decade.

Electoral Populism in the Centre

One of the most important political figures that rose to the presidency after the fall of Suharto is Megawati Sukarnoputri, the daughter of the charismatic first president of Indonesia, Sukarno. In 1999, during the initial election campaign after the fall of Suharto, Megawati, who was a staunch opponent of Suharto during the New Order, led the nationalistic party, Indonesian Democratic Party of Struggle (PDIP) and presented herself as a populist figure by envisioning a "new" Indonesia that was free from corruption, collusion, and nepotism and also by emphasising the interests of "weak people" as her father did.

When she became president in 2001, she showed little populist inclination. Megawati Sukarnoputri is an upper middle class woman with little exposure to the real lives of the "weak people". She had limited interest in policy making, and was unenthusiastic about addressing the public. Neoliberal bureaucrats stabilised the macro economy, while she preferred to cooperate with the military to achieve political stability and even supported retired generals running for governorships. She did little to combat government corruption and her popularity steadily declined, with an opinion poll in June 2003 showing that only 15 per cent of the voters supported her re-election as president. She was just an electoral populist in the sense that she pretended to be a populist only during the election campaign.

The second figure we will consider is Susilo Bambang Yudhoyono, known as SBY, a retired military officer. When direct presidential election was instituted for the first time in Indonesia in 2004, he ran for the presidency from a small, new party and gained victory for a number of reasons. First of all, he drew the sympathy of the electorate when he was kicked out

Figure 8-1 SBY Carving an Image for Himself

of office as the coordinating minister of politics and security by President Megawati because he had revealed his ambition to run for the presidency, making Megawati furious. Second, distrust toward political parties was on the rise during the Megawati period and the electorate was seeking a figure who was not involved with the corrupt major parties. SBY fitted the bill. Third, his large stature and baritone voice made him appealing to the electorate. Fourth, he was a military officer, but was regarded as a reformist officer with a good track record, and so could sell himself as a clean candidate. Fifth, he chose the campaign strategy of direct appeal to the public. He went to see poor fishermen and peasants, discussing their issues and problems with them. He watched movies with street children and showed his compassion for them. Subsequently, he published a full-colour biography with the front cover showing a smiling "cool" SBY in a black leather jacket (see Figure 8-1).

But, again, when he became president in 2004, his leadership and actual policies were not so populist. He showed no clear commitment to improve the lives of the rural or urban poor, but tried to appease all sectors of society. He was not clear in decision making and failed to convey clear-cut and appealing messages to the public. His Cabinet made efforts to combat corruption but the results did not satisfy the public.[1] He too was an electoral populist.

As these two examples demonstrate, Indonesian leaders promote themselves as populists during election campaigns, yet are decidedly less populist when governing the country. The Cabinet is almost always an accommodative coalition including the major parties, and the politics of patronage and corruption is the norm. These politics are not just a result of the personal characters involved. There also seems to be four socio-structural and institutional reasons why leaders in power cannot behave as populists, or are not obliged to act as populists.

First of all, in the post-Suharto politics of democratic transition, the New Order's oligarchs such as Habibie, Akbar Tandjung, and Ginandjar Kartasasmita shrewdly won out over the radical, leftist, and populist streams. They chose a moderate path for the country and for their own interests, and since this crucial transition period they have wielded the politico-economic power at the centre.[2] As Robison and Hadiz noted, "The essential power relations of oligarchy and the hegemonic position of many of the main players themselves have been preserved and reassembled in a remarkable metamorphosis within the political and economic wreckage of the post-Suharto era."[3] There was no room for a populist to emerge as national leader. There was no opportunity for radical change of the state ideology of Pancasila either towards an Islamist or leftist direction. For example, an Islamist movement to amend the Constitution to include a requirement for Muslims to follow Sharia law was not accepted by the majority of the members of parliament. When the third president, Abdurrachman Wahid (1999–2001) tried to overturn an assembly resolution to prohibit the dissemination of Marxism and communism, the majority of the national parliamentarians opposed the president's move on grounds that the rise of communism could endanger the normal politics of moderation. Finally Wahid's liberal attitude towards political thought of all kinds, and his abrupt, ad hoc style of governance outraged parliamentarians, resulting in him being impeached in parliament and ousted from the presidency.

Second, Indonesia is a religiously and ethnically segmented society. Muslims are in the majority, but they belong to various factions such as the Nahdlatul Ulama or Muhammadiyah which often have their own political identities. This diversity tends to motivate the politicians at the centre to choose the politics of consensus or balance.

Third, the class divide between rich and poor is extremely sharp and each Cabinet avoids the risks of taking sides with one class. The industry-based economic structure in Java is quite different from the natural resource-based economic structure in the outer islands, and this difference has been a cause of conflict over economic policy. Currently, no national leader has managed to fashion an attractive political rhetoric that could draw support from the majority. It is hard for a national leader to construct a populist rhetoric that can attract a majority of Indonesia's diverse population.

Fourth, these social divisions are easily articulated as political and social movements, so national leaders avoid taking stances that might deepen existing social schisms.

While these four factors obstruct the rise of populism in national politics, the situation is different at the regional and local level. Recent decentralisation has given local governments wider authority. Local leaders have leeway to allocate these local government budgets for populist and other aims. The next section sketches the decentralisation scheme and then presents a case study of a local leader who combined entrepreneurship and populism.

Politics of Local Entrepreneurship and Populism

A Big Bang Approach to Decentralisation

Indonesia started decentralisation in 2001, marking a major break from the centralised pattern of government during the New Order. The World Bank called the change a Big Bang approach. The central government delegated administrative authority in all sectors except foreign affairs, defence and security, the judiciary, monetary and finance matters, and religion. Some 1.9 million officials were transferred to local governments, increasing their staff from around 700,000 to 2.6 million. Local parliaments were granted the authority to choose their local heads — governor of a province, head (*bupati*) of a district, and mayor of a town. These local heads have almost complete authority over local civil servants. These radical institutional changes brought into being a new style of local politics. Local politicians can now gain politico-economic power with less reliance on the support and patronage of central government. The jargon of "good governance", about participation, transparency and accountability, has become popular as local heads seek ways to legitimise their authority and sustain their hold on power. Populist appeals and populist schemes, such as low credit schemes for small-scale companies and poor peasants, and cheap or free education and health service, have also become common.

The decentralisation scheme was adjusted several times. The central government tried to recentralise but the attempt faced resistance and had to be abandoned halfway. From 2004, all local government heads were selected by direct elections. This further stimulated local politicians to sell themselves with populist policies during elections, and to implement such schemes in order to retain their popularity and their chances of re-election. Fadel Muhammad, the governor of Gorontalo Province, represents a new type of local leader now emerging in decentralised Indonesia.

Table 8-1 Business Interests of Fadel Muhammad

Companies or Groups headed by Fadel	Period
1 Arco Chemical Indonesia Co. Ltd/Lyondell Indonesia Co. Ltd/ Bayer Urethanes Indonesia Co. Ltd (petrochemical industry)	1987–2004
2 Dowell Anadrill Schlumberger Indonesia Co. Ltd (oil and gas services)	1985–2004
3 Gema Baker Nusantara Co. Ltd/Dwi Sentana Prima Co. Ltd	1983–2003
4 Gema Sembrown Co. Ltd/Sembawang Maritime Oilfield Engineering Co. Ltd (steel fabricator for oil and gas industry)	1988–now
5 Nesic Bukaka (telecommunication)	1993–now
6 Intan Group (insurance and finance)	1995–2004
7 Warta Group (publishing)	1989–now
8 Sierad Group (food industry)	1994–9
9 President of Bukaka Group (heavy industry)	1987–7
10 Batavindo Group (petrochemical industry)	1995–2000

Source: Fadel Muhammad, *Biodata Fadel Muhammad*, pp. 2–3.

Fadel's Rise in the New Order

Fadel Muhammad became governor of Gorontalo province in Sulawesi in 2001. He calls himself an "entrepreneurial governor", and calls Gorontalo an "entrepreneurial province". The place has become quite famous for his unique style of local governance.

Fadel was born in 1952 in Ternate, Maluku Province, and grew up there until graduation from high school. His parents were from Gorontalo. In 1972 he entered the Faculty of Physics and Engineering at Bandung Institute of Technology, one of Indonesia's most prestigious universities, and won prizes as a model student. After graduation, he entered the world of business by establishing an auto repair shop, PT. Bukaka Teknik Utama, with six employees. PT. Bukaka developed rapidly and within ten years became a leading company in the infrastructure, engineering, and construction sectors.[4] This success partly reflected the founder's entrepreneurial skill, but also benefited greatly from state policies during the Suharto period. Economic nationalists such as Sudharmono and Ginandjar Kartasasmita were unhappy about the economic dominance of the ethnic Chinese and launched a policy of affirmative action to promote indigenous (*pribumi*) businessmen. The *pribumi* entrepreneurs received preferential treatment from the government in procurement for development projects. Several of them such as Arifin Panigoro, Fahmi Idris, Sarwono Kusumaatmadja, Hasyim Joyohadikusumo, and Abdul Latief were able to grow their businesses successfully.[5] Fadel was among these. In the 1990s, he headed many large companies (see Table 8-1). He became a member of the central board of the chamber of commerce and industry.

As his companies began to grow, Fadel joined national politics through the corridor of the government party, Golkar, in order to "save companies from predation and increase his own political power" with the realisation that "the relationship between politics and business was quite close and an entrepreneur could not receive any opportunity from the government without any links with Golkar because the government controlled everything at that time (during the Suharto period)".[6] He became a member of the People's Consultative Assembly, the highest governing body in 1992 and a division head for cooperative and private enterprises on the central board of Golkar in 1993. Just a year after the fall of Suharto, he was treasurer of the Golkar central board.

Fadel is a pious Muslim and has been active in Islamic society. He is a member of Al-Khairaat, an Islamic social organisation that has wide influence in the eastern part of Indonesia. When President Suharto established the association of Indonesian Islamic Intellectuals in order to co-opt Islamic groups in 1990, Fadel became one of the founders.

The Asian economic crisis of 1997–8 hit Fadel's companies hard. PT. Bukaka Teknik was saddled with debts of 100 billion rupiah.[7] Fadel was declared bankrupt, but he survived. He abandoned PT. Bukaka, established a new business vehicle called Gema Group, and was released from bankruptcy by a ruling of the Supreme Court in 2004.

This brief biography shows that Fadel was not a pure neoliberal entrepreneur but rather an entrepreneur facilitated by the state's affirmative policies. This probably explains why his own political policies were a mix of promoting corporate management and providing affirmative assistance. On the one hand, he tried to promote business by establishing a brand image for Gorontalo province. On the other hand, he used public funds to offer guaranteed minimum prices for agricultural products and to provide selective assistance to a limited number of entrepreneurs.

The Birth of the Entrepreneurial Governor in Gorontalo

Gorontalo province lies at the northern edge of Sulawesi Island (see Figure 8-2). It has a total population of 890,000 (as of year 2000), of which

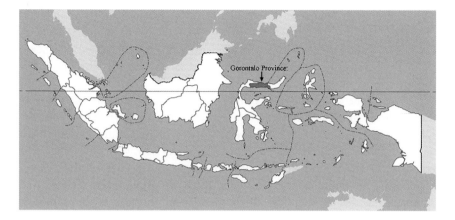

Figure 8-2 Location of Gorontalo Province

98.2 per cent are Muslim, and 90.4 per cent returned themselves as ethnic Gorontalo, according to the census in 2000. The Gorontalo area was separated from North Sulawesi as a new province in October 2000 mainly as a result of demonstrations and lobbying by young intellectuals and businessmen of Gorontalo origin.[8] Gorontalo province is an economically poor agricultural region, with 30.2 per cent of the regional GDP deriving from the primary sector, and 55.7 per cent of the workforce (above the age of 15) working in the primary sector.

When the movement to establish a new province started, Fadel had no interest at all. However, he suddenly changed his stance and considered running for the governorship after the province was established. Maybe he was looking for a solution to his company's debt problems and needed the financial benefit of the governorship.

In 2000, direct election of the regional head was not yet in force. The governor was elected by members of the provincial parliament. Fadel would win the election if he became the candidate from the Golkar party because the party held 25 out of the total 45 seats. However, he had no political base in the province and there were several local Golkar politicians who wanted to run for the governorship. The strongest rival to Fadel was Ahmad Pakaya, the district head of Gorontalo and the provincial branch head of Golkar. He was a rich contractor and was nicknamed the political commander of Gorontalo (*Panglima Politik Gorontalo*) because of his strong political base in the province.[9] He was said to have a strong desire to be the first governor even if his governorship lasted only a minute.[10]

Fadel used two strategies. First of all, he lobbied the central board of Golkar because the central board had the final say in choosing Golkar's candidate. Fadel had good access to the central board and exerted significant influence because he himself was a treasurer of the board. He did get the support from Jakarta.

Second, he avoided direct conflict with the local politicians by ignoring them. He differentiated himself from other candidate by talking about the future of Gorontalo. He wrote several articles on the future development of the province in the local newspaper, *Gorontalo Post*, with titles like "The potential of the Gorontalo economy from the perspective of the ocean", "Economic development is a challenge for each autonomous region", and "Accelerating the development of Gorontalo: agribusiness is the economic base".[11] These articles offered a vivid future vision for the province. One article argued that the provincial government must take an entrepreneurial role in development, and another emphasised the importance of corn and agribusiness in the Gorontalo economy. The Gorontalo province was a new political unit. Under the New Order, it had been impossible to discuss the future of the area as a unit. Fadel's concrete vision for the future was something new for the Gorontalo people. Established local politicians, including Ahmad Pakaya, failed to offer alternative visions of comparable attractiveness.[12] Everyone could realise the difference between Fadel and the old mundane oligarchies of local bureaucrats and politicians. Fadel made speeches on the future of Gorontalo to the young members of Al-Khairaat and other audiences.[13] He started to draw support from young intellectuals in the province, and began to have contacts and influence within the provincial branch of Golkar.[14]

When the provincial branch of Golkar started to discuss its candidate for governor, Fadel made a highly visible self-promotion by using a half page of a local newspaper with the headline, "Let's develop the Gorontalo society, an independent, entrepreneurial, and religious society with a rich culture" (see Figure 8-3).

Opinion polls favoured Fadel. In a poll published by the *Gorontalo Post*, Fadel was by far the most popular figure for the governorship.[15]

Finally, Pakaya gave up the gubernatorial race and Fadel was chosen as the candidate from Golkar. The provincial parliament then selected Fadel as the first governor of Gorontalo province on 12 September 2001. One consolation for Pakaya was that his relative, Gusnar Ismail, became vice-governor.

The Politics of Implementing Entrepreneurship

Fadel said, "The management of a local government is the same as the management of a company."[16] This remark reminds us of the neoliberal

Hanya dengan bersatu dan dengan dipandu oleh semangat Patriotisme 23 Januari 1942 serta warisan sikap keteladanan, kepahlawanan Nani Wartabone, kita mewujudkan percepatan pembangunan

Provinsi Gorontalo

menuju masyarakat yang bermartabat, terhormat, maju & sederajat dengan daerah lain"

bersama **Ir. Hi. FADEL MUHAMMAD.**

"mari kita membangun masyarakat Gorontalo yang *mandiri, berbudaya, entrepreneur,* bersandar pada moralitas agama"

Figure 8-3 Fadel Campaigns for Governor

populist prime minister of Thailand, Thaksin Shinawatra.[17] Fadel dubbed himself as an "entrepreneurial governor", styled his provincial government as an "entrepreneurial government", and tried to "manage" the government. This idea of "management" comes from his experience as a corporate manager and also from the idea of new public management (NPM). He was a political outsider in Gorontalo and was relatively free from the vested politico-economic interests of the province. This freedom gave him the room to introduce a new politics of entrepreneurship.

According to Fadel, a local government needs to pursue benefits (= the rise of human welfare) that are worth their costs (= public expenditure). Development programmes need to deliver quantifiable results.[18] He reformed the budget procedure. Under the old system, everyone involved in approving a project would receive an honorarium. The governor could collect an honorarium from every project, resulting in quite a large sum. Fadel abolished this system and introduced a scale of rewards and bonuses based upon performance.

Fadel believed that the province needed to specialise in order to develop successfully, and that managing this specialisation was the role of local government. As soon as he assumed the governorship, he unveiled the concept of an *agropolitan* that would achieve economic development based on the primary sector. The term *agropolitan* was coined by combining agribusiness and metropolitan.[19] The three major programmes of the *agropolitan* concept were: development of agricultural production, mainly corn; promotion of the fishing industry; and human resource development.

There were several reasons why he took a "back to basics" strategy of prioritising agriculture with a special focus on corn production, both in practice and in rhetoric. First, the domestic demand for corn was high, and Indonesia was a net importer. Second, corn was in short supply in the international market because of rising demand for energy crops. Third, the Gorontalo people were accustomed to cultivating and eating corn.

Fadel proudly announced "the movement to produce 1 million ton of corn",[20] meaning a plan to expand corn production from 70,000 tons in 2001 to 1 million tons by 2006. The components of the plan were: recruitment of capable people as top provincial government officials; setting a minimum purchase price of corn by governor's decree; converting to high-yielding hybrid corn; low-interest loans for farmers; an incentive system for sub-district heads to widen the corn production area; and infrastructure development, especially road construction, to transport corn from the production areas.

In truth, it is not clear to what extent these strategies helped to raise the income of poor peasants. The selling price of corn rose above the governor's minimum purchase price because of high global demand for corn, and the benefits were shared among various groups involved in corn production and distribution.

Politics of Promoting Entrepreneurship

In parallel with these concrete policies, Fadel implemented a marketing strategy to promote himself and Gorontalo province. Referring to the book, *The Marketing of Nations* written by the U.S. business scholar, Philip Kotler, Fadel set out to establish a brand image for Gorontalo province.[21] The centrepiece of this brand was corn. He boldly said, "The people will follow me if I speak about the importance of corn again and again."[22] Fadel himself acted as a drumbeater and seized every opportunity to implant the image of "Gorontalo = corn" in everyone's mind. When he was given a chance to talk to a community or make a speech to government officials in Jakarta, he always talked about corn and the *agropolitan* concept in Gorontalo. He introduced a corn festival and harvest festival and even held an international conference on corn. Taking advantage of his strong network with the Jakarta oligarchs, he often invited the president, ministers, or senior government officials to Gorontalo, and invariably conducted them to a corn field in order to get their support for the corn development strategy and to ensure Gorontalo would get funds from the central budget for corn development in the future. Even the President of Zambia visited the corn fields in Gorontalo in June 2005.[23] This brand-building policy bore fruit. Gorontalo province began to be known as "the corn province" in Indonesia even though Gorontalo contributed only 2.14 per cent of Indonesia's total corn production of 11.22 million tons in 2004.

In Gorontalo province, he established a direct dialogue with the people. His speech, with a distinctive, husky voice, was mystifying and "modern" in rural Gorontalo. He profusely used jargon words from business English such as parity, corporate culture, brand image, marketing of nations, strategic resources, and core competency. He had previously delivered speeches at national and international seminars, and this style proved attractive among the Gorontalo people. Fadel's speech came over as cool and of international standard. Many young intellectuals, peasants, and fishermen loved it just because the contents were totally different from their daily conversation. No other Gorontalo oligarchs could match this.

Fadel enthusiastically promoted himself and his policy through the media. In rural Gorontalo, the most effective medium to reach people is local radio. According to a survey done in November 2006 by the polling institution, LSI, 65.6 per cent of respondents knew Fadel Muhammad from radio programmes. He knew Parni Hadi, the director of Radio Republik Indonesia (RRI) in Jakarta and approached the Gorontalo branch of RRI two months after he became the governor in 2001. He used the local government budget to improve the equipment of the Gorontalo branch of RRI, thereby getting the support of the radio announcers and reporters. He made sure that every activity of Fadel as governor was covered live on radio. The Gorontalo branch of RRI and its employees were persuaded to support him. He also approached the local newspapers, again using the local government budget. Four million rupiah (around US$400) per month bought space to cover the daily activities of Fadel in the *Gorontalo Post*, the most popular local newspaper.[24] When Fadel invited a senior government official to Gorontalo and brought him to a corn field to harvest corn together, local newspapers announced the visit with banner headlines and pictures of Fadel and the officer harvesting the crop (see Figure 8-4).

Figure 8-4 Harvest Festival with Chief Justice of the Supreme Court

He issued a tabloid titled *Agropolitan* and opened a website on "Gorontalo — Agropolitan Province". By 2006, he had also published four books about himself in collaboration with Asep Sabar, a local newspaper journalist. The titles are *Fadel Muhammad: Concept and Idea to Develop Sulawesi* (2004), *Report from the Field: Fadel Muhammad, Gorontalo, and Sulawesi* (2005), *Fadel: Mr. Entrepreneur* (2005), and *Fadel: Precise Solution for Regional Development* (2006).

Politics of Financing Entrepreneurial Government

Gorontalo is a small province of 890,000 people (0.4 per cent of Indonesia's total population) with a limited local budget. Fadel mobilised his political and bureaucratic network in Jakarta to bring national budget funds to Gorontalo. Between FY2001 and FY2006 the amount and percentage of national budget allocated to Gorontalo province steadily increased (see Table 8-2). Even though the Department of Agriculture's total allocation to the provinces declined from FY2004 to FY2005, the percentage allocated to Gorontalo rose from 1.4 per cent in FY2004 to 1.9 per cent in FY2006. This percentage is quite high given Gorontalo's 0.4 per cent share of total population in Indonesia.

Table 8-2 National Budget Allocation to Gorontalo Province, 2001–6

Fiscal Year	Million Rupiah
2001	73,384
2002	248,361
2003	419,966
2004	436,864
2005	773,423
2006	1,026,965

Source: Bappeda Provinsi Gorontalo, *LPJK-Gubernur Gorontalo 2001–2006*, p. III-76.

The *agropolitan* programme was generously supported by both the central departments (see Table 8-3) and the provincial government (see Table 8-4). It seems that the large increase of budget allocation from the central government from FY2004 to FY2005 resulted from a realignment of political alliances following the direct presidential election in 2004. SBY became the president, with Jusuf Kalla of Golkar as vice president, and Golkar became

Table 8-3 Total National Budget to Support the *Agropolitan* Programme, 2001–5

Fiscal Year	Billion Rupiah
2001	16.34
2002	11.66
2003	17.65
2004	18.97
2005	33.79

Source: <http://pde.gorontaloprov.go.id/lain/program.pdf>

Table 8-4 Total Provincial Budget to Support the *Agropolitan* Programme, 2002–5

Fiscal Year	Billion Rupiah
2002	7.55
2003	5.95
2004	7.49
2005	6.83

Source: <http://pde.gorontaloprov.go.id/lain/program.pdf>

the largest party in the government coalition. Fadel was a member of the Golkar central board. From this position, he could easily lobby the central government to gain an increase in the budget allocation for his province.

The Politics of Good Performance

The economy of Gorontalo province performed well. Corn production increased from around 70,000 tons in 2001 to around 440,000 tons in 2006. According to the Central Bureau of Statistics (BPS), the provincial economic growth rate rose from 5.38 per cent in 2001 to 7.06 per cent in 2006, the third highest provincial growth rate of all Indonesia. The gross regional domestic product per capita rose from 2.16 million rupiah in 2001 to 3.72 million rupiah in 2006.[25]

Furthermore, Fadel quickly supported the central government's idea of adopting a budgeting system based on performance, and had Gorontalo designated as one of the pilot provinces for the scheme in 2004. He successfully promoted the idea of a national corn committee and became its first chairman.

These and other achievements, and his efforts to publicise them, were rewarded with many awards to him and his government. In November 2004, he was the only person in the government sector to receive the "Entrepreneur Agribusiness Award" from the journal *InfoBisnis*. In December 2004, he received an award from the central government for his contribution to food security. The total number of awards given to him and his government reached around 34 within six years.

His achievements and his publicity made him popular within Gorontalo province. When LSI conducted an opinion poll on the popularity of each candidate for the Gorontalo provincial governorship in the middle of November 2006, 82.1 per cent of respondents answered that they would support Fadel as governor if an election was held on that day. His performance as governor was rated positively by 93.3 per cent. The agropolitan programme was rated as successful by 86.5 per cent. Of all respondents 96.9 per cent liked Fadel; 92.4 per cent said he had the capability to govern the province and paid due attention to the people; 89.7 per cent regarded him as a governor who made good decisions; 70.5 per cent thought he was free from corruption, collusion, and nepotism; 93.5 per cent said he was smart, and 87.6 per cent said he was honest.

At the direct election for Gorontalo provincial governor in November 2006, Fadel won a landslide victory with 82 per cent of the total votes, the highest among all gubernatorial elections in Indonesia. His ambition did not stop there. He took a PhD course on public administration at Gadjah

Mada University, graduating cum laude in October 2007. The dissertation is about himself and his "successful" experience as the governor of Gorontalo province. Next year he published the revised dissertation titled "Reinventing Local Government: Experience from the Region." He declared that he was prepared to be the vice president if Sultan Hamangku Buwono X, a charismatic Javanese sultan, ran for the presidency. This declaration came before he was listed as one of ten bad debtors who had failed to repay billions of dollars owed to the state. During the Asian economic crisis, Fadel had borrowed from the badly administered Bank Indonesia Liquidity Assistance scheme to support his now-defunct Bank Intan. He had repaid only Rp 4.9 billion out of Rp 88.2 billion owed.[26] The legacy of the Suharto regime still haunts Fadel Muhammad.

Other Examples of Local Populism

Fadel is not alone. Following decentralisation, local politics in Indonesia has thrown up several populist leaders, with varying characters and styles.

Basuki Purnama is the son of a Chinese businessman in the sand export business. He became the district head (*bupati*) of East Belitung district, Bangka-Belitung province.[27] East Belitung district was established in 2003 by separating from Belitung district. The total population was around 88,000 in 2004. Basuki became the first Chinese local government head in Indonesia. He became politically conscious in 2001, following the unstable political conditions and riots against the Chinese in Jakarta and other cities. In 2004 he decided to jump into the election race for the East Belitung district parliament as the candidate of the new and small New Indonesian Association Party (Partai Perhimpunan Indonesia Baru, PPIB) led by Sjahril, a famous economist. He was branch head of PPIB in East Belitung district.

He knew little about politics or election campaigning, and followed the normal style of electioneering. He visited villages, met the people, and gave them everything they demanded such as T-shirts, soccer balls, and money for repairing mosques. He spent around 1.2 billion rupiah, yet PPIB won only two seats in the district parliament. The cost-benefit ratio was bad, but he became a parliamentarian. He rejected all the bribes and even the official travel expenses. He went to the parliament almost every day of duty and listened to the grievances of the people. He was not so popular among his fellows in the parliament but became popular among the people because he projected a clean image.

At elections for the district head in June 2005, he decided to run. His campaign motto was quite simple, "Just give us the chance." He emphasised

six factors using a mnemonic of "Smart plus M": Strong connected (strong
network with every sector); Middle-aged (35–50 years old); Actuated (vision,
mission and programmes that are easily understandable by the people); Rich
(economically rich); Talented (high leadership ability); and Moral (high
morals and ethics).[28]

Basuki ran a unique campaign. He did not visit the villages, but invited
village people to his house to listen to him making speeches criticising the
current local administration. He said, "I don't want to be a *bupati*, but the
leader of a revolution (*pemimpin revolusi*)." This rhetoric, his clean image
and his staunch criticism of the local government won him the election with
35 per cent of the votes at a total cost of only 800 million rupiah. He was
39 years old at that time.

His first address to the district officials began with the following
sentence:

> I am not a *bupati*. I am a commoner with the *bupati* cloth. I hate all of
> you. Be careful with me. First of all, I don't need any allocation (*jatah*)
> [from budget projects]. I don't need any travel expense. I don't want your
> wives to bring some cakes to my house ....

He launched some populist policies. He allocated around 2.5 billion
rupiah from the local budget to introduce a free health service in collaboration with ASKES (a health insurance company) in 2006.[29] He made tuition
free in high schools.[30] He passed on 10 per cent of the local government's
allocation from central funds directly to the villages. He increased the salaries
of village officials, raising village heads from 750,000 rupiah in 2005 to 2.5
million rupiah per month in 2006.[31] He gave grants of 500,000 rupiah for
bereavement and 200,000 for birth allowance. He made his hand-phone
number public so that people could easily complain if any government
service was unsatisfactory.[32] He announced in public, "even if contractors
get profits from the district government projects, don't reserve a part of
these profits for the *bupati*, not even a penny".[33] People appreciated these
schemes, as well as Basuki's clean image. After a year and eight months in
duty, he resigned as the *bupati* and ran for the governorship of Bangka-
Belitung province in February 2007. He lost the election by a slim margin.
Maybe he was too politically ambitious.

Other *bupati* have followed him, scaling the ladder from *bupati* to
candidate for the governorship on the basis of populist appeal. Some have
succeeded and some failed.

Gamawan Fauzi, gained popularity as *bupati* of Solok district in West
Sumatra province for being clean and fighting corruption. With this support,

he successfully ran for the governorship of West Sumatra province. In 2000, Rustrinignsih ran for *bupati* of Kebumen in Central Java province as the PDIP candidate, and won victory by two votes. She started a radio programme and SMS service for constituents to send their petitions and complaints. Her commitment to reform the Kebumen district government raised her popularity. She was re-elected as *bupati* and later elected as vice-governor of Central Java province.[34] I Gede Winasa, *bupati* of Jembrana district in Bali province, started an inexpensive education system for the poor, was re-elected as *bupati*, and ran for the governorship in Bali province but failed to gain the support from the dominant political party, PDIP, and lost the game.

Epilogue

There appear to be two different types of leadership in Indonesia. At the national level, leaders tend to be bland and not distinctive. Megawati and SBY promoted themselves as populist leaders only during their election campaigns, but once in power tended to form coalition cabinets that included major political parties, and failed to exert any strong and distinctive leadership. They are accommodative and conciliatory and as such are not so popular among the people. I believe this is a function of the fragmented nature of Indonesia's national society, the resulting complexity of its politics which demands conciliation and compromise, and the success of the old oligarchs in retaining power in the crucial post-Suharto transition period.

At the provincial and local level, a new and different style of leadership is emerging. Fadel Muhammad shaped a strong and highly distinctive leadership marrying elements of entrepreneurship and populism. He proposed a future vision for Gorontalo which caught the public imagination. He delivered on this vision by accelerating corn production under his *agropolitan* programme. He won enthusiastic support among the Gorontalo people. How did Fadel do all this?

First of all, the decentralisation scheme opened up the institutional possibility for each local leader to exert strong leadership. Especially after the introduction of direct elections for the regional head in 2004, candidates needed to build a wide base of support. Second, Gorontalo province is a rather homogeneous rural and agricultural society. It is not so difficult for a local leader to build wide support by appealing to the common denominator of the population. Third, Gorontalo province is a newly born political unit so people, especially young intellectuals, were seeking a fresh leader. Fadel was suitable for them. Fadel himself became a symbol of the clear break from the old, traditional, and unprogressive past of Gorontalo. Fourth, Fadel was a totally new player with no vested interests. He could launch a new style of politics without considering the locally embedded politico-economic structures. He could leverage his links with the central government, especially through Golkar, to obtain national budget support for his *agropolitan* programme. Fifth, Fadel projected himself as an entrepreneur, though in truth his own commercial success owed a great deal to the New Order's affirmative policies. In like fashion, he projected a concept of "entrepreneurial government", yet used protectionist policies such as floor-pricing to win the support of corn farmers. Sixth, Fadel tirelessly publicised himself, his policy, and the province through the media.

Fadel is not a typical populist, but represents a new type of local leader — a child of the age of democratisation and decentralisation. These new leaders are experimenting with methods to marshal political support, including populist appeals as well as promises of "entrepreneurial government". The revised law on local government in 2008 allows independent candidates with no affiliation to any political party to run in the elections for local heads. This change may increase the numbers of leaders of this new type.

Notes

[1]   The government is showing better performance on corruption in local government. A World Bank report entitled "Fight against Corruption in Decentralized Indonesia" (*Memerangi Korupsi di Indonesia yang Terdesentralisasi*) in May 2007 detailed corruption cases involving DPRD members and local heads. Based on the data from all the high public prosecutors' offices from the year 2002 to September 2006, there were 265 corruption cases by DPRD members. In all, 967 DPRD members were suspected, accused, or condemned by 29 high public prosecutors' offices. During the same period, permits were issued to investigate 327 provincial DPRD members and 735 district/municipal DPRD members. There were also 46 corruption cases involving 63 local heads as either suspects, accused, or condemned. Based on Department of Home Affairs data from 2004 to early 2006, permits were issued to investigate seven governors and 60 *bupati*/mayors or vice *bupati*/mayors. See Taufik Rinaldi, Marini Purnomo and Dewi Damayanti, *Memerangi Korupsi di Indonesia yang Terdesentralisasi: Studi Kasus Penanganan Korupsi Pemerintahan Daerah* (Jakarta: Justice for the Poor Project: Bank Dunia, 2007), p. 2.

[2]   In his dissertation on the survival of Golkar, Akbar Tandjung, head of Golkar at that time, described how the Golkar party tried to choose the moderate way during the transition period. See Akbar Tandjung, *Partai Golkar di Tengah*

Turbulensi Politik Era Transisi [The Golkar Way: Survival in the Turbulent Politics of Transition] (Jakarta: Gramedia Pustaka Utama, 2007).

3   R. Robison and V. Hadiz, *Reorganizing Power in Indonesia: The Politics of Oligarchy in An Age of Markets* (London and New York: Routledge Curzon, 2004), p. 13.

4   The biography of Fadel is in Fadel Muhammad, *Biodata Fadel Muhammad* (n.p., 2005?); <http://www.tokohindonesia.com/ensiklopedi/f/fadel-muhammad/index. shtml>; and the website of PT. Bukaka Teknik Utama, <http://www.bukaka. com/AboutUs.php>.

5   Adam Schwartz, *A Nation in Waiting: Indonesia's Search for Stability* (Singapore: Talisman, 2004), pp. 117–20. Fadel himself evaluated this era as the "old but unforgettable era" and justified the policies because those who benefited from the policies were the real entrepreneurs. See Asep Sabar, ed., *Fadel Muhammad: Gagasan & Pemikiran Membangun Sulawesi* (Gorontalo: Puslitbang Gorontalo Post, 2004), p. 320.

6   Asep Sabar, *Fadel: Sang Entrepreneur* (Jakarta: Arena Seni, 2005), pp. 111, 311.

7   *Gorontalo Post*, 29 Aug. 2001.

8   The reasons behind the separation was economic backwardness and ethnic difference.

9   Interview with Lala, ex-journalist of *Manado Pos*, 19 July 2006.

10   Interview with a young intellectual, 18 July 2006.

11   *Gorontalo Post*, 17 April 2001; 20 June 2001; 21 June 2001; 28 June 2001; 29 June 2001.

12   Pakaya once wrote an article, "The Direction of Political Party Strategy in Gorontalo", but it had no concrete ideas (*Gorontalo Post*, 18 and 19 April 2001).

13   *Gorontalo Post*, 25 June 2001.

14   Interview with Arusdine Bone, a young cadre of the Golkar provincial branch, 21 July 2006; and interview with Elnino, a young local journalist, 23 Aug. 2005.

15   *Gorontalo Post*, 4 Aug. 2001.

16   Interview with Fadel Muhammad, 3 April 2006.

17   Pasuk Phongpaichit and Chris Baker, *Thaksin: The Business of Politics in Thailand* (Chiang Mai: Silkworm Books, 2004), p. 101.

18   Asep Sabar, *Fadel Muhammad*, pp. 31–2.

19   The term itself was not coined by Fadel Muhammad but by the human resources development agency at the Department of Agriculture in 2000 or in 2001 (interview with Jamaluddin, ex-provincial department head of agriculture, 7 Jan. 2006). But Fadel shrewdly presented the term as if it was coined by himself.

20   The movement officially started on 15 April 2004, see *Bulletin Agropolitan Gorontalo* Edisi I Thn I Juli 2005, p. 5.

21   Asep Sabar, *Fadel Muhammad*, p. 24.

22   Interview with Fadel Muhammad, 3 April 2006.

23   *Bulletin Agropolitan Gorontalo* Edisi I Thn Juli 2005, p. 8.

24   Interview with a journalist, 28 Jan. 2008.

25   Bappeda Provinsi Gorontalo, *LPJK-Gubernur Gorontalo 2001–2006* (Gorontalo: Provinsi Gorontalo, 2006), p. III-79.

26   *Jakarta Post*, 16 Feb. 2008.

27   The following information on Basuki was based on the interviews with Basuki Purnama, 7 July 2007, and with Adi (a journalist of *Pos Belitung*), 14 Feb. 2008.

28   *Bangka Pos*, 25 June 2005.

29   *Pos Belitung*, 26 Jan. 2006, 15 Feb. 2006.

30   The central government subsidised the fee for elementary schools and junior high schools under the budget item called *dana BOS* (bantuan operasional sekolah) (the helping fund for school operations).

31   *Pos Belitung*, 18 July 2006.

32   *Pos Belitung*, 10 Oct. 2005.

33   *Bangka Pos*, 16 May 2006.

34   *Gatra*, 26 March 2008, p. 17.

PART II
Populism in Northeast Asia

CHAPTER 9

A Populist with Obsolete Ideas: The Failure of Roh Moo-hyun

Kan Kimura

> The president has recently been a sandbag. I consider this my fault, as well as a cost of democracy, and accept it. But there are those who are allowed to criticise the president, and those who are not. If those who are not allowed to do so punch the president like a sandbag, I feel deeply sorry and sometimes even feel frustrated.[1]

On 26 December 2006, the South Korean president, Roh Moo-hyun, made the above statement in a Cabinet meeting at the presidential palace. Clearly it was an unusual statement for a president to make. He showed an aggressive attitude towards public opinion and influential politicians who had fiercely criticised the president. In the same meeting he said, "I have been silent and patient with a number of criticisms, but from now on I will explain point by point."

Behind the scenes, the Roh Moo-hyun regime had already become a lame duck even though more than a year remained until the expiration of Roh's term in February 2008. According to an opinion poll conducted by the Korea Society Opinion Institute in December 2006, the approval rate for the president's performance had fallen to just 5.7 per cent, and the approval rate for the ruling Yeollin Uri Party to 9.6 per cent.[2] This approval rate was the worst in Korean political history since democratisation in 1987. The Yeollin Uri Party and its leading politicians seriously started to differentiate themselves from the collapsing Roh regime, further aggravating relations between Roh Moo-hyun and the party. Roh's statement in Cabinet, quoted above, was principally directed against Goh Kun, a former prime minister and the interim head of state.

How did the Roh regime arrive in such a situation? The first reason is a provision in the South Korean constitution which forbids re-election of the president. Owing to this rule, it is common for a president to become a lame duck at the end of his term. Yet the constitution has remained unchanged since 1987 and hence all presidents since that date have operated under the same conditions as Roh Moo-hyun. It is true that earlier presidents of the democratisation era such as Roh Tae-woo, Kim Young-sam, and Kim Dae-jung became lame ducks at the end of their terms, but not to the same extent or for as long a time as Roh.[3]

The second reason is that Roh had no solid base of popularity. Unlike previous presidents, he drew no support from the regionalism which had characterised South Korean politics since democratisation in 1987.

Roh thus differed from his predecessors in that the decline in his popularity began earlier and fell more steeply. Within only half a year after taking office in February 2003, his approval rating had fallen to about 20 per cent. Although his popularity rating recovered to around 50 per cent during the debate over his impeachment in 2005, because public opinion felt the impeachment was based on weak grounds, it plummeted again to about 20 per cent in the second half of 2005, and stayed low from then onwards. In short, after only a brief spell at the start of his term, Roh's public approval rating was abysmal throughout.[4]

As we will see later, Roh could not rely on a political party to regain support. As a result, his leadership had to be very "populistic", in the sense that he tried to appeal to the public directly, not via his party, as a strategy to win popularity.[5] He very often appeared on TV and sent many messages on the website of the presidential office. As a reformist politician, he launched many "reform plans" without showing any grand design for changing the society as a whole.

One of the tactics Roh used to boost his low popularity was heavy resort to nationalistic rhetoric. It is not clear whether this nationalistic rhetoric stemmed from Roh's political convictions, or was simply a political strategy. Yet he had earlier showed some skill in wielding this weapon. In 2002, when two South Korean schoolgirls were run over and killed by a U.S. military vehicle, provoking strong anti-American sentiments, Roh capitalised on these sentiments in his presidential election campaign, propelling himself into the presidency in December 2002.

This kind of nationalistic populism was seen in other East Asian countries, especially in Japan and Taiwan. Jun'ichiro Koizumi, prime minister in Japan, Chen Shui-bian, president of the Republic of China (Taiwan), and Roh Moo-hyun are sometimes regarded as the same type of nationalistic populists because they appealed directly to the people when popular support for their political parties had weakened.

However, the results were not the same. Although Koizumi retained his personal popularity until the day of his retirement as a prime minister, Roh and Chen had to struggle with the "too early lame duck phenomenon" for a long time. Why did this situation arise in East Asia, especially in South Korea? This chapter examines this question through the experience of Roh Moo-hyun.

The Wave of Nationalistic Populism in Northeast Asian Countries

Around the time that Roh Moon-Hyun was elected president, rather similar political leaders came to power in other Northeast Asian countries.

These three political leaders had totally different backgrounds. Roh and Koizumi were elected as leaders of the ruling parties in their countries, while Chen won power as an opposition candidate. Koizumi is from a conservative family, with both his father and grandfather being prominent figures in Japanese public affairs, while Roh and Chen emerged through participation in democratic movements.

Yet these three leaders share four similarities. First, all their regimes had strong intentions for "reform". Second, they all relied on their individual popularity rather than traditional party systems in order to win office and to maintain their political support. Third, they all therefore emphasised direct communication with their people through the mass media, the Internet, and simple and persuasive discourse. Fourth, nationalistic rhetoric played an important role in their attempts to maintain this individual popularity. A regime which is nationalistically coloured and based on individual popularity is defined here as a "nationalistic populist" regime.[6]

Why did these nationalistic populist regimes emerge simultaneously in Japan, South Korea, and Taiwan at this specific time? There were three important factors shaping the historical context. First, these three countries experienced rapid economic growth after the Second World War. Second, in each nation an elite group of bureaucrats or conservative politicians are considered to have played a vital role in this process of economic growth. Third, all these countries went through an economic slump in the 1990s, though in different ways, and it became apparent by the year 2000 that they were no longer able to achieve the high economic growth of earlier years.

These commonalities across Japan, South Korea, and Taiwan created similar situations in the three countries. Economic decline in the 1990s seriously undermined public trust in the governments and ruling parties that had maintained their political authority in the past because of their record in promoting economic growth. Economic decline also undermined public trust in the elites that occupied a central place in these governments and ruling parties. Growing suspicion towards political elites also overflowed into distrust of opposition parties, and resulted in distrust of politics as a whole, whether ruling parties or opposition.[7]

The collapse of trust in the existing political party system meant that old ruling parties were unable to depend on the authority of the party for winning elections. All parties sought to elect leaders who were able to build a personal base of support owing to their own highly assertive and unique characters, rather than being dependent on the traditional party system. The politicians with such characters had previously tended to be marginalised in the party systems. As a consequence, each party came to be dependent on its leader's individual popularity.

At the same time, the decline in economic growth generated an argument that the existing state-led political and economic system should be reviewed. The new political leaders in Northeast Asian countries thus began to propose reformist messages to their people. Although Roh, Koizumi, and Chen had totally different backgrounds (Koizumi emerged from a major faction in a ruling party; Roh emerged from a marginalised position in a ruling party; and Chen was a leader of the main opposition party which had a long history of democratic activism), they all adopted strong reformist ideas and took a critical attitude towards traditional elites.[8] Even though these leaders might belong to an influential family of conservative politicians, or be a Cabinet member, or hail from an elite university with a high reputation in the society, they behaved and even were expected to behave as if they were different from conservative politicians, elite bureaucrats, or those who graduated from an elite university — in short, as if they were a totally new type of political leader.

The end of high economic growth in the 1990s also stimulated nationalism in the three Northeast Asian countries. In all three countries, the high economic growth that started in the 1950s and the 1960s was seen as a cause of the "greatness" of the nation. Declining growth in the 1990s not only undermined the prestige of the elites in each country but hurt the pride of the nation as a whole. Opinion surveys in Japan and South Korea showed steep decreases in the number of people who stated they were proud of their own nation.[9]

The end of the high economic growth era urged nations to reconstruct grounds to explain the greatness of their own nation. Nationalism in each country sought new grounds for national pride. In Japan, a so-called "neoliberal view of history" emerged. In South Korea there were debates between "the progressive view of history" and conservative views. A "New Right Movement" started in 2004 and engaged in intensive dispute against "progressive factions". In Taiwan also, there was fierce debate over the history and role of the Kuomintang, especially focusing on the 228 incident.[10] In all three countries, people voiced doubts about the political and economic systems which sustained their country until the 1980s, and sought new ways to understand the past and project the future.

In this situation, the political leaders of Japan, South Korea, and Taiwan focused on crafting new forms of nationalism. The new political leaders all achieved their leadership by emphasising reformist messages appropriate to the new political and economic circumstances created in the 1990s. However, these leaders lacked full and detailed plans on how to translate aspirations for reform into concrete reality. Koizumi made privatisation of the postal service "the core of reform" and argued as if this one measure was the solution to all the problems in Japan. In Taiwan, Chen Shui-bian tried to give "the issue of a fourth nuclear power plan" more meaning than just an environmental issue.[11] Roh Moo-hyun waxed eloquent about the importance of reform but could not display any comprehensive plan. Instead he insisted that moving the capital from Seoul and "reform of the old media" were essential for the future.

The leaders in all three countries faced great difficulties in presenting a grand design of reform that was unique, attractive, and suitable for their country's situation in the globalising world, where major counter-ideologies such as Marxism had lost influence and where market liberalisation seemed the only way to generate economic growth. Instead all three leaders came up with very partial plans for reform but claimed they were a complete programme. Their proposals were a collection of scraps stitched together like patchwork quilts.

Nationalism played a crucial role in this process, because the new nationalisms of this period and the reform policies of the three political leaders headed in the same direction. The important point is that all three leaders criticised the same three things — traditional political systems, old elites, and the old ideologies which had supported the old systems and given legitimacy to the old elites.

Koizumi resolutely continued his visits to the Yasukuni Shrine in order to show that he was a "reformist" who "challenged taboos", while at the same time adopting a liberal stance in his general diplomacy. In a similar way, all three political leaders sporadically resorted to nationalistic rhetoric to show that they were challengers against old taboos.

Roh, Koizumi, and Chen were mainly focused on domestic "reform" and all were relatively unconcerned with diplomacy. They never made the issue of diplomatic policy an important part of their campaigns in the major elections. Public interest in each country was also directed to domestic issues such as the economy and political corruption. Nonetheless, nationalistic statements by each leader greatly influenced the neighbouring countries and eventually led to deterioration in the international relations among the Northeast Asian countries of Japan, South Korea, Taiwan, and China.

What was the role of nationalistic discourse in the Roh Moo-hyun regime?

Genealogy of the "Outsiders"

The deaths of two South Korean schoolgirls run over by a U.S. military vehicle in 2002 and the consequent anti-U.S. movement, greatly contributed to the establishment of the Roh Moo-hyun government. The association between Roh Moo-hyun and the anti-U.S. movement was not coincidental. The roots lay in Roh's political career.

Roh Moo-hyun was born in 1946 in today's Gimhae city in Gyeonsamnam-do, near South Korea's second largest city of Busan. He was a son of a poor farmer. After graduating from Busan Commercial High School, he passed the bar exam at the age of 29 and set up his own legal practice after serving as a judge. He gained a reputation as a "human rights lawyer" as a result of defending students who were detained and tortured by the authoritarian Chun Doo-hwan government in the so-called Burim Incident of 1981 because they had studied leftist ideologies.

In 1987, the Chun Doo-hwan government was overthrown by the democratisation movement, establishing the Sixth Republic which continues to this day. Roh entered politics at the invitation of Kim Young-sam, one of the most important figures in South Korean democratisation along with Kim Dae-jung, and the most popular politician in the Gyeonsamnam-do region. Roh was elected to the 13th National Assembly as a candidate of the opposition Democratic Party, defeating Ho Sam-Su, a powerful candidate of the ruling party who used to be influential in the Chun Doo-hwan regime. As a member of the National Assembly, Roh Moo-hyun took an active part in hearings about corruption during the Chun Doo-hwan government and about the Kwangju massacre, and thus came into the political limelight.

Roh Moo-hyun's career has led him far away from these activist beginnings. In 1990, Kim Young-sam, the leader of the Democratic Party, had ambitions to win the next presidential election in 1992. He decided to dissolve his party, and merge with the ruling Democratic Justice Party of President Roh Tae-woo, and the New Democratic Republican Party of Kim Jong-Phie, to establish the Democratic Liberal Party. The merged party won an absolute majority in the National Assembly. This party elected Kim Young-sam as the party leader later in 1992.

Roh Moo-hyun objected to the dissolution and merger. He re-established the Democratic Party with a small number of parliament members, and criticised Kim Young-sam's dissolution of his party as nothing more than a political "illicit union" to get the presidential seat. Cutting his ties with Kim Young-sam, who had unparalleled influence in Gyeonsamnam-do and Busan, severely weakened Roh's political position in these areas.

To counter the size of the merged Democratic Liberal Party, Roh merged his party with the Peace and Democratic Party of Kim Dae-jung to form a new United Democratic Party. Roh became the spokesman of the opposition, but Kim Dae-jung dominated the merged United Democratic Party, and Roh's faction had only a minority weight. In Gyeonsamnam-do, Roh and his allies from the former Democratic Party had difficulty hanging onto their seats in national and other elections against the candidates of Kim Young-sam's Democratic Liberal Party, which was later renamed as the New Korea Party. Roh Moo-hyun lost his seat in the National Assembly at the 1992 election, and then ran unsuccessfully for mayor of Busan city in 1995 in the first mayoral election in South Korea for 35 years. He failed yet again to be elected at the 1996 national election.

Despite his repeated failures at elections, Roh's weak position in the United Democratic Party forged a bond between Roh and a force which would later propel him to the presidency. This force is known as the Outsiders.[12] To understand the roles of the Outsiders, we need to look back at the political history after democratisation in 1987.

After the 1987 democratisation, the participants in the democratic movement divided into three groups. Some joined the Democratic Party of Kim Young-sam; some joined the Party for Peace and Democracy led by Kim Dae-jung; and others remained as Outsiders, or "Jaeya" people, not belonging to any of the established political parties. Kim Young-sam and Kim Dae-jung had been members of political factions with their roots in the conservative Democratic Party, the ruling party during the Second Republic (1960–1). Their groups entered the National Assembly through elections, but the Outsiders did not. The Outsiders included several relatively socialist people who had engaged in civil movements and labour movements. Lee Boo-young and Kim Geun-tae, who had long careers as democracy campaigners with a strong anti-U.S. slant during the 1960s or the 1970s, were typical of the Outsiders.

The Outsiders regarded the 1987 democratisation as insufficient as it had led to the regime of Roh Tae-woo who had been involved in the 1979 coup which smashed the "Seoul Spring" and restored authoritarianism. The Outsiders also saw the merger which created Kim Young-sam's Democratic Liberal Party as an "unprincipled alliance", based on political calculation, between the old privileged class which had supported the Chun Doo-hwan regime and a conservative part of the opposition, led by Kim Young-sam. As a result, the Outsiders opposed the "illicit union" with street protests in 1990.

But the street campaigns of the Outsiders at this time were criticised by the general people and the Outsiders lost support. After a long period of authoritarian government, the people were happy to see the return of direct presidential election and were interested in political, economic, and social stability rather than further political reform at this stage.

The Outsiders were thus forced to change their strategy. Some entered the "political sphere", meaning the political world revolving around the National Assembly. Several joined the United Democratic Party since it was in opposition to the Democratic Liberal Party which they had earlier opposed on the streets. They adapted themselves to this form of politics and occupied the most leftist position in the political sphere.[13]

Roh Moo-hyun was not an original member of the Outsiders but had shared similar experiences as them. Both Roh and the Outsiders had failed to counter the rise of Kim Young-sam's Democratic Liberal Party and eventually been integrated into the opposition force led by Kim Dae-jung. However both had only minority weight in this opposition coalition because of Kim Dae-jung's powerful position. In this situation, the relations between Roh Moo-hyun and the Outsiders gradually became very close. Yet Roh was very different from the mainstream of the Outsiders. He had been drafted into politics by Kim Young-sam. He had repeatedly run for elections. He was a practical politician rather than an ideologist. Even so, in the context of their common position, Roh Moo-hyun came to perform a role as spokesman of their combined interests.

The Millennium Democratic Party was formed in 2000 after another merger. Roh became its chief advisor. In 2002, he resolved to compete for the party's nomination as candidate in the 2002 presidential election, and was strongly supported by the Outsiders. Starting as a minor candidate, Roh became popular for his soft way of speaking, commitment to "reform", and his nationalistic appeals to anti-U.S. sentiment. He promised to establish peace and prosperity in the Korean peninsula "by the hand of the Korean people".[14]

Against this background of nationalistic feeling, he won the party nomination against a conservative, Lee In-jae, and won the presidency in 2002 against another conservative, Lee Hoi-chang. This victory was proclaimed as a "revolution" by Roh Moo-hyun and the Outsiders against conservative forces. In 2003, Roh formed a new Yeollin Uri Party (Our Open Party), purportedly to represent this new trend of reform, deliberately excluding the conservatives from his old party, and thus making the Outsiders a major force in the new ruling party.

The fact that the Roh Moo-hyun government was established with the political support of the Outsiders had a great influence on its direction and performance. In the 1987 democratic movement, the Outsiders had represented socialistic ideas and anti-U.S. nationalism. The 2002 presidential election had taken place in another phase of heightened nationalism. In the financial crisis of 1997, South Korea had been obliged to accept advice from the IMF and open up its economy further to foreign capital. The feeling of national humiliation fed into strong nationalism at the time of the 2002 World Cup football tournament, which was co-hosted by South Korea and Japan. The death of the two schoolgirls and acquittal of the American soldiers completed this picture. The Roh regime began with an image of nationalism.

Obsolete Nationalism

Such nationalistic feelings under globalisation create the conditions for the rise of a politician with reformist and nationalistic messages. In this respect, South Korea does not differ vastly from Japan and Taiwan. Yet the nationalism and reform policies of the Roh Moo-hyun regime were not the same as those of the other countries. Roh Moo-hyun was strongly influenced by the Outsiders. The Outsiders provided Roh with an ideology and a roster of ideas for reform. Roh had the ability to translate these "heavy" ideas into simple messages and to make them appealing to the general public because of his soft image. Thus Roh had a rather well-formed ideology underlying his reform policies. Koizumi and Chen had no comparable grand vision of reform backed by a coherent ideology. But ideology turned out to be a liability for the Roh administration in practice.

The problem was that the reform ideology of the Roh administration had been fundamentally generated in the democratic movement in the 1980s. It was based on the conditions of South Korea around 1987. Arguments made by the Outsiders during the democratic movement of the 1980s re-surfaced in the thoughts of Roh Moo-hyun as president two decades later. For example, Roh stated on 28 December 2006:

In respect to this issue, some people ask me, for instance, why you do not clearly show anti-U.S. attitudes. On the other hand, other people criticise me for not taking a clear stand against North Korea.

However, can we open the way to the future by clarifying an anti-North Korean position? Can anyone deal with future events by clearly expressing anti-U.S. attitudes? The United States now accounts for 20 per cent of the entire world economy, but its percentage is estimated to decrease to 10 per cent by 2050. On the other hand, South Korea will become a country with more than 60 thousand dollar income by 2050 and be one of the great powers in the world.

Therefore, we should at least achieve a good standard of autonomy and live up to the name of an independent state. In order to do so, we should pursue autonomous and balanced diplomacy and gradual change.[15]

The statement made two contradictory points. Roh expressed an optimistic view that South Korea "will become one of the great powers in the world", while at the same time emphasising the powerlessness of South Korea in that moment. Behind this contradiction lay frustration at Korea's present position as inferior to the United States, and at the fact that this situation could not easily be changed. The optimistic vision of the future was offered to cover up this frustration. Roh had anti-U.S. sentiments and would like to have acted upon them, but in practice this was impossible. As a result, he had to be patient, accept the current position of the country, maintain its authority, and prepare for a future when South Korea could become a "great power" and be able to openly express its "anti-U.S." attitudes. Such ideas reflected the political anguish of some Outsiders who used to engage in a radical anti-U.S. movement. but who eventually became more moderate.

This same contradiction had prevailed at the time of the democratic movement. On the one hand, activists berated the U.S. for supporting the Chun Doo-hwan regime; on the other, they appealed to the U.S. to support their democratic movement. Activists of that era were strongly influenced by dependency theory. Because the authoritarian regimes in South Korea were maintained by American imperialism, it was necessary to fight against the United States. Yet in strategic terms South Korea depended heavily on the U.S. in the context of the Cold War.

As a result, South Korea's democratic movement had a severely bifurcated view of the U.S. On the one hand the activists viewed the U.S. as an imperialistic country which pursued its own interests with all the assets of a great power. On the other they saw the U.S. as an idealistic nation which started with the Puritan Movement and pursued "freedom and democracy". Activists did not see their movement as "anti-U.S." but as "critical of the U.S.", and they were hopeful that the U.S. could be nudged back towards its original path as a result of such criticism. The activists knew it would be impossible to overthrow the U.S., yet they hoped that, if the American people understood the South Korean position, that could lead to changes in the direction of U.S. policy that would result in more autonomy for South Korea. Under this framework of thinking, the activists allied a nationalistic impulse which longed for the independence of South Korea with a "small country minded" perception[16] of reality.

The nationalism of the Outsiders was imbued with this "small country minded" perception. In fact this has been a distinctive characteristic of South Korean nationalism since Syngman Rhee (president, 1948–60). This consciousness directly affects thinking on appeasement policy towards North Korea. North Korea, which is struggling with its stagnant economy, is also "a small country", and actually smaller than South Korea in relation to the United States. Thus the world should pay attention not only to North Korea's aggressive attitudes but also to the difficult situation in which North Korea is placed, and should avoid driving the North into a corner. Roh Moo-hyun spoke to CNN on 16 September 2005 as follows.

> I do not think the United States unconditionally denies North Korea's right to the peaceful use of nuclear energy. I think the United States denies it because they cannot trust North Korea. We should understand the current situation in this way. Therefore, if dialogue between the two countries develops and if the United States increases confidence in North Korea, and if certain conditions are agreed, the United States could approve of North Korea's right to peaceful use of nuclear energy, which is a legitimate right of a sovereign state.[17]

Such nationalism based on dependency theory and the "small country minded" perception led the Roh Moo-hyun government into contradictory policies. The government sent troops to Iraq and allowed the U.S. to build a new base on its territory to aid the U.S. troop redeployment, while at the same time professing anti-U.S. sentiments for public consumption. These contradictory policies undermined the public support for the Roh Moo-hyun administration. The Roh Moo-hyun regime could not retain the support of people who thought of themselves as anti-U.S.

There was another problem embedded in the ideology of the Roh regime. The economic thinking of the Outsiders was shaped by their opposition to the Park Chung-hee regime which took power by coup in 1961.

The Park regime espoused the strategy of top-down developmentalism that had originated in Japan. Subsequent regimes continued the trend, arguing that all national resources, including aid from overseas earmarked for other purposes, should be concentrated on achieving "development" and "modernisation" rather than pursuing national independence, equal distribution of wealth and rights, and greater democracy. The Outsiders harshly criticised this "developmentalism" which emphasised economic growth. They also drew on dependency theory to explain why South Korea found itself in this position. According to this view, South Korea could not achieve democratisation or even true economic development because it was dependent on the United States. Hence the priority was to achieve independence from the United States in order to lead South Korea to further economic development. This was the South Korean Outsiders additional contribution to dependency theory. But in practice, South Korea was incapable of breaking free of U.S. influence. At best it could establish a cooperative relationship, and dream of the U.S. returning to its founding principles.[18]

But dependency theory and a "small country-minded" nationalism were not appealing in South Korea in the 2000s. In a survey conducted by the Korea Research Company in January 2007, 56 per cent thought that "economic growth and job creation" should be the priority of the next president. Other issues scored much lower: "alleviation of the gap between the rich and the poor, and better welfare system" (23.2 per cent), "alleviation of local conflicts" (7.3 per cent), "political reform and combat of corruption" (7.3 per cent), and "improvement of North-South relations and diplomatic security" (5.5 per cent). These were the kind of issues emphasised by the Roh government.[19]

The Roh regime was tied to an ideology that had been forged in the democratisation movement of the 1980s, but rendered obsolete by the changes of the intervening years.

Conclusion

The economic globalisation of the 1990s resulted in the 1997 financial crisis in South Korea, and drastic economic reforms by the Kim Dae-jung government. The end of the era of high economic growth undermined the authority of the old political system that had overseen that growth. As a result, Roh Moo-hyun and the Outsiders, who had earlier been marginalised in South Korean politics, took power in the 2002 presidential election. At the outset, the Roh Moo-hyun government, with its emphasis on reform of the old political, economic, and social systems, seemed perfect for South Korea at a turning point amid globalisation.

This promise very quickly disintegrated. The reform policies which Roh Moo-hyun proposed were not generated by the actual conditions of South Korea in 2002, but originated in the ideas of the Outsiders in the democratic movement in the 1980s and early 1990s. Their anti-Americanism, "small country minded" nationalism, economic views emphasising distribution rather than growth, and a worldview based on dependency theory were outdated.

Both inside South Korea and in the international community, Roh Moo-hyun rapidly lost credibility. His words sounded beautiful as an "Outsider", yet his message on closer examination was irrelevant. South Korea wanted a political leader that would sustain a democratic, prosperous, and peaceful society.

The true mood of the people was shown on 9 October 2006 when North Korea carried out a nuclear test. The majority of South Korean people were not distressed about the failure of appeasement policies, or an escalation of the crisis that could delay Korean unification, or the possibility of a response by Japan or some other nuclear power. What the South Korean people really feared was a decline in foreign investment and a second financial crisis.[20]

South Korea longs for both independence and foreign investment, but desires investment more than independence. Ordinary South Koreans aspire to maintain a peaceful, stable, and prosperous life, and could not see how this would be achieved by the nationalism, dependency theory, and "small country consciousness" promoted by Roh Moo-hyun and the Outsiders. They believe foreign investment will contribute to prosperity. Roh and the Outsiders were perfectly capable of seeing the mismatch between their ideology and the people's aspirations, but Roh was hide-bound by his own statements and political promises in the past. Roh Moo-hyun was stuck with his "old idealism", and his failure paved the way for the return of an old way of thinking.

At the presidential election in 2007, a "CEO-turned politician", Lee Myung-bak of the Grand National Party, won against Chung Dong-young of the pro-government United New Democratic Party. Lee Myung-bak represented a return of the very "developmentalism" that the idealism of Roh Moo-hyun and the Outsiders had been crafted to oppose.

Notes

[1]   *Chosun-Ilbo*, 27 Dec. 2006.
[2]   *Donga-Ilbo*, 6 Dec. 2006.

3   Choi Jang-jib, *Hangug minjujueuiwa jedojeog sircheoneuroseoeui minjujueui* [Democratisation in Korea and Institutional Practice] (Seoul: Minjuhwaun-donggineomsaeophoi, 2006).

4   *Chosun-Ilbo* , 2 Jan., 2007; "yeoronjosa jaryochir", Donga-Ilbo website, <http://www.donga.com/news/poll.html> [accessed 8 July 2008].

5   On populism as a strategy of politicians, see Kurt Weyland, "Classifying a Con-tested Concept: Populism in the Study of Latin American Politics", *Comparative Politics* 34, 2 (2001).

6   Kimura Kan, "Nationalistic Populism in Democratic Countries of East Asia", *Journal of Korean Politics* 16, 2 (2007).

7   Kimura, "Nationalistic Populism"; Asian Barometer Survey, <http://www.asianbarometer.org, undated> [accessed 8 July 2008].

8   Cheongwadae, <http://www.president.go.kr/> [accessed 15 Feb. 2007]; Government Information Office, <http://www.gio.gov.tw/>, undated [accessed 15 Feb. 2007]; Office of the President, <http://www.president.gov.tw/>, undated [accessed 15 Feb. 2007]; *Shusho Kantei*, <http://www.kantei.go.jp/>, undated [accessed 15 Feb. 2007].

9   Kimura, "Nationalistic Populism"; World Values Survey, <http://www.worldvaluessurvey.org/>, undated [accessed 8 July 2008].

10   An anti-government uprising in 1947 that was bloodily suppressed by the ruling Kuomintang. The title "228" refers to 28 February, the day on which the uprising began.

11   Toru Sakai, *Taiwan: Shitatakana Rinjin* (Tokyo: Syuuei-sya Shinsyo, 2006).

12   Yi Jeong-heui, "Jaeya jeongchijibdaneui minjuhwa undong: jeongchiideorrogi, jungsimseryeog, jeonchigwoneui gwangaereur jungsimeuro" [Democratisation Movement by the Outsiders: Ideology, Central Forces and Relations with Insiders], *Gatorrigsahoigwahagyeonggu*, 1999.

13   Seo Yeoung-seog, "Sisagihoig — Goncheoneur tonghae bon 14dae chongseongudo: minjudang jaeyaibdangpaeui gongchensirtae" [Endorsement and the 14th General Election: Endorsement of Outsiders by Democratic Party], *Worgan sahoi pyeongron*, 92–3 (1992).

14   Cheongwadae, <http://www.president.go.kr/> [accessed 15 Feb. 2007].

15   *Chosun-Ilbo*, 2 Jan. 2007.

16   On the "small country minded" perception in South Korea, see Kimura Kan, *Chosen/Kankoku nashonarizumu to shokoku ishiki* (Kyoto: Mineruba Shobo, 2000).

17   Cheongwadae, <http://www.president.go.kr/> [accessed 15 Feb. 2007].

18   Kimura, "Nationalistic Populism".

19   *Seoul Kyeongje*, 1 Jan. 2007.

20   *Phuri Nyuseu*, 12 Oct. 2006.

CHAPTER 10

Populism and Nationalism in Taiwan: The Rise and Decline of Chen Shui-bian

Mitsutoyo Matsumoto

Introduction

In the presidential election of 2000, Chen Shui-bian achieved the first major change in Taiwan's government by displacing the Kuomintang which had ruled Taiwan since its inception. Chen enjoyed a massive personal popularity at this stage. Although his approval rate dropped later[1] because he could not promote reforms under a divided government, he narrowly achieved re-election in 2004 by appealing to Taiwanese identity. Numerous scandals inside the government were exposed in 2005–6. The First Lady of President Chen was indicted, and Chen himself was pressed to resign in autumn 2006. He survived until 2008, although his approval rate was very low throughout the period, and then suffered defeat at the hands of a revived KMT at elections in 2008. The clue to understand Chen's dramatic rise and decline is in his populism.

Chen was a populist leader who emerged from a counter elite, the Democratic Progressive Party (DPP). Based on Otake's classification (see Introduction), Chen's leadership style was populist, and was also similar to "neopopulism" in Latin America. In Taiwan, two popularly elected presidents, Lee Teng-hui and Chen Shui-bian, have been characterised as populists by some local observers and news commentators. Huang studied how Chen deployed his political skills to mobilise the Taiwanese and hence be elected and re-elected.[2] Shyu shows that Taiwan's electoral politics have given rise to a populist-democratic culture in which Taiwanese politicians bring up populist issues rather than the rational policy debates of an electoral democracy.[3] Mizuno and Pasuk (see Introduction to this volume) point out that many Asian populists have been "electoral populists", and have tend to accept neoliberalism. Chen was a populist leader who emerged in electoral politics. His election victories raised his own authority and his political influence inside the DPP. But Chen did not embrace neoliberalism. The values of populism vary according to the context, the character of the elite, and the dominant political discourse.[4] Chen's populism was first anti-privilege, and later pro-nationalism.

Chen's populism was also shaped by party politics. He developed a direct and quasi-personal relationship with his followers, bypassing established intermediary organisations, or subordinating them to his personal will.[5]

This chapter analyses Chen Shui-bian's populism to understand his rise and decline. The first two sections discuss the background to the growth of populism in Taiwan. The third plots the development of Chen's populism, showing how he subordinated the DPP to his personal will, and how his agenda changed considerably during his presidency. The conclusion discusses some possible reason for the failure of Chen's populism.

Emergence of an "Unorganised Mass"

Kurt Weyland argues that "neopopulism" in Latin America arose for two main reasons. First, the increasing modernisation of society began to weaken established mechanisms of elite control, particularly clientelism and corporatism, thus rendering unorganised masses of people available for political mobilisation. Second, the severe economic problems plaguing several Latin America countries during the 1980s delegitimated the established political elite, making new charismatic leaders attractive to a large number of people. Under these circumstances, neopopulist leaders managed to win office thanks to their personalistic relationship with largely unorganised masses of followers.[6]

In Taiwan, the established structure of power in Taiwan was the nationalist Kuomintang (KMT) regime. After the Second World War, the KMT was defeated in the Chinese Civil War with the Chinese Communist Party (CCP) on the Chinese mainland, and retreated to Taiwan where it established an authoritarian regime under a single dominant party. This regime was a political and economic monopoly by the minority Mainlander elite, excluding the Taiwanese from power. The KMT authoritarian regime effectively controlled the state and society through a quasi-Leninist party organisation. Lacking a strong social base in Taiwan, the immigrant KMT regime tried to launch social reform projects and use local elections to help strengthen its legitimacy and organisational penetration. Social groups, such as farmers, labourers, businessmen, and students were all organised into a party-infiltrated, hierarchical structure of state-licensed and state-sponsored associations — an exclusionary state corporatism. The KMT adopted cliente-lism to build a ruling coalition in partnership with local elites and their factions. The KMT kept control at the centre, while rewarding local factions with political and economical privileges. There were two levels of clientelism at work here: one between the KMT and local factions, and the other be-tween local factions and voters.[7]

Economic growth, sometimes described as "a miracle", was achieved under KMT authoritarian rule. As a result of lasting economic development and accompanying social development, the KMT's control of society through clientelism and corporatism was weakened, and an "unorganised mass" emerged in Taiwan. A middle class which was outside the corporatist structure expanded in the process of economic development. Clientelist mobilisation for elections became less effective. Yet inflation was successfully restrained and income distribution seemed to be fair during rapid economic growth, so most Taiwanese people were satisfied with the economic performance of the KMT-led government. Economic problems did not become political issues, and there was no political mobilisation on class and economic issues.[8] Unlike most other new democracies, Taiwan's democratic transition was not accompanied by any major economic crisis. The damage of the 1997 crisis was not so severe, compared with Korea. The authoritarian KMT government could be proud of its economic performance, and was not threatened with ejection for economic mismanagement.

It was not an economic crisis that undermined the legitimacy of the established political elite and created the space for a populist leader to emerge, but a diplomatic crisis. In the early 1970s, the international envi-ronment changed drastically for Taiwan. The Republic of China (ROC) lost its seat in the United Nations to the People's Republic of China (PRC). Subsequently the ROC did not receive formal recognition from other nations. The ROC lost its status as a sovereign state in international society and the KMT government was isolated. As a result, the prestige and legitimacy of the Mainlander elite was damaged. The Chinese nationalism, which had been the dominant idea and value of society in post-war Taiwan, lost its appeal, while Taiwanese nationalism rose in its place. Taiwanese people gained confidence through economic success and aspired for international status and recognition of Taiwan's achievement.

In this situation, the *Dangwai* (opposition) grew by winning local elections, and can be considered a counter elite. In elections before the democratic opening in 1987, the major campaign issues of the opposition were for changes in the power structure, such as democratic reform and majority rule. From the 1980s, the opposition began to appeal to Taiwanese nationalism in order to mobilise mass support under the slogan of "popular self-determination". They demanded that the destiny of Taiwan should be determined by the Taiwanese people themselves. Under the KMT's authoritarian rule, the opposition was never allowed to organise political parties, so *Dangwai* politicians appealed directly to the people to win votes in local elections. Their political style was populist, and a prototype of populism was nurtured in local politics, but could not emerge at the national level because, under martial law, legislative elections at the national level were suspended, and any mass movements were strictly banned.

Democratisation paved the way for charismatic leaders and opened the door for the counter elite to emerge on a national political stage.

Seeds of Populism

How does a populist leader evoke emotional responses from people and mobilise their support? In Taiwan what were the issues and emotions that a populist leader could appeal to? The answers to these questions lie in the interplay between Taiwan's international status and the ethnic composition of its population.

Taiwan embarked on a democratic transition in 1986, when the opposition *Dangwai* decided to form the DPP, the first meaningful but then illegal opposition party. In 1987, President Chiang Ching-kuo lifted martial law. After Chiang's death a year later, Lee Teng-hui became the first Taiwanese to occupy the presidency. In 1991, the constitution was revised. From that point onwards, the people of Taiwan have been able to elect their government and leaders at the national level, and the ROC's central institutions represent only the people living on Taiwan and its surrounding islands. "The ROC on Taiwan" in Lee Teng-hui's phrase, became a *de facto* Taiwanese state.

The process of Taiwan's democratic transition led by the KMT proceeded peacefully but gradually. The success of the process diluted the DPP's appeal as a vanguard for democratic reform. The issue of democratic reform declined in electoral appeal. The reconsideration of "a history of the past", addressing past human rights wrongs by the state, did not proceed very far, and the privileges of the KMT were retained. The Taiwanese suffered infringements of human rights as well as losing private property to the authoritarian KMT government.

"Transitional justice" refers to a range of approaches that states may use to address past human rights wrongs in order to meet society's desire to rebuild social trust and establish a democratic system. In a period of democratic transition, transitional justice has often provided opportunities for the society to address past human rights abuses, mass atrocities, or other forms of severe trauma in order to facilitate a smooth transition into a more democratic or peaceful future. However, for Taiwan, transitional justice was not fully realised,[9] and resentment towards the KMT, including Chiang Kai-shek, remained.

Furthermore, in the process of democratisation in Taiwan, money politics became more serious. The KMT was called "the richest party in the world" because of its vast assets including party-owned enterprises.[10] The KMT assets were seen as the main reason behind money politics. Most of these assets had been left behind by the Japanese, and would normally have been requisitioned for the state by the government, but instead were shared out among various agencies including the KMT. People came to be more discontented with money politics, corruption, and the privileged position of the KMT, and to distrust politics, especially political parties.

To put populism in its context in Taiwan, it is necessary to consider the established structure of power in society, not only domestically, but also internationally. Many countries have not recognised Taiwan or the Republic of China (ROC) as a sovereign state. In a globalising world, people in Taiwan became more frustrated with the fact that Taiwan was not a member of the United Nations. They asked why international society would not recognise their country although it had realised two universal values of economic development and political democratisation. After Taiwan's transition to democracy, the Taiwanese pointed to the "inconsistency" of international society on this issue.

For historical reasons, democratisation was inevitably accompanied by "Taiwanisation" or indigenisation, and brought about a conflict over national identity. This conflict revolved around the projected future of Taiwan — whether the country would be unified with China or remain independent. In the post-war era, the KMT government promoted Chinese nation-building in Taiwan. A Chinese identity, rooted in mainland China, was imposed on the residents of Taiwan by the KMT government through formal socialisation channels. The residents of Taiwan were told to think of themselves as Chinese, and as citizens of the sole legitimate China, namely the ROC. In the process of democratisation, this old identity lost its appeal, but nothing appeared to take its place.

Lee Teng-hui, the first Taiwanese president, reasoned that there was no future for Taiwan unless its people could establish a new identity, yet at the same time it was risky to dissolve the ROC.[11] The PRC considered Taiwan an inseparable part of China — the "One China" principle — and

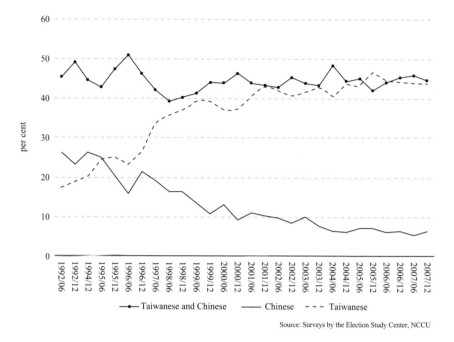

Source: Surveys by the Election Study Center, NCCU

Figure 10-1   Changes in Identity as Taiwanese/Chinese in Taiwan, 1992–2007

maintained a policy of resorting to force if Taiwan showed signs of moving towards independence. With the end of the Cold War and the rapid progress of globalisation, the PRC became more threatening towards Taiwan, both politically and economically. The United States opposed any one-sided alteration of the situation in the Taiwan Straits, and did not support the independence of Taiwan.

Lee aimed to build a framework for coexistence of the ROC on Taiwan and Taiwanese identity by democratising the political system, and by promoting a "moderate" Taiwanese identity as opposed to a "radical" Taiwanese nationalism (demanding independence). Ogasawara argues that Taiwanese identity is a political group consciousness demanding Taiwan's autonomy, and its ultimate form is Taiwanese nationalism. Taiwanese nationalism is a demand that an independent sovereign state must be established in Taiwan in contradiction of the "One China" principle; it implies the ultimate dissolution of the ROC, and the establishment of the Republic of Taiwan, a Taiwanese nation, and Taiwanese culture.[12] After Lee took this initiative, the KMT appealed to the masses by emphasising Taiwanese identity while insisting on maintaining the *status quo* across the Taiwan Straits, though the

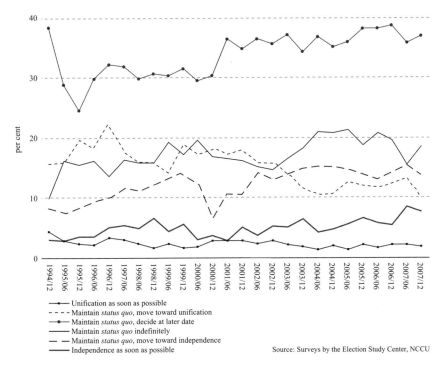

Figure 10-2   Stance on Unification or Independence in Taiwan, 1994–2007

party still retained the ultimate aim of unification with mainland China in the future.

Along with broadening political freedom and increasing interactions with people across the Taiwan Straits, more Taiwanese became gradually more conscious of their identity as Taiwanese rather than Chinese. More called themselves "Taiwanese". Especially from 1995, the proportion of the population who identified themselves as "Taiwanese" increased steadily, while those identifying themselves as solely "Chinese" dwindled (see Figure 10-1). At the same time, most people were still oriented to maintaining the *status quo* in relations with the PRC (see Figure 10-2). They wished to maintain the "ROC on Taiwan" as a *de facto* Taiwanese state, while at the same time seeing their own identity as "Taiwanese".

Moreover, democratisation awoke an ethnic consciousness which had been repressed until that time. Relations among ethnic groups became more complicated.

Taiwan is a society composed of four ethnic groups: the majority *Minnan*, *Hakka*, Mainlanders, and indigenous people.[13] *Minnan, Hakka,* and Mainlander are all *Han* people, and together make up around 98 per cent of the population. *Han* people from China's coastal provinces of Fujian and Guangdong began immigrating to Taiwan in the seventeenth century. These earlier arrivals called themselves *Minnan* (literally meaning southern Fujian), and constitute about 70 per cent of Taiwan's population today. Another 12–15 per cent of the population belongs to the *Hakka* minority, also immigrants from China. The *Minnan* and *Hakka* groups, whose ancestors experienced Japanese colonial rule, along with indigenous peoples, are identified as "Taiwanese". In 1949, when the Chinese Communist Party took over mainland China, the retreat of the KMT government from China to Taiwan brought a new influx of *Han* immigrants hailing from various provinces in China. Those who immigrated to Taiwan in 1949 or later are identified as Mainlanders. This group constitutes about 13–15 per cent of Taiwan's population.[14]

The resulting society can be divided in various ways — between Taiwanese and Mainlanders, between *Minnan* and *Hakka* who belong to the *Han* peoples, and between the *Han* and indigenous people. Though the main division is that between Taiwanese and Mainlanders,[15] the more the influence of the *Minnan* increases, the more other groups such as the *Hakka* and indigenous peoples feel resentment and fear. Lee Teng-hui promoted the unity of the "New Taiwanese", beyond ethnic differences. The new Taiwanese were those who opposed China's threat to assimilate Taiwan, and who would strive for the future of Taiwan regardless of when they came to reside on Taiwan. Lee intended to unify the people living on Taiwan as the "nation" of the democratised ROC on Taiwan, whose central institutions represented only the residents of Taiwan.

In short, the "seeds of populism" in Taiwan lay in the resentment against the KMT, the growing distrust of established politics, the discontent with the treatment of Taiwan in the international area, and social divisions over national identity and along lines of ethnicity.

Chen Shui-bian and the DPP

In the 2000 presidential election, Taiwan for the first time elected a national leader from the counter elite, Chen Shui-bian, the brightest political star in the DPP. Chen came from an impoverished background. He was born to a tenant farming family in Tainan County, a northern part of Taiwan, belonging to the *Minnan* ethnicity. He had been an academically bright student since youth and graduated from a prestigious senior high school with honours. In 1969, he was admitted to National Taiwan University. He passed the bar exams before the completion of his junior year with the highest score, earning him the distinction of being Taiwan's youngest lawyer. Chen became involved in politics in 1980 when he defended the participants of the Kaohsiung Incident[16] in a military court. In 1981, he won a seat in the Taipei City Council as a candidate of *Dangwai*, an opposition movement. On 12 January 1985, Chen was sentenced to a year in prison for libel as an editor of *Neo-Formosa* magazine. While Chen was in prison, his wife Wu Shu-chen was elected to the parliament, the Legislative Yuan. On his release, Chen practised law and served as her legislative assistant. In 1989, Chen was elected to the Legislative Yuan and re-elected to another three year term in 1992. He resigned in 1994 and rose to national prominence by winning election as mayor of Taipei against a KMT opponent. From that point he became the brightest political star in the DPP.[17]

The 2000 presidential election presented a good opportunity for the DPP because the ruling KMT was split. Lee Teng-hui as chairman of the party handpicked his former vice-president Lien Chan as the KMT presidential candidate rather than the more popular James Soong who thus decided to run as an independent candidate. Vehement competition between Lien and Soong split the KMT party's support.

The DPP made two major changes in order to grasp this opportunity. First, it changed the party rules to allow Chen to stand as its candidate. Under the DPP's internal rules, a party member could stand for no more than one executive position within four years, and Chen had stood for mayor of Taipei in 1998. But the rule was changed. Second, the DPP passed a "Resolution Regarding Taiwan's Future" in May 1999 and for the first time grudgingly accepting the legitimacy of the ROC. In its party constitution, the DPP stated that its aim was to establish the Republic of Taiwan as a new and independent nation. However, this was not an election-winning issue (see Figure 10-2). In fact, the party had suffered a crushing defeat in the presidential election of 1996 when it campaigned on the independence issue. To gain broad support among the electorate, the DPP had to avoid highlighting problems related to national identity. Chen's most serious problem was how to convince Taiwan's voters that he was realistic and flexible enough to manage the cross-Straits relationship. The change from advocating Taiwanese independence to accepting the *status quo* was justified by claiming that Taiwan already was independent and thus there was no need to declare independence a second time. The resolution was passed at the same meeting that selected Chen as the DPP's presidential candidate. Yoking these two issues was intended to allay popular fears about the nature of the DPP and portray Chen as moderate and realistic.

Anti-privilege Populism

Chen ran for the presidency in 2000 on a populist strategy. There seem to be various reasons why he took this strategy. A popular distrust of politics, especially of the political parties, was then growing, so it was rational for Chen to rely on his personal popularity more than on party organisation. Besides, the party organisation of the DPP was weak, so Chen could not draw on a strong organisation as KMT presidential candidates had in the past. In addition, there was an institutional reason. Taiwan's constitution is a French-style semi-presidential system, so the candidate is more important than the party organisation in an election campaign.[18] During the campaign, Chen Shui-bian made great efforts to reach beyond the DPP's traditional supporters. Chen presented himself to the electorate as "a child of Taiwan", coming from a poor family in Tainan and being ethnically Taiwanese and *Minnan*. He cultivated an image of a "clean" politician who spoke for the interests of the Taiwanese and the average person. At the same time, he talked of "a harmony of ethnicity" and "the new moderate line" which insisted on the *status quo* across the Taiwan Straits, in order to get broad support among the electorate beyond the core base of the DPP.

Instead of nationalism, he emphasised the problem of "black and gold", referring to money and gangster politics and political corruption in Taiwan. Money politics and corruption has deep roots in Taiwan,[19] but Chen argued that political corruption had grown worse under the KMT rule and caused widespread public discontent. He vigorously attacked the KMT as privileged, emphasising the antagonism between "corrupted", "privileged elites" and the "common people". He claimed that a change of government would end "black and gold". For Chen's populism, the "internal enemy" was the KMT.

The presidential race was exciting from start to finish. James Soong, running as an independent candidate split from the KMT, received the bulk of the KMT vote and registered 36.8 per cent of total votes cast, while the official KMT candidate Lian Chan garnered a mere 23.1 per cent. Both were defeated by Chen, who received 39.3 per cent of the ballots.

Though he had defeated the KMT, Chen's power base was very weak because he received only a minority vote. In addition, the DPP occupied only about 30 per cent of the 225 seats in the Legislative Yuan while the KMT had 115, an absolute majority. Under the ROC's constitution, the president has the power to appoint the prime minister without the consent of the parliament, but did not have the power to dissolve the Legislative Yuan without the Legislative Yuan first passing a motion of no confidence in the Cabinet. So President Chen could not build on his momentum to dissolve the Legislative Yuan and gain a majority there. Though he had defeated the old power structure at the presidency level, it was only a partial victory.

In this situation, Chen maintained his populist strategy in an attempt to establish his own authority. He dubbed himself "the president of the people", and declared that he had distanced himself from the activities of the DPP. He also positioned the new government as "the government of the people" and aimed to select talented people from the opposition in order to establish a government which represented the whole population of Taiwan. Chen appointed Tang Fei, defence minister in the outgoing KMT government, as prime minister, but only on an independent, non-party basis, to which Tang agreed. Many former KMT Cabinet members, including close friends and advisers to Lee Teng-hui, were recruited into the Tang Fei government on the same basis.

In his inaugural address, Chen promised his allegiance to "the new moderate line" by announcing the "Five Nos". He would not declare Taiwan independence, not change the name of the ROC, not insert Lee Teng-hui's "special state-to-state thesis"[20] into the constitution, not hold a referendum on the unification-independence question, and not abolish the National Unification Guidelines and the National Unification Council[21] as long as mainland China abstained from using force against Taiwan. The declaration impressed the international community favourably, and the approval rate of President Chen reached 70 to 80 per cent at the inauguration of his administration. Furthermore, Chen insisted on reforms to end "black and gold", principally by liquidating the KMT's vast assets, a symbol of the privileged and corrupted nature of the KMT and the origin of money politics in Taiwan.

However, "the government of the people" collapsed after just five months. In autumn of 2000, the DPP, which had long upheld a pro-environmental stance, made an abrupt request to halt the construction of a fourth nuclear power plant. This move resulted in a serious confrontation between the DPP and the premier, Tang Fei. The DPP had long been a fervent opponent of the KMT government's nuclear policy, to the extent that an anti-nuclear clause had been inserted into the party's platform. Tang Fei remained committed to the nuclear plant project and eventually was forced to resign as a result. The DPP's insistence on scrapping the project caused Chen to lose a prime minister who had played a crucial role in smoothing the transfer of power. The DPP then formed a minority Cabinet and halted the construction of the nuclear plant. The forceful style of the DPP angered the KMT which eventually resolved to impeach President Chen.

During this period, the political structure changed substantially. The forces in the political arena were reorganised into a "pan-green" party camp and a "pan-blue" party camp, divided basically over the issue of Taiwanese independence versus unification with China. The KMT allied with two splinter parties, James Soong's People First Party (PFP) and the New Party (NP), which was the most stridently pro-unification.[22] These three parties formed a united opposition in the Legislative Yuan that effectively stymied the DPP government's actions. Lee Teng-hui, who had been forced to resign from the KMT after the 2000 election defeat, launched a new party, the Taiwan Solidarity Union (TSU) committed to a stance of Taiwanese independence. The TSU gave its support to President Chen, and helped him to consolidate the government's indigenisation line and resist the unification pressure from Beijing. The media named the DPP and the TSU as the "pan-green" camp, and the KMT, PFP, and NP as the "pan-blue" camp, emphasising the confrontation between them. At the same time, the media also divided in alignment with the two camps.

Elections for the Legislative Yuan in 2001 were an opportunity for the "pan-green" camp to end this divided government by winning a majority in the parliament. At the polls, the DPP became the largest party in the Legislative Yuan, but the "pan-green" camp failed to achieve a majority. The "pan-blue" camp still held a majority in the parliament. President Chen thus faced the prospect of a divided power structure for the remainder of his term of office. The DPP's failure to win control of the legislature meant Chen was not in a position to deliver on political reform, especially the promise to liquidate the KMT's vast assets.

The Turn to Nationalistic Populism

Weyland suggests that, in more consolidated party systems, neopopulist leaders emerge by taking over parties of populist origin, undermining the established party apparatus, and subordinating these weakly institutionalised organisations to their personal control. He also points out that the relationship between leaders and the party remains populist as long as the party has low levels of institutionalisation and leaves leaders wide latitude to dominate and shape its organisation.[23] Chen's relationship with the DPP fits Weyland's description. The DPP was a decentralised and weakly institutionalised party; in practice, the party chairman operated under tight constraints and most had been unable to exercise decisive leadership because influential faction-leaders controlled more political resources than the chairmen. The DPP's factionalism was a product of its history. The party evolved from a collection of anti-KMT political forces, the *Dangwai*. The factions existed before the party came into being, and the party's founding institutionalised the factional structure. The factions within the DPP reflected successive generations of *Dangwai* politicians and activists. Chen was leader of one faction, the Justice Alliance, and won factional competition within the DPP.

By winning the 2000 presidential election, Chen gained charisma as the first president from the party. Yes like many charismatic leaders, he made no attempt to reform the party apparatus to remove restrictions on the leader's authority.[24] He assumed the DPP chairmanship in 2002, but introduced no reforms to centralize control over the party. Rather, he relied upon his authority as the president to evade the restrictions on his power within the party, and to manoeuvre within the factional politics of the DPP, particularly by balancing the influence of rival factions. Roberts suggests that partisan vehicles are inevitably instruments that serve a populist leaders' interests, given the weight of his personalistic authority.[25] The real basis of Chen's authority was his status as the president, and he exercised this authority to defang the DPP, and subordinate the party to his personal control.

Chen maintained his populist electoral strategy in order to seek re-election to the presidency in 2004. But he dropped the attack on money politics and the privileged position of the KMT, and based his appeal more than ever on popular identification with Taiwanese identity. Two factors brought about such a turn. First, the divided government led to a political stalemate. The opposition accused Chen's government of causing economic depression and political disorder, and Chen's approval rate continued to fall. Meanwhile, the PRC government adopted a generally unfriendly stance, refusing to enter into a political dialogue with Chen's administration unless it would accept the principle of "One China". Second, electoral alliances tied Chen's hands. In spring 2003, the KMT and the PFP made a pact to cooperate in the presidential election due the following year. The two candidates who had lost to Chen in 2000 agreed to run on a joint ticket with the KMT chairman Lien Chan as the presidential candidate and the PFP chairman James Soong as the vice presidential candidate.

Chen was obliged to alter his strategy. He decided to mobilise support on nationalist issues. The crisis over the SARS epidemic provided an opportunity. The PRC reaction to the crisis aroused hostility and nationalist feeling in Taiwan. Chen's government and the DPP seized the opportunity to lay out several new policies and agendas which emphasised Taiwan's autonomy and Taiwanese identity.[26] In particular, President Chen proposed to hold referendums on national political issues. This proposal played an important role in Chen's re-election strategy. Chen hoped the proposal would not only mobilise the DPP party base but also attract new supporters aroused by patriotic emotions. He also expected that holding the referendum at the same time as the presidential election would allow enthusiasm for the referendum to spill over into the presidential race.

The "pan-blue" camp was cautious about a referendum that could be seen as a first step towards independence. Chen attacked the "pan-blue" camp with the rhetorical question, "Do you deny the legitimate action of a sovereign state?" When a Referendum Law was passed by the "pan-blue" camp's initiative, Chen declared that he would hold a referendum to allow people to express their opposition to China's deployment of missiles aimed at Taiwan. The referendum would be voted on the same day as the presidential election. When the PRC and other countries such as the United States and Japan declared themselves against the implementation of this referendum, Chen promoted himself as a president who would never submit to outside pressure. He campaigned for the referendum stating, "If you love Taiwan, support the referendum!"

On the approach of the election, opinion polls gave the "pan-blue" camp an edge. On 19 March 2004, the day before the election, there was a gunshot attack on Chen. The polls went ahead and the "pan-green" ticket garnered a slight majority of 29,518 votes out of about 13 million ballots cast. Some believe the shooting incident tipped the result. However, the referendum failed because of a successful boycott campaign by the "pan-blue" camp. With this narrow victory, Chen was inaugurated for a second term of office on 20 May.

The main cause of Chen's victory lay in his strategy of appealing to a Taiwanese identity.[27] But this strategy proved to be a double-edged sword as it raised emotions both of sympathy and antipathy. There was a growing acceptance of a Taiwanese identity in broad terms. But bringing this issue of Taiwanese identity into the political spotlight risked exposing the many differences of opinion over the matter. Some felt strongly about Taiwanese identity and some less so. Some were strongly conscious of an identity as *Minnan*, and others opposed them. Chen himself was a divisive force for personal reasons. Coming from Tainan, belonging to the *Minnan* ethnicity, and leading the DPP that was often seen as a spokesman for the Taiwanese, especially the *Minnan*, he tended to alienate those of other ethnic origins and political proclivities. Some were concerned that politicisation of the identity issue would result in ethnic disharmony, and threaten the *status quo* across the Taiwan Straits. Therefore, Chen's excessive populist appeal to Taiwanese identity tended to provoke social division as well as intense confrontation between the two political camps. In the election to the Legislative Yuan in December 2004, Chen appealed for continued support by playing up the identity issue, but the DPP failed to win a majority. The opposition continued to control the legislature, and again Chen faced the prospect of a divided government all through his term of office.

After inaugurating his second term, Chen Shui-bian came under joint pressure from the PRC and the "pan-blue" camp. To break the deadlock of a divided government, Chen offered "reconciliation" to the opposition and people in a speech celebrating the New Year in 2005. However, far from responding to Chen's call, the opposition parties put pressure on him in cooperation with the PRC. In March 2005, the Chinese People's National Congress in the PRC promulgated an Anti-Secession Law which threatened "non-peaceful measures" if Taiwan made a formal declaration of independence or continued to resist national reunification. After that, the "pan-blue" camp established direct ties with the Chinese Communist Party (CCP). The leader of the CCP, Hu Jin-tao, invited Taiwan's opposition leaders to visit Beijing, including the chairman of the KMT, Lian Chan, in April, and the chairman of the PFP, James Soong, in May. Lien and Soong openly sided with their Chinese host in recognising the so-called 1992 consensus accepting the principle of "One China". [28] At the same time, the PRC government still refused to enter into a political dialogue with Chen's administration. The opposition was eager to advertise an improvement in relations with the PRC. In reaction, Chen Shui-bian attacked the "pan-blue" camp as "the internal enemy inside" and the PRC as "the external enemy". He linked these external and internal enemies by claiming that "Lien Chan and James Soong were conspiring with the PRC to rule Taiwan". This led to a more serious confrontation between the ruling party and the opposition, and to a deepening of social divisions.

Furthermore, numerous money scandals were exposed inside Chen's administration. In autumn 2005, a high-ranking officer in the Presidential Office, who had been on Chen's staff and a member of the DPP, was prosecuted for corruption over illegal money trading. In 2006, Chen's son-in-law and other family members were accused of being involved in illegal insider-trading in the stock market and receiving bribes. Wu Shu-chen, the First Lady of President Chen, who had long been seriously criticised for abusing political privileges and accepting bribes or gifts, was charged in autumn 2006, along with three high-ranking officials under the Presidential Office, with embezzling NT$14.8 million of Presidential Office secret funds by using forged documents. President Chen was also investigated but avoided prosecution under the constitutional prerogative of the president.

This succession of corruption scandals greatly disappointed those who held a clean image of Chen and the DPP. Chen's approval rate dropped sharply and he was pressed to resign. The opposition parties stirred up mass demands for "clean politics" to impeach President Chen. The KMT not only gathered great numbers of people on the streets to demand that the president resign, but the former DPP chairman Shid Ming-the also launched a campaign under the title, "Million voices, against corruption, President Chen must go".

Chen countered with his populist strategy of appealing to a Taiwanese identity in an attempt to restore the prestige and credibility of himself and the DPP. He adopted a more radical stance that seemed to be moving towards a declaration of independence. In February 2006, he stated that he would "cease to apply" the Guidelines for National Unification, and that the National Unification Council would "cease to function". From 2006 to 2007, he activated a "Correcting Naming" movement which replaced "China" with "Taiwan" in the names of government offices and companies. Chen had become increasingly dependent on the so-called "deep green" end of the political spectrum, consisting of those who gave unwavering support to Taiwanese independence. To please this core constituency, he kept issuing outlandish and provocative political proclamations. Each time, Chen came very close to nullifying at least one of the "Five Nos", the pledge that he had made at his first inauguration in 2000 to assure the United States that Taiwan would not take unilateral action to change the *status quo* in the Taiwan Straits. Chen repeatedly appealed to a Taiwanese identity, while the DPP mobilised people against those who demanded that the president resign on a platform of "Save Taiwan". The "pan-green" reiterated that the crisis of President Chen was a crisis for Taiwan, and that those who loved Taiwan had no choice but to save Chen in order to save Taiwan.

As Roberts points out, the followers of a populist leaders are required not only to vote in elections, but may also be mobilised for rallies, demonstrations, strikes, and occupations, and even called on to take up arms to defend their leader in times of peril.[29] For the cause of saving Taiwan, those who felt strongly about Taiwanese identity were mobilised for a "democratic civil war", in Lee Teng-hui's phrase.

As a result, Chen survived this crisis, and was immediately faced by elections for the Legislative Yuan and the presidency in 2008. Chen was barred from standing again due to a two-term limit, but used his position as president to spearhead the DPP campaign. He suggested measures to dilute the prestige of Chiang Kai-shek by removing Chiang's statue from public places and by renaming places named after Chiang.[30] From the point of view of the Taiwanese, Chiang is a dictator who violated their human rights, and deprived them of their property. Chen insisted that these measures symbolised the achievement of transitional justice. During the election campaign for the Legislative Yuan, Chen pronounced that "a victory for the KMT is a victory for China" and aroused a sense of impending crisis among the electorate.

In March 2007, Chen announced the "Four Imperatives and One Non-Issue",[31] superseding the "Five Nos". Subsequently, the DPP passed a "Normal Nation Resolution",[32] embracing Chen's nationalist programme, and Chen promoted the idea of a referendum on joining the UN in the name of Taiwan. The PRC criticised this idea as a first step towards independence. The United States also decisively opposed the move as a unilateral action to change the *status quo* in the Taiwan Straits. People were distressed by the loss of Taiwan's international credibility, and also with economic stagnation and political corruption under Chen's administration.

At the election for the Legislative Yuan in January 2008, the "pan-blue" coalition won a clear majority, handing the DPP a "historical defeat". Chen resigned as chairman of the party. In March, Ma Ying-jeou was elected president on the KMT ticket, handing the DPP another defeat. Chen's nationalist populist strategy had ended in failure.

Concluding Remarks

Chen Shui-bian's populism was first focused against privilege, and then changed to promoting nationalism. In the first stage, Chen promised political reform but was unable to deliver because of the divided government. Throughout Chen's term in the presidency, the DPP failed to win power in the legislature. The only powers available to Chen were those exercised by the president and the Cabinet, not those of the legislature. He began to appeal to Taiwanese identity to secure re-election in 2004, and then took up nationalism to survive adversity and maintain his political influence in the face of pressures from the PRC and the opposition alliance. Chen was driven by the logic of his position towards a more aggressive and radical form of Taiwanese nationalism, favouring the independence of Taiwan.

His nationalistic populism tended to increase division within society. Chen himself was a divisive force for personal reasons. Coming from Tainan, belonging to the *Minnan* ethnicity, and leading a party that was often seen as a spokesman for the Taiwanese, especially the *Minnan*, he tended to alienate those of other ethnic origins and political proclivities. Although he succeeded in gaining election in 2004 by appealing to Taiwanese identity, his growing radicalism alienated the electorate and brought about his downfall four years later.

Chen was brought down by shifts both in the international and domestic arenas. Taiwan used to appeal to the U.S. by presenting itself as a democracy in contrast to the PRC's militaristic party state. But the U.S. and the PRC had converged on maintaining the *status quo* in the Taiwan Straits, and the U.S. gave greater priority to this international agenda rather than to Taiwan's domestic circumstances. In that context, Chen's nominally "democratic" proposal to hold a referendum on the UN issue could be seen as an attempt to alter the *status quo*.[33] Wary of the increasing international pressure on Taiwan, the voters applied the brakes on Chen's radicalism. Both inside Taiwan and in the international community, Chen lost credibility.

On the other hand, Chen was squeezed by the "Taiwanisation" or indigenisation of the KMT. Ma Ying-jeou, a Mainlander, former KMT chairman, and presidential candidate at the 2008 election, insisted on "giving priority to Taiwan" and taking a "Taiwan-centred" stance in policies, while not abandoning the ultimate goal of unification with the mainland. Ma and the KMT asserted a moderate line which included maintaining the *status quo* in the Taiwan Straits and improving China–Taiwan relations. This line was designed to appeal to the centrist portion of the electorate. As Chen became more radical, the KMT shifted to appeal to the mainstream voters who wanted to maintain the ROC on Taiwan and a Taiwanese identity.

Chen Shui-bian intended to mobilise support by arousing antagonism against his opponents. The situation escalated to the stage of a "democratic civil war", in Lee Teng-hui's phrase. People tired of the sense of crisis, and lost faith in Chen, while the KMT shifted itself to capture mainstream opinion. Electors who embraced a Taiwanese identity were given another choice. Not only the United States and the PRC, but also most Taiwanese came to consider Chen Shui-bian too risky, with the result that his populist politics ended in failure.

Notes

[1]   The approval rate of President Chen was 77 per cent at his inauguration, but fell sharply to 37 per cent when it was decided to halt the construction of a fourth nuclear power plant in autumn 2000. Though it rose to 51 per cent two years after his inauguration, it then fell to a level of 30 per cent. When Wu Shu-chen, the First Lady of President Chen, was indicted, the approval rate of President Chen fell to 16 per cent from 23 per cent the previous month (*United Daily*, 4 Nov. 2007).

[2]   K.K. Huang, *On Populism Destroying Taiwan Revisited* (Taipei: Democratic Action Alliance, 2004) (in Chinese).

3   Huoyan Shyu, "Populism in Taiwan: The Rise of a Populist-Democratic Culture in a Democratising Society", *Asian Journal of Political Science* 16, 2 (2008): 130–50.

4   Margaret Canovan, "Trust the People! Populism and the Two Faces of Democracy", *Political Studies* 47 (1999): 2–16.

5   Kurt Weyland, "Classifying a Contested Concept: Populism in the Study of Latin American Politics", *Comparative Politics* 34, 2 (2001): 1–22.

6   Kurt Weyland, "The Politics of Corruption in Latin America", *Journal of Democracy* 9, 2 (1998): 108–21.

7   Lin Chia-lung, "Paths to Democracy: Taiwan in Comparative Perspective", PhD dissertation, Yale University, 1998.

8   Shelley Rigger, *From Opposition to Power: Taiwan's Democratic Progressive Party* (Boulder: Lynne Rienner, 2001).

9   Vincent Wei-cheng Wang and Samuel Chang-yung Ku, "Transitional Justice and Prospect of Democratic Consolidation in Taiwan: Democracy and Justice in Newly Democratized Countries", *National Development Studies* 4, 2 (2005): 1–38.

10   The KMT's net worth peaked in the 1990s at T\$60 billion (US\$1.8 billion) but had fallen to T\$27.7 billion in 2006 (*Financial Times*, 31 Oct. 2006). See Matsumoto Mitsutoyo, *A Study of the KMT Party-owned Enterprises* (Tokyo: Japan Association for Asian Studies, 2002) (in Japanese); and "Taiwan: 'Dual Transition' and 'Black and Gold Politics'", in *Akusesu Chiiki Kenkyu 1*, ed. Takeshi Kishikawa and Masahiro Iwasaki (Tokyo: Nihon Keizai Hyoronsha, 2004) (in Japanese), pp.133–54.

11   Lee Teng-hui, *The Insistence of Taiwan* (Tokyo: PHP, 1999) (in Japanese).

12   Ogasawara distinguished the terms "Taiwanese identity" from "Taiwanese nationalism". In this essay, the terms are used following his argument. See Ogasawara Yoshiyuki, "An Analysis of the Presidential Election of 2004: The Re-election of Chen Shui-bian and the Taiwanese identity", *Nihon Taiwan Gakkaihou* 7 (2005): 44–68 (in Japanese).

13   The indigenous minority is composed of 13 groups. Today, people of predominantly *Han* extraction make up around 98 per cent of the population, while those of Austronesian ancestry comprise roughly 2 per cent (*Taiwan Year Book 2007*: <http://www.gio.gov.tw/taiwan-website/5-gp/yearbook/>).

14   Government Information Office, *Taiwan Yearbook 2007*, at <http://www.gio.gov. tw/taiwan-website/5-gp/yearbook/>; Shyu, "Populism in Taiwan".

15   The "2-28 Incident", a brutal confrontation between Taiwanese and mainlanders, has been the source of socio-political trauma for the Taiwanese people. The incident was an anti-government uprising in Taiwan that began on 28 Feb. 1947, and was violently suppressed by the KMT government resulting in many civilian deaths.

16   After a demonstration on Human Rights Day, 10 Dec. 1979, police arrested many opposition figures. After trials in 1980, 8 were sentenced to prison terms ranging from 12 years to life, and around 50 others to lesser terms.

17 Four year later, Chen lost his political base when the KMT regained the Taipei mayoralty and Ma Ying-jeou became the mayor of Taipei.

18 David J. Samuels, "Presidentialized Parties: The Separation of Powers and Party Organization and Behavior", *Comparative Political Studies* 35, 4 (2002): 461–83.

19 Rigger, *From Opposition to Power*.

20 On 9 July 1999, Lee Teng-hui declared to Germany's *Deutsche Welle* news programme: "Since the introduction of its constitutional reforms in 1991 [the Republic of China] has redefined its relationship with mainland China as being state-to-state relations or at least special state-to-state relations." Lee's statement set off a new confrontation with the PRC, and the US government for the first time ascribed the responsibility for increasing tensions across the Taiwan Straits to Taiwan.

21 The National Unification Council, established in 1990, is an advisory body set up to look into eventual reunification with the mainland. The National Unification Guidelines were the guideline for future reunification made by the Council in 1991. The existence of the Council and the guidelines show the intention of eventual reunification with the mainland and no intention of independence.

22 The NP splintered from the KMT in 1993 and James Soong gathered those who had supported him in the 2000 presidential election into the PFP, so the three parties have the same roots.

23 Weyland, "Classifying a Contested Concept".

24 Angelo Panebianco, *Political Parties* (Cambridge: Cambridge University Press, 1988).

25 Kenneth M. Roberts, "Populism, Political Conflict, and Grass-Roots Organization in Latin America", *Comparative Politics* 38, 2 (2006): 127–48.

26 The Taiwanese identity is a broad concept encompassing Taiwan's autonomy, including the Taiwanese consciousness, anti-China consciousness, correcting names for "Taiwan", the establishment of a new constitution, promoting the international status of Taiwan, "loving Taiwan", and so on. See Ogasawara, "An Analysis of the Presidential Election of 2004".

27 Ogasawara, "An Analysis of the Presidential Election of 2004".

28 In 1992, the practical need for Taipei and Beijing to enter into some kind of functional dialogue over issues prompted the two sides to reach a interim agreement on their conflicting sovereignty claims. Both were in favour of "One China", even though they had different versions of that "One China", and this was called "One China with different interpretations" (*Yige Zhongguo gezi biaoshu*). Beijing insisted that the PRC was the sole legitimate China, while Taipei claimed that the ROC was the one China.

29 Roberts, "Populism, Political Conflict, and Grass-Roots Organization in Latin America".

30 For example, the National Chiang Kai-shek Memorial Hall, a monument erected in memory of Chiang Kai-shek, was renamed as the National Taiwan Democracy Memorial Hall on 19 May 2007.

31　　The Four Imperatives are: independence; rectification of names; a new Constitution; and development. The One Non-Issue states that Taiwan faces no problem of leftist or rightist policy lines.

32　　The Resolution announced: "In order for Taiwan to become a normal nation, we need to actively promote and implement name-rectification, promulgate a new constitution, and accede to the United Nations. In addition, we must realise transitional justice and restore a Taiwan-centric identity, with the ultimate goal of transforming Taiwan into a normal nation" (<http://www.dpp.org.tw/upload/news_letter/20071101174527_data_1.pdf>).

33　　Ito Tsuyoshi, "Is This not 'Same Bed, Different Dreams,' but 'Different Bed, Same Dreams'?: Difference of Interpretation of 'democracy' on the U.S.-Taiwan Relation", *East Asia* 488 (2008): 22–9.

CHAPTER 11

Neoliberal Populism in Japanese Politics: A Study of Prime Minister Koizumi in Comparison with President Reagan

Hideo Otake

In the spring of 2001, Jun'ichiro Koizumi surprisingly gained massive grass-root support in his bid for the presidency of the Liberal Democratic Party (LDP), and became prime minister of Japan. He was regarded by political observers as a lone wolf in the LDP, and even seen as somewhat eccentric. He showed no interest in patronage politics, partly because he was a third generation Dietmember and enjoyed solid constituency support. He had long advocated the privatisation of the postal service, which was taboo in the LDP because the association of post office managers across the country was one of the strongest LDP supporting organisations and vigorously opposed privatisation. Prior to the election, almost no one expected his ascendancy to the prime ministership.

During his campaign for the LDP presidency, he vigorously attacked the mainstream leaders of the LDP and was willing to sacrifice the break-up of the party if necessary for his reform project to succeed. He espoused drastic dismantling of the iron triangles of politicians, bureaucrats, and business associations, including the one surrounding the postal service. Another lone wolf in the LDP, Makiko Tanaka, the daughter of ex-premier Kakuei Tanaka, encouraged Koizumi to run for the presidency, and was even more outspoken in her criticism of the LDP leadership.

Koizumi and Tanaka both attracted large numbers of people in the streets of Japan whenever they organised rallies for the election. The audiences for their campaign TV programmes were at record levels. TV producers competed to have them appear on their programmes. Koizumi thus won unprecedented popularity in his election to the LDP presidency and led the LDP to a landslide victory in the Upper House election a few months later.

Until the fall of 2005, Koizumi's popularity gradually declined — as he had expected and had previously stated. It fell sharply when he dismissed Tanaka from her position as foreign minister after her repeated thoughtless misconduct. Tanaka created unnecessary conflicts within the government, yet at the time was still quite popular among the ordinary electorate. She appeared convincing in her TV appearances, and succeeded in concealing her misconduct from the public, while presenting herself as an aggressive reformer of the scandal-ridden Foreign Ministry. Nonetheless, Koizumi achieved a safe victory in his second bid for the LDP presidency in September 2003, and led the LDP to victory in the Lower House election in November. Two years later, in September 2005, he led the LDP to massive victory in the Lower House elections, once again to the great surprise of most political observers in Japan. In these election campaigns, he revealed his uncompromising stance toward "reforms", and asked the electorate to allow him to continue his reform efforts. These included the privatisation of postal services and the dismantling of the semi-public Highway Corporation, both of which Koizumi felt symbolised the iron-triangles in Japanese politics.

Mass media portrayed the popular support for Koizumi and Tanaka as "populism", and contrasted this style with the traditional patronage politics long conducted by the mainstream LDP leaders. Many believed this populism was a new phenomenon in Japanese politics. This author, however, believes Koizumi's political strategy has historical precedents in Japanese post-war politics and contains numerous similarities to the style of former U.S. president, Ronald Reagan. In this chapter, I will examine Koizumi's leadership style in this context.

A Quarter Century of Populism in Japan

We can detect an almost regular rhythm in Japanese politics since the latter half of the 1970s (see Figure 11-1). Against a background of declining trust in party politicians and public officials, expectations for a particular political leader rose rapidly and then equally abruptly fell. This pattern was repeated several times.

The decline of political trust is a common phenomenon widely observed in advanced nations since the latter half of the 1960s.[1] It is particularly conspicuous in Japan. For instance, an opinion survey conducted in the spring of 1993 by TBS, a major television company, revealed a striking result. When asked the question, "Do you trust politicians", only 8.7 per cent responded "Yes", while 90.2 per cent responded "No".[2] Nevertheless, a continuing downward trend of political trust in Japan has been intermittently

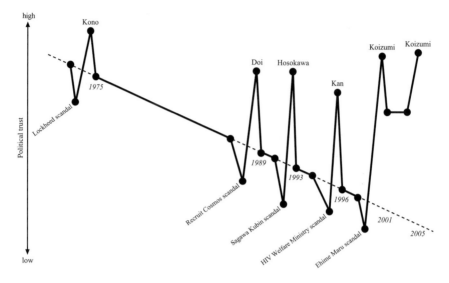

Figure 11-1   Cycles of Political Scandal and Populist Expectation in Japan

punctuated by sharp rises in people's expectations from politics despite repeated betrayals of trust. Those politicians who enjoyed massive (though short lived) support include the following:

1.   Kono Yohei and his New Liberal Club split from the LDP (which had enjoyed a majority in both Houses since 1955) during the public outcry over the Lockheed scandal in 1976. In the next general election, the New Party gained wide support, particularly in the metropolitan area, and brought the LDP's majority control to a temporary end.

2.   Takako Doi, the first female politician elected to the presidency of the Japan Socialist Party (JSP), the major opposition party until 1993, led a large group of female candidates in the Upper House Election of 1989, bringing a landslide victory to the JSP.

3.   Morihiro Hosokawa formed his Japan New Party in 1992, immediately after the Sagawa Kyubin scandal was exposed. He gained nation-wide support in the general election of 1993, and was subsequently elected prime minister. Hosokawa enjoyed unprecedented popularity until his own scandal was revealed.

4.   Jun'ichiro Koizumi challenged the Hashimoto faction in the election for the LDP presidency in the spring of 2001. The Hashimoto faction has been the most powerful and dominant player in the LDP since the

1970s. Koizumi received a great deal of unexpected support from the rank-and-file of LDP members, and won a landslide victory.

5. Makiko Tanaka, whose active support of Koizumi was crucial to his election, attracted very large audiences in a series of political gatherings and frequent TV appearances with her outspoken criticism of LDP leaders.

6. Finally, the well-known governor of Tokyo, Shintaro Ishihara, maintains popularity with his policies and provocative public statements. He was regarded as a possible candidate to become LDP president, and hence prime minister, around the year 2000.

Similar phenomena can be observed at the local level as well. To take only a few prominent examples, two comedians, Yukio Aoshima and Nock Yokoyama, were elected to the position of governor in Tokyo and Osaka respectively in 1995; and Yasuo Tanaka, a writer and a NGO activist, won the governorship of Nagano in the fall of 2000. More recently, a comedian, Hideo Higashikokubara became governor of Miyazaki. It is noteworthy that all of these politicians won election as governor with the backing of spontaneously organised citizens' movements.

The cause of the temporary increase in popularity of these politicians, national as well as local, is nearly always non-partisan support from the new middle class in metropolitan areas (Yasuo Tanaka and Hideo Higashikokubara are exceptions in that their support bases are not in the metropolis). These politicians' basic strategy is to distance themselves from all political parties, including their own, as well as from government offices. By making political parties and the government appear the enemy of the people, these politicians can most vocally advocate eliminating corruption through "reforms", whatever "reform" may mean. It should be emphasised that favourable news coverage — often favourable to an extreme degree — plays a critical role in contributing to these victories.

This cycle of political trust and mistrust can be found in Japanese politics throughout the past 30 years. At times when public distrust emerges along with criticism of scandalous party politicians in general, the trust of the voters is directed to an individual political leader, who is expected to carry out radical reforms of existing institutions. Reform proposals carry weight because of the moral integrity of these leaders, rather than for any intrinsic features of the reform. For example, the 1994 introduction of an electoral system combining single-member territorial constituencies and proportional representation for the Lower House was supported by the media and public because those who advocated the new system were trusted, although the system was not clearly understood by the general public.

These reformers, however, lost the public's trust either when their repu-
tations were damaged by a scandal about themselves (in the case of Hosokawa),
or when the people began to think their reform efforts had faded away (in
the case of Doi in her effort to reform the JSP), or when their popularity
simply decreased as time passed (in the case of Kono). This loss of trust
usually occurred within a couple of years; popular enthusiasm faded and the
normalcy of mistrust returned with additional suspicion.

Koizumi was the only exception as far as national level politics is
concerned. He enjoyed relatively high popularity throughout his five year
premiership, and won another massive victory in the general election of
2005. This was in large part due to his exceptional ability of Machiavellian,
often cold-blooded, manoeuvring against the LDP political bosses as well as
the general public.[3]

Ironically and most importantly, wariness about the institution of parliamentary democracy is practically non-existent in Japan. Despite increasing
political distrust, confidence in representative democracy is quite firmly held
and stable. The legitimacy of this system is globally accepted, especially with
the fall of socialist countries, and the collapse of the new left utopianism
which was rampant during the late sixties and the early seventies.[4] Japan is
no exception. In contrast to some West European countries where new right,
often racist, movements have gained some degree of popular support, right-
wing extremism is almost non-existent in Japan (with a possible exception
of the Tokyo governor, Ishihara). As a result, popular trust in the existing
system remains high and stable. Political misgivings in contemporary Japan
are not deep-rooted, especially when compared to the pre-war period of
rising fascism and militarism, the immediate post-war period of rampant
anti-systemic opposition to representative democracy, or the turbulent years
of the late 1960s when students and young workers challenged the existing
political, economic, and social systems.

Examination of Populism as a Political Science Concept

I will now examine the occasional eruptions of popular expectation which
suddenly emerged in Japan against the background of general political distrust, using the concept of "populism". Populism has been applied to various
political phenomena and thus must be clearly defined. I will then analyse the
characteristics of populism in Japan, focusing on prime minister Jun'ichiro
Koizumi in comparison with former U.S. president Ronald Reagan.

As was already mentioned, the leadership style of Koizumi has often
been called populist by the Japanese media. The term populism is sometimes

linked with concern over the revival of the mass mobilisation techniques and rightist rhetoric of fascism.[5] Some of Koizumi's campaign statements aroused this concern in Japan's neighbouring countries, particularly his intention to visit the Yasukuni Shrine on the anniversary of Japan's defeat in 1945. Accusations of populism are more frequent in the case of Tokyo governor, Shintaro Ishihara, whose frequent provocative, racist, or anti-American statements became the target of widespread attention and criticism. In recent years, however, populism refers to irresponsible "sweet" policies designed to attract voters. In this case, populism does not mean mass mobilisation through rightist (or leftist) rhetoric, but implies political opportunism or flattery of the public, one type of pathology of mass democracy.

In political science literature, populism has at least two distinct historical backgrounds. The first refers to the movement in the late nineteenth century in the United States in which farmers, artisans, and workers organised the People's Party in order to defend their interests against monopolistic capitalism embodied by industries such as giant railway companies.[6] The second refers to the authoritarian regimes in Latin American countries including Mexico, Brazil, and Argentina, which successfully mobilised mass support during the 1930s and 1950s.[7] Latin American populism is mostly characterised as a movement from the top-down, beginning with a leader and trickling down to the people. Until recently, populism was commonly used in Japanese political science literature only in this second meaning, very similar to the concept of fascism.

In contrast, populism in U.S. history has been characterised as a movement from the bottom-up, beginning first with the people and then rising up to leaders. Although it is sometimes observed that the U.S. movement has elements of irrationality, populism has been evaluated positively as a democratic movement in the name of the people.[8] This brand of populism was foreign to Japanese political scientists until quite recently but has a number of similarities to modern Japanese populism. As time passed, U.S. politicians in power, often those on the right, began to circumvent the populist tradition and mobilise the people through the media. Senator Joseph McCarthy and President Ronald Reagan are often cited as typical examples of this type of U.S. politician.

Both traditions of populism, the Latin American variety and the U.S. variety, see politics not as an arena in which different interests are bridged and conflict is mitigated, but as a drama in which the good guy fights for the interests of the people against the bad guys. This view of politics not only has a dramatic element, but also a moral element. In this drama, a hero embodies the moral superiority of the common people and fights a meta-phorical war against the villain who symbolises privileges such as "money power", that are denied to the people. Despite contextual differences, this moralist interpretation has appeared in many countries many different times.

Let us examine the concept of populism more thoroughly, focusing upon the tradition of American populism, which seems comparatively similar to the Japanese populism. For this purpose, I will rely mostly on the work of Michael Kazin.[9] According to his argument, the core of populist rhetoric is the dualistic conflict of the powerful vs. the powerless, the wealthy vs. the poor, the privileged class vs. the ordinary citizen, or the selfish elites vs. the virtuous people. This dualist interpretation of politics is combined with a moralist view of politics. The dualist-moralist view has been a standard ploy in journalism, cultivated and circulated throughout the media. It should be noted here that this moralist interpretation conceals potential conflicts within the people, and makes it possible to draw support from the widest spectrum.

According to the populist tradition in the U.S., the "ordinary people" embody American democratic virtue, while the powerful ignore, corrupt, and betray this democratic ideal. This image is based on a naive trust in the institution of American democracy. The populists are adverse to both extreme right and left, which ignore the values of the American liberal democratic tradition. This naive trust has a healthy optimism, which softens its political agitation.[10] This combination of trust in democratic institu-tions and scepticism of acting politicians is also observable in contemporary Japan. In fact, this is a crucial ingredient of populism in contrast to revo-lutionary ideologies.

Populist movements have appeared repeatedly throughout U.S. history, but took on new characteristics during the 1960s and the 1970s. This new variant of populism is commonly called the "New Right". The New Right found its enemy in big government, personified by liberal presidents and liberal welfare bureaucrats. It fought for the rights of "the people", personi-fied by white workers and the urban middle class. George Wallace, the first leader of this new populist movement, ran for president in 1964, 1968, and again in 1972. He ran on a platform of traditional democracy governed by the ordinary people rather than the autocracy of the Federal Government and the Federal Courts.

Wallace felt the government was dominated by liberals who gave too much preference to the African American minority. He made so many out-spoken statements tainted by racial prejudice that he simply could not obtain favourable media coverage, hampering his campaign. The same was true of candidates from the Christian Right, which emerged as a political force in the later half of the 1970s.

Unlike Wallace, Ronald Reagan carefully presented himself as the representative of the middle, not the extreme right, and thus emerged as a truly successful populist. He was known as the "Great Communicator" due to his exceptional mastery of communication. He argued that the populist tradition was deeply rooted in America. He was an outsider of professional politics and wanted to promote the interests of the ordinary people whom he felt had been neglected until that time. Reagan targeted the middle class, and thus appealed to the majority of the American people. The middle class were a "silent majority", and Reagan sold himself as their spokesman.[11]

Against a background of ever-increasing taxes, Reagan played up the dualism of the middle class versus the wealthy. On the one hand, there was the taxpayer who worked hard and paid taxes honestly, and on the other hand was the wealthy man who enjoyed a close connection to the government and succeeded in evading taxes. In addition, there were politicians and bureaucrats who spent public monies for their own benefit, and liberals who dispersed precious taxpayers' money to minority groups who were often viewed as dependant on the welfare system.

Although Kazin did not explicitly state it, the neoliberalism of the Reagan administration represents a reappearance of traditional American populism. I will therefore call it "neoliberal populism". Reagan's rhetoric helped unite "ordinary Americans" and groups in the American public against the "Washington establishment" and Wall Street. The way Reagan executed his strategy concealed the existence of class conflict, racial conflict, and gender conflict. His balance of dualism at the international level performed a similar function. He portrayed a virtuous America defending its ideals against an evil Soviet Empire. This is populist strategy, masterfully implemented.

In the post-Reagan years, we can detect a departure from the neoliberal tendency in the political climate.[12] George Bush Sr. moved toward a "warm conservatism", showing more concern for the weak sections of society, while Bill Clinton moved further to the "Third Way, American Style". Nevertheless, both Bush and Clinton inherited Reagan's dualist rhetoric of the ordinary American versus the Washington establishment.

Adopting the new left ideology, American radicals either emphasised the class conflict within the ordinary people or regarded the ordinary people as wrongdoers or accomplices of The Establishment against the minorities. Reagan and his followers tended to evade thorny moral questions which the radicals raised about such matters as abortion or affirmative action. Reagan consciously paid more attention to the concerns of the ordinary people, namely the white middle and working classes, such as unemployment and inflation.

The populist tradition arises from the cleavage between the American ideal and political reality. Americans are discontented with the current political situation because it deviates from an American ideal as the people understand it, and they are sceptical of politicians who are presumed to be responsible for this deviation. American history thus displays a repeated rise and fall of populism with different policy orientations depending upon the historical context. Reagan's populism reflected the dominant neoliberal political climate after the eighties.

Reagan skilfully presented himself as a hero, one who challenged enemies both at home and abroad. Despite his huge wealth, he succeeded in making the people identify with him as their fellow citizen. His career and inherent talent fitted nicely to the "theatrical" political show. He mobilised the electorate through the media, instead of organising and controlling the movement itself.

In sum, populism in the American tradition reflects political mistrust of politicians and public officials, but at the same time enshrines a basic trust in the constituent principles of the existing political system. Its reformist stance is fundamentally different from the revolutionary project in that American populism does not pursue any institutional reforms of "the system". It simply mobilises hostility toward perceived enemies (liberals, Wall Street, big government) in order to raise support for a particular individual.

A Comparison of Koizumi and Reagan

On the basis of the above discussion, I will now examine the characteristics of Koizumi's populism in comparison with Reagan, who may be regarded as the most successful populist in the twentieth century. Koizumi's populism has many similarities to the populism of Hoshokawa in 1993–4, and Koichi Kato, who failed to gain momentum in 2000. In this sense, Koizumi represents a type of Japanese populism in existence since the 1990s.[13]

Like Reagan, Koizumi's political style as a reformer reflected the neoliberal political climate of its time. The nucleus of Koizumi's ideology was neoliberal criticism of the government and politics. He tried to introduce such neoliberal strategies as privatisation, deregulation, and decentralisation. A goal of this neoliberalism was to deconstruct the powerful iron triangles consisting of LDP politicians, bureaucrats, and interest groups. Koizumi was striving for "small government" and was repeatedly quoted as saying, "entrust to the private sector whatever the private sector can perform".

Moreover, Koizumi tried to mobilise the urban new middle class, which was neglected by the LDP. Despite the fact that both Reagan and Koizumi leveraged the middle class's resentment and discontent towards the government, their rhetoric lacked the sensational and xenophobic slogans which extreme rightists commonly rely upon. In other words, their neoliberal populism was more moderate.

There are two important differences between Reagan's and Koizumi's ideology, however, reflecting the differences in the neoliberalism of the United States and of Japan.

First, in Japan, neoliberalism was not accepted by politicians or the general public as a systematic ideology. Prescriptions both for and against neoliberalism were discussed only in forums of opinion leaders. Among a wider public, political corruption became the main issue in the latter half of the 1970s, and remains an issue until today. Neoliberal causes such as small government and privatisation were advocated and accepted mostly as a means to eliminate corruption. The neoliberal reforms by the Nakasone Cabinet (1981–6) dismantled the radical labour movement in the public sector through privatisation. The basic task during the 1990s was to reform the vested interests in the LDP and its government. This is the major reason why the Democratic Party of Japan was sympathetic to Koizumi's reforms and expressed its readiness to support Koizumi and his group within the LDP during the first year of his prime ministership. Koizumi targeted constituency services by the LDP, the practice of parachuting by high level civil servants to large private or semi-public corporations, and luxurious gifts and entertainment offered by business corporations to public officials. Unlike the Nakasone period, the ideology of Japanese reformers since 1990 has almost lost the anti-labour element and is no longer systematically neoliberal in character. The populist reforms have often been expressed simply as efforts to eliminate bureaucratic waste and political "fat" and thus to promote effectiveness and simplicity.

The most salient issue raised by Koizumi was the privatisation of postal services. His aim was not simply to restructure the postal service, but to reform the spending of huge postal savings by the government. Postal savings were poured into various semi-governmental "special corporations", including the Highway Corporation whose budget was the target of clientelistic politics. LDP Dietmembers competed to build highways in their constituency and distribute the Highway Corporation's large budget to local construction companies. These corporations then provided lucrative executive positions to retired bureaucrats. In sum, the postal service was pinpointed as the core of structural corruption. Koizumi argued that the most important problems for

Japanese politics were administrative and budgetary reforms and that these problems stemmed mostly from the postal savings.[14] Koizumi ran for LDP president for the first time in 1995, and made this issue almost a single slogan. His neoliberalism derived not from systematic ideological thought, but from his awareness of a fiscal crisis and his critical attitudes toward other LDP members and public officials. In other words, his reform projects hardly reflected the philosophy of neoliberalism. Most other reformers in Japan have shared the same characteristics. The possible exceptions are Yasuhiro Nakasone and Ichiro Ozawa.

The second difference is that Koizumi's populism is far less sensational than that of Reagan. Koizumi is much more moderate. Reagan's populist ideology is said to contain two elements distinct to American history.[15] One is "civil religion" or "national pride"; Americans believe that America is the special country chosen by God. The other is strong concern for national security; increasingly, Americans tend to feel the United States is threatened by outside enemies. This threat is imagined not as an ideology like fascism or communism, but as individual leaders who symbolise the political institutions of hostile nations. These two characteristics are, however, not unique to the United States. In other countries also, neoliberalism is associated with nationalist aspirations and a harsh attitude toward those who disturb the public (that is, capitalist) order. An example is Margaret Thatcher's mobilisation of nationalism in the United Kingdom during the Falklands War.

Koizumi's neoliberal populism was almost totally lacking in those two elements. This means that while Reagan was a "positive populist" who gave dreams and hopes to his fellow people,[16] Koizumi was a "negative populist" who almost exclusively criticised and attacked domestic enemies.

Both Koizumi and Reagan skilfully manipulated the media — television in particular — and appealed directly to the general public. Both played the role of hero in a drama that is carefully conceived and performed. In Japan, the style is commonly called *Gekijo gata seiji*, or "theatrical politics".

However, the distinct characteristics of media politics in the two countries contribute to important differences between the two. Unlike Reagan, Koizumi did not rely on a professional team who fully utilised the techniques of public relations. Koizumi gained sudden popularity through the very negative reaction of the public against prime minister Yoshiro Mori, his immediate predecessor. In addition to the semi-illegitimate selection of prime minister Mori by the "Big Five" (LDP bosses) behind the scenes, the general public had many reasons to have strong distrust and abhorrence toward Mori. These reasons included a series of imprudent statements, his careless mishandling of the tragic sinking of the Ehime-maru ship hit by an American submarine, and finally a scandal over his golf club membership.

Koizumi's contrasting image with Mori spontaneously gave him popularity. In other words, Koizumi gained his popularity without much conscious effort and ironically, his popularity derived from an image that he did not flatter the people. Koizumi himself abhorred opportunistic attitudes toward the people.

In contrast, Reagan was trained as a public relations man, first as a movie star in Hollywood, then as a speechmaker travelling the country. He accumulated techniques to attract the public. Furthermore, it was standard practice in the United States to apply the sophisticated technique of commercial marketing in political campaigning. The Reagan team made use of these techniques to the fullest extent.[17] It is known that Ishao Iijima, Koizumi's first secretary, introduced various techniques to create favourable media coverage. However, his efforts were rudimentary in comparison with the professionalism of the Reagan team. Therefore, Koizumi had difficulty maintaining his popularity, especially once it began to decline. Nonetheless, Koizumi maintained relatively high popularity due to his own exceptional talent in TV performances. This was shown most clearly in his campaign at the Lower House election in 2005, which gave him one more massive victory.

Reagan was an extremely eloquent speaker who used anecdotes ingeniously. An analyst pointed out that he was an effeminate leader, despite the common image of his cowboy style.[18] In contrast, Koizumi presented himself as a traditional samurai, a man of few words. He expressed his opinion or sentiment in short, sharp, and impressive terms. For this reason, some called his style "one phrase politics". It seems that the domestic political culture and the style of TV broadcasting in each country determines which type looks more attractive on television — an eloquent speechmaker, or a reticent leader. Koizumi's style was as attractive to the Japanese audience as Reagan's was to the Americans.

A far more important difference between Reagan and Koizumi lies in the institutional setting of the country where each performed his leadership role. In the United States, the president is elected to a 4-year term, as is a governor in Japan. In contrast, the Japanese prime minister is continually threatened by the risk of being unseated, even during his tenure as party president. This is in part due to the difference of the presidential system and the parliamentary system, but also to the fact that major Japanese parties do not have a centralised structure that guarantees some security for the elected party leader. In the early 1990s, Ichiro Ozawa attempted to build a party system that would guarantee a fixed term, but so far it has not materialised. Furthermore, in order to be re-elected, the LDP president needs support from Dietmembers in addition to the support from rank-and-file party members. This lack of stability seriously hampers a prime minister's reform efforts, as he cannot introduce policy innovations that would alienate his fellow Dietmembers. More than the American president and the Japanese prefectural governors, the Japanese prime minister has to take into consideration the interests of the Dietmembers in order to remain in power through to the end of his term, not to mention to secure re-election.

Koizumi obviously began to take re-election into consideration one year after his first election. This is evident from the fact that once he entered the second year of his presidency, nearly all his reforms lost dynamism and began to stall. In September 2003 he was re-elected, making tacit concessions to some of the oppositional LDP leaders, while maintaining his image as a reformer in public. He showed his talent for Machiavellian manoeuvring in this process, and he seems to have secured the second three-year term ahead. Freed from the concern of re-election, he engaged in serious reforms, confronting the resisting forces in bureaucracy and the LDP with moderately high popularity. This resulted in the privatisation of postal services in 2005, a really unprecedented achievement in the history of the LDP. This led to a massive electoral landslide in the election of 2005.

Concluding Remarks

There is one more populist prime minister in post-war Japan whom I have not mentioned so far, Kakuei Tanaka. His popularity suddenly erupted when he became prime minister in 1972. However, he was forced to retire in 1974 after a public outcry against him over charges of corruption. Compared to Koizumi, Tanaka had a very different base of support, namely farmers and small businessmen, and these supporters expected him to practice redistributive politics rather than trying to "reform" them. Since the later half of the 1970s, reformers, including his daughter Makiko Tanaka, have challenged "the LDP politics of Tanaka style"[19] which he and his followers established. Tanaka's "reshuffle project of Japanese archipelago" was essentially an attempt to redistribute wealth from the metropolis to rural areas, and from the large corporations to the small. In this sense, Tanaka's project and Koizumi's reforms both conceal the conflict between large cities and the countryside, and between big business and their employees on one hand, and small business and farming on the other. The popularity of Tanaka and Koizumi (nearly 70 to 80 per cent of the public supported their Cabinets at the beginning) implies that each took care not to reveal this potential conflict, and attracted the Japanese electorate not by concrete policy proposals, but by personality, vague slogans emphasising "change", and attacks against the enemy (in Tanaka's case, bureaucratic dominance). Herein lies the secrecy of their populism, and populism in general.

It should be noted, however, that their leadership styles differ. This gap reflects the difference between Tanaka's politics of interest and Koizumi's politics of morality, reprised by other Japanese populists since 1976. All the populist reformers since the later half of 1970s attempted to eliminate "the politics of Tanaka" with the backing of the metropolitan new middle class. This was the essence of Koizumi's challenge against the most powerful faction, the Hashimoto faction, which was the descendent of the Tanaka faction. In fact, this is one battle in a long series between the urban interest and the rural interest in disguise.

Notes

1. Joseph S. Nye, Philip D. Zelikow, and David C. King, ed., *Why People Don't Trust Government* (Cambridge, Mass.: Harvard University Press, 1997); Susan J. Pharr and Robert D. Putnam, ed., *Disaffected Democracies: What's Troubling the Trilateral Countries* (Princeton: Princeton University Press, 2000).

2. Tetsuya Chikusi, *Tajisouron — Media to Kenryoku* (Tokyo: Shinchosya, 1994), p. 162.

3. Hideo Otake, *Koizumi Jun'ichiro: A Study of Populism* (Tokyo: Toyokeizai Shimposha, 2006).

4. Andrew Wroe, "Trust in Government: A Crisis of Democracy?", in *Controversies in American Politics and Society*, ed. David McKay, David Houghton, and Andrew Wroe (Oxford: Blackwell, 2002); Hans-Dieter Kingemann and Dieter Fuchs, ed., *Citizens and the State* (Oxford: Oxford University Press, 1995), chapter 11.

5. Shin Sakata, *Koizumi Jun'ichiro no Shisou* (Tokyo: Iwanami Shoten, 2001).

6. Jun Furuya, *Americanism — 'Fuhen Kokka' no Nashonarisumu* (Tokyo: Tokyo Daigaku Syuppankai, 2002).

7. Ruth Berins Collier and David Collier, *Shaping the Political Arena: Critical Junctures, the Labor Movement, and Regime Dynamics in Latin America* (Indiana: University of Notre Dame Press, 2002).

8. Christopher Lasch, *The Revolt of the Elites* (New York: W.W. Norton, 1995), chapter 5.

9. Michael Kazin, *The Populist Persuasion: An American History* (New York: Basic Books, 1995).

10. Kazin, *The Populist Persuasion*, pp. 1–2.

11. The catch word, the silent majority, was first used by Nixon in U.S. politics during the late 1960s.

12. The concept of "political climate" is expressed in various terms with nuances and implications such as "tide of reform" (Light), and "policy mood" (Stimson). Phillips, 1990, conceptualises this notion in relation to the rise and fall of

political mistrust. See Paul C. Light, *The Tide of Reform* (New Haven: Yale University Press, 1997); James A. Stimson, *Public Opinion in America: Moods, Cycles and Swings*, 2nd ed. (Boulder: Westview Press, 1999).

13 Some recent populists, such as Takako Doi, Naoto Kan, and Yasuo Tanaka, do not belong in this category. Their ideology is not tainted by neoliberalism, and they are new left populists who advocate citizen participation. In contrast, Shintaro Ishihara belongs to a third category, nationalist populists, a rare species in Japanese politics. Nonetheless, all these populists draw support from the urban new middle class.

14 Jun'ichiro Koizumi, *Kanryou Oukoku Kaitairon — Nihon no Kiki wo Sukuu Hou* (Tokyo: Koubunsya, 1996).

15 Michael Weiler and W. Barnett Pearce, "Ceremonial Discourse: The Rhetorical Ecology of the Reagan Administration", in *Reagan and Public Discourse in America*, ed. Michael Weiler and W. Barnett Pearce (Tuscaloosa: University of Alabama Press, 1992).

16 Weiler and Pearce, "Ceremonial Discourse", p. 20.

17 Hedrick Smith, *The Power Game: How Washington Works* (New York: Random House, 1988).

18 Kathleen Hall Jamieson, *Eloquence in an Electronic Age: The Transformation of Political Speechmaking* (Oxford: Oxford University Press, 1988), cited in Weiler and Pearce, "Ceremonial Discourse", p. 37.

19 Takashi Tachibana, *Tanaka Makiko Kenkyuu* (Tokyo: Bungei Syunju, 2002).

CHAPTER 12

Afterword

Benedict Anderson

Today, populism in Southeast Asia is attached to current events, and often treated as if it had no antecedents. But it has a history. The first real populists were certain anticolonial nationalists, exemplified by U Nu and Sukarno — with counterparts elsewhere like Nkrumah, Touré, Mandela, and so on. They had to be populist, since under colonial conditions they had few political resources except mobilised popular support.

Here are two matters of interest about these anticolonial populists. The first is limned by Ernesto Laclau when he writes that populist movements are best defined by their enemies. In the colonies they were easily identified, because they were "white". The second is that after managing to get their countries to be independent, free of the white rulers, they usually came to bad ends — imprisonment, exile, or assassination. Once in power, they teetered towards authoritarianism, made trouble for themselves by vanity and megalomania, overspent their budgets, and so on, and were eventually overthrown, very often by young militaries. This suggests that Laclau is right when he argues that it is very difficult to sustain populist movements over a long term, especially if the original enemies have disappeared. Victory always means taking over the "target" position of the former enemy, that is, as controllers of the state.

Laclau explains why. Everyone who joins a populist movement engages with the movement in two ways. First, each person has their own particularist demand or complaint — about unjust treatment, unfair taxes, poor services, not enough schools, and so on. These demands are all very different. But second, populism allows each person to look at all these other people with their different demands and realise that in some way they are all brothers and sisters. Everyone is being blocked, or mistreated, or poorly served in the same way. Laclau calls this equivalence. The problem for a populist move-ment is that once power is achieved, this equivalence tends to disappear, yet all the particularist demands are still there. People are still complaining about schools, taxes, health care, and so on, and they still feel the state is not attentive to their particular problem. Perón is the classic case. Once in power, he faced more and more concrete demands by different groups. The uniting factor of a drive against a common enemy, an exterior force, had been undermined. In many cases, populist leaders in this type of situation react by trying to invent a new external enemy. Sukarno is a case in point. As internal conflicts increased, he claimed foreigners were trying to overthrow him and destroy Indonesia. But typically this manoeuvre does not work.

This pattern raises the question of whether there is something inherently unstable about populist rule, and I think there probably is. As a result, many populist leaders either get very quickly overthrown, or they turn towards some kind of authoritarianism.

* * *

Let me now move to the present-day context of populism. Perhaps the proper way to pose the former point about instability is by thinking of a cycle. The dominating factors in the present-day politics of Southeast Asia are closed national oligarchies. Power is shared in a small circle. Top people queue for a turn at lucrative posts. Nobody wants to disturb these cosy arrangements. An air of passivity reigns. Think of the Philippines in the 1950s when anyone of any importance had a turn at being president or vice-president, and everybody understood that they should not break the rules — until Marcos came along. Look today at Badawi in Malaysia, Arroyo in the Philippines, and SBY in Indonesia. Yet occasionally, a challenge appears. Mahathir was very hungry for power, and really disliked the old Malay aristocracy. Thaksin believed he could shake up Thailand's old parliamentary regime where all the ministries and pay-offs were shared around. The crash of 1997 had made the old system a sitting target. Thaksin did not like the old Bangkok elite, and quite a few of the people around him were quietly opposed to the monarchy. (I am not convinced that Estrada truly belongs to this club. He wanted to play at being an oligarch himself. He was certainly popular, but not a populist, since he never formulated a clear enemy.)

But once these challengers are in power, the cycle turns. The challengers congeal into oligarchy. The arteries of the body politic gradually get clogged up; opportunities are shared out; barriers to participation rise; the insiders make all the deals among themselves; and these all have political and economic consequences that end up in a crisis, a new opportunity for populist challenge, and another turn of the wheel.

* * *

Populism is inevitably culturally specific. Each populist leader draws on symbols and cultural attributes from a specific context. Joel Rocamora describes how Estrada fashioned charisma out of drinking, womanising, and other habits that appealed in the Philippines' macho culture. The same formula would not work in Indonesia. What works in Malaysia would not work in the Philippines.

These symbols and attributes come out of the older historical formation of the country. Take for example the Philippines. The class structure of the country is very obvious, and yet few except the politically engaged notice it and talk about it. Instead the society is described as being divided between rich and poor, implying that the difference is just a matter of luck or fortune, not a radical difference born out of the culture of a feudal past. If you see a rich man as a poor man who has happened to become rich, then he is not very different. But if you see him as a noble or a king, then he is radically different from you in the local cultural formation, and populist antagonism becomes more likely. One striking feature of world politics since the early twentieth century has been the destruction of monarchies. They have been replaced not only by democracies but — much more significantly — by republics. Behind Laclau's idea of equivalence, the ability to realise that my grievance is equivalent to everyone else's grievance, is the idea of the nation, the idea of a society which ought to be equal, where no-one is looked down upon, humiliated, or marginalised. The appeal of populism to this vague but radical egalitarianism is rooted deep in the idea of the nation.

It is instructive to look at the language used by people who are afraid of populism. In Thailand, intellectuals are prepared to be contemptuous of rural people in public. These intellectuals have an inflated idea of their own moral and political value, because they are so close to the state. This openly contemptuous language would not be possible in a republic. When Thaksin launched his populist policies, ex-prime minister Anand Panyarachun criticised such policies by claiming it was wrong to give money to peasants because they would not know how to use it and would waste it on such things as mobile phones. Inherent in this language is a clear sense of distance. I am not like a peasant, and the peasants are not like me — as if the two were members of different countries.

In Indonesia, attitudes to the police conceal a similar attitude. Most ordinary people dislike and distrust the police because they are oppressive, corrupt, lazy, and brutal. But above a certain level of society, the police become friends because in the end the police are a necessary force for protection against other citizens. In the first 30 years of Indonesia's history, the people were accorded great symbolic respect — as *Rakyat* with a capital R —

because the people were the foundation of Indonesian nationalism. But the word has since disappeared, replaced by *masa*. This word too used to have a positive meaning, that is, the human material for vast political mobilisations. But now it has changed to mean the unorganised, brutal, greedy, looting, burning masses — the nightmare of the middle class.

Talking about the mass of the people in a way which positions them miles away is a powerful form of distancing in the imaginary of the state, which in some ways is a response to the fear that large social distances actually create. Real oligarchs, of course, are not afraid of the people. But the urban middle class — especially the Chinese middle class — are very afraid, and that is why they do not trouble the oligarchs or the police. They fear they will become the victims of subaltern rage, greed, and envy. In a city like Bangkok, this feeling is palpable. The fine talk about democratic values, the separation of the powers, respect for the judiciary, and the rule of law conceals a big hypocrisy. The middle class talk about democracy but when challenged politically they resort to wholly undemocratic methods, and are capable of terrifying brutality.

CONTRIBUTORS

Benedict Anderson is Aaron L. Binenkorb Professor of International Studies Emeritus at Cornell University. He is editor of the journal *Indonesia* and author of *Imagined Communities: Reflections on the Origins and Spread of Nationalism*, *Language and Power: Exploring Political Cultures in Indonesia*, *Under Three Flags*, *The Spectre of Comparisons* and *Java in a Time of Revolution*.

Chris Baker is a writer, editor, and translator. He has a doctorate in history from Cambridge University, and has published on Thailand's history, political economy, and current affairs.

Boo Teik Khoo, associate professor, School of Social Sciences, Universiti Sains Malaysia, is the author of *Paradoxes of Mahathirism: An Intellectual Biography of Mahathir Mohamad* (Oxford University Press, 1995) and *Beyond Mahathir: Malaysian Politics and its Discontents* (Zed Books, 2003), and co-editor (with Francis Loh Kok Wah) of *Democracy in Malaysia: Discourses and Practices* (Curzon Press, 2002).

Kan Kimura is a professor at the Graduate School of International Cooperation Studies, Kobe University. He received an L.L.D from Kyoto University in 2001 for a book on Korean nationalism. He has been a Visiting Scholar at the Fairbank Center for East Asian Research at Harvard University, the Asiatic Research Center of Korea University, the Sejong Institute, and the Faculty of Asian Studies of the Australian National University. He has published in Japanese, Korean, and English on Korean history and politics.

Mitsutoyo Matsumoto is associate professor of the Faculty of Foreign Languages at Nagasaki University of Foreign Studies. He is the author of *The Study of the KMT Party-Owned Enterprises* (Japan Association for Asian Studies, 2002), a contributor to *An Introduction to Asian Political Economy* (Yuhikaku, 2006), and the author of several chapters and articles about the political economy and democratic politics of Taiwan.

Hiroshi Matsushita is professor at Kyoto Woman's University, and professor emeritus at Kobe University. He has a PhD from the University of Cuyo (Argentina), and conducted research and taught at the Universities of Nanzan and Kobe. His publications include *Movimiento obrero Argentino 1930–45* (Buenos Aires: Siglo veinte, 1983) and *Peronism, Authoritarianism and Dependency* (in Japanese; Tokyo: Yushindou, 1987), which won the Ohira Masayoshi prize.

Kosuke Mizuno is a professor of development studies, Center for Southeast Asian Studies, Kyoto University, and currently director of the Center. His interests cover organisations, institutions, and economic development in Indonesia based on extensive fieldwork. His publications include *Rural Industrialization in Indonesia: A Case Study on the Community Based Weaving Industry in West Java* (Institute of Developing Economies, 1996), which won the IDE prize for the Japanese version. He is the Japanese representative on the JSPS-NRCT Core University Programme between Thammasat University and CSEAS Kyoto University titled "Making Region in East Asia".

Masaaki Okamoto is associate professor at the Center for Southeast Asian Studies, Kyoto University, specialising in the local politics of Indonesia. His recent publications include *Violent Groups and Local Bosses in the Reformation Era in Indonesia* (in Indonesian, coedited with Abdur Rozaki, IRE Press, Yogyakarta), and "Jawara in Power, 1998–2007", in *Indonesia* 86 (Oct. 2008).

Hideo Otake is professor of political science at Doshisha Women's College. He received a PhD from the University of Tokyo, and has conducted research at the University of Chicago (1970–3), Hamburg University (1983–5) and Science Po in Paris (1999–2000). He has published more than fifteen books, including *Nihongata Popyurizumu* (Populism, Japanese Style, 2003), and *Koizumi Jun'ichiro: Popyurizumu no Kenkyu* (Jun'ichiro Koizumi: A Study of Populism, 2006).

Pasuk Phongpaichit is professor and chair of the Political Economy Centre at the Faculty of Economics, Chulalongkorn University. She has a doctorate in economics from Cambridge University, and has published widely on the Thai political economy, corruption, illegal economies, social movements, and regional issues. She has been a visiting professor at Kyoto University, Tokyo University, John Hopkins SAIS, University of Washington, and Griffith University.

Joel Rocamora is a research associate at the Institute for Popular Democracy, Manila. He is also a political "practitioner", being chairman of Akbayan, a progressive political party. He received his PhD in politics at Cornell University.

Yoshifumi Tamada is professor at the Graduate School of Asian and African Area Studies, Kyoto University. He is the author of *Myths and Realities: The Democratization of Thai Politics* (Kyoto University Press, 2008), and co-editor (with Funatsu Tsuruyo) of *Thailand in Motion: Political and Administrative Changes, 1991–2006* (in Japanese, IDE-JETRO, 2008).

Nualnoi Treerat is associate professor of economics and former director of Political Economy Centre, Faculty of Economics, Chulalongkorn University. Her research interests and publications are in the fields of corruption and good governance, and public policy.

INDEX